Contents

Kicking Butt with MIDP and MSA

The Java™ Series

Kicking Butt with MIDP and MSA

Creating Great
Mobile Applications

Jonathan Knudsen

✦Addison-Wesley

Boston • San Francisco • New York • Toronto • Montreal
London • Munich • Paris • Madrid
Capetown • Sydney • Tokyo • Singapore • Mexico City

This Book Is Safari Enabled

The Safari® Enabled icon on the cover of your favorite technology book means the book is available through Safari Bookshelf. When you buy this book, you get free access to the online edition for 45 days.

Safari Bookshelf is an electronic reference library that lets you easily search thousands of technical books, find code samples, download chapters, and access technical information whenever and wherever you need it.

To gain 45-day Safari Enabled access to this book:

- Go to http://www.awprofessional.com/safarienabled
- Complete the brief registration form
- Enter the coupon code A7JL-TRJK-DN4T-39KB-UBZ5

If you have difficulty registering on Safari Bookshelf or accessing the online edition, please e-mail customer-service@safaribooksonline.com.

Visit us on the Web: www.awprofessional.com

Library of Congress Cataloging-in-Publication Data

Knudsen, Jonathan.
  Kicking butt with MIDP and MSA : creating great mobile applications / Jonathan Knudsen.
    p. cm.
  Includes index.
  ISBN 0-321-46342-0 (pbk. : alk. paper)
  1. Mobile computing. 2. Application software—Development. 3. Smartphones. 4. Pocket computers.
I. Title. II. Title: Kicking butt with Mobile Information Device Profile and Mobile Service Architecture.

  QA76.59.K657 2008
  004.16—dc22   2007045477

ISBN 13: 978-0-321-46342-5
ISBN 10:   0-321-46342-0
Text printed in the United States on recycled paper at RR Donnelley in Crawfordsville, Indiana.
First printing, December 2007

For Kristen, my true love

Foreword

THE progress of cell phones as application development platforms has been truly staggering over the past eight years. Even the primitive early cell phones proved to be exciting despite early difficulties with performance and interoperability. But the platforms have grown and matured significantly, and they're growing beyond their early successes in games. The Mobile Information Device Profile (MIDP) is currently widely deployed in its second generation. Layered on top of it are APIs that significantly enrich the developer's environment: first JTWI (Java Technology for the Wireless Industry) and now the most recent, MSA (the Mobile Services Architecture).

This book is a wonderful companion for developers wanting to write software for these modern platforms. It is not a reference manual: it is a hands-on guide that is best used with a computer in front of you so that you can work through the numerous examples with the help of the associated Web site. One of the great features of this book is that it goes beyond the APIs and explains how to use the mobile development features in NetBeans to quickly and easily develop and debug sophisticated applications.

Cell phones don't need to be limited to running small, local applications and games: enabled by MIDP2 and the associated APIs, they can be full-fledged participants in the network. This book shows you how to construct such applications easily and efficiently.

—James Gosling

Preface

THIS book is about creating applications for cell phones and other small devices.

Help Me Help You

The best way to learn programming is by doing it. Try something, and if it works, tweak it and try again. A good book gives you lots of things to try and tweak.

If you just read the text of this book, you'll miss about half of the content. I put just as much sweat into making the examples clear and instructive as I put into writing the text. The best way to read this book is sitting in front of your computer, trying out the examples as you go along. You can download the source code for the book from the Web site:

> http://kickbutt.jonathanknudsen.com/download.html

The examples are available for NetBeans Mobility and the Sun Java Wireless Toolkit. You can read about these tools in Chapter 2. The following instructions describe how to load and run a chapter's sample code in either tool.

Running Examples Using NetBeans Mobility

Download the zip file for the chapter. Unzip it to a location of your choice. In NetBeans, choose **File > Open Project...** from the menu. Navigate to the project and open it. You can run the project by choosing **Run > Run Main Project**.

Running Examples Using the Sun Java Wireless Toolkit

Download the zip file for the chapter. Unzip it to the apps folder under the toolkit's installation directory. For example, if the toolkit is installed in c:\WTK2.5.1, and you've downloaded the examples from Chapter 11, unzip the file to create the directory c:\WTK2.5.1\apps\kb-ch11.

Now, in KToolbar, open the kb-ch11 project. Run the project by clicking **Run**.

Finding API Documentation

As you read through this book, you should also have immediate access to the relevant API documentation. This book explains how to use APIs in practical terms, while the API documentation is a definitive reference for classes and methods.

Documentation for many of the APIs discussed in this book is online here:

> http://java.sun.com/javame/reference/apis.jsp

For the remaining APIs, you can download the relevant specifications from the Java Community Process Web site:

> http://jcp.org/

The Real World

Many of the APIs described in this book are quite new. The MSA specification is so new that real devices do not yet implement it, and the MSA subset is just beginning to make its way to the real world. That means that some of the features described in this book will be available to you only in the desktop emulator, at least in the near term. Whenever possible, I have tested the examples in this book on the real devices I have available.

Acknowledgments

THE first person who got this book rolling is Monica Pawlan, who used to be my boss at Sun Microsystems. I'm grateful to her for getting me connected with the Java Series people, including Myrna Rivera at Sun and Greg Doench and Michelle Housley at Addison-Wesley.

I'd like to thank my technical reviewers, Sang Shin and Joe Bowbeer, for working their way through the book and providing feedback to improve the book. Joe went far beyond the call of duty in providing detailed comments, pragmatic suggestions, sample code, and links for more information.

I'd also like to thank Dan Sears and Martin Brehovsky for comments on specific parts of the book.

My family gets a huge thank you for helping me through another book. My wife, Kristen, deserves a parade in her honor for being so patient with me. My children, Daphne, Luke, Andrew, and Elena, were terrific about cheering me on. I'm really looking forward to having more time with all of you.

About the Author

JONATHAN Knudsen is the author of several books and more than one hundred articles about Java technology and mobile robots. He is the husband of the most glorious woman ever to walk the Earth, the father of four amazing children, a decent piano player, and the scourge of many Bonsai trees. When Jonathan grows up, he wants to be a cowboy.

Section I

Getting Started

1

Overview

J AVA TECHNOLOGY IS enjoying a rock star career in the mobile phone industry. After starting in Japan in 1999 as NTT DoCoMo's i-mode service, the lead singer of the band, the Mobile Information Device Profile (MIDP) is now deployed on over 2.1billion mobile devices worldwide (according to information available at http://java.sun.com/javaone/sf/2007/articles/mobilitygeneralsession.jsp).

This chapter explains why MIDP is such a good fit for mobile devices and describes how MIDP and the rest of the band fit together to form a powerful platform for mobile applications.

1.1 Not Plastics, but Wireless

In an updated version of the 1967 classic *The Graduate*, the young hero of the film would be urged to get involved in the wireless industry. The revolution of desktop computers has come and gone. The new revolution is wireless devices, which provide a cheap, lightweight, and often stylish portal to the full power of the Internet.

Mobile phones already outnumber desktop computers as a method of connecting to the Internet, and the trend will only continue. With more and more applications moving from the desktop to the Internet, a mobile phone is a much simpler and more convenient alternative to a desktop computer or even a laptop.

The wireless networks of today are still slow compared to cable modem and DSL technologies that are available in many homes. Nevertheless, much useful work can be done with a wireless device. Faster networks, which will open up new worlds of applications, are deployed in some parts of the world and will become widespread in the next couple of years.

1.2 MIDP, the Heart and Soul of Mobile Java Technology

MIDP is the foundation of most Java technology mobile applications today. This might change in the future, as you'll see later, but for the moment, MIDP dominates the world of Java technology on mobile devices.

MIDP is a specification defined by a consortium of interested companies and individuals through the Java Community Process (JCP). Specifications defined through the JCP are called Java Specification Requests (JSRs), and each is assigned a number.

The first MIDP specification was JSR 37, published in September 2000. MIDP 1.0 defines a complete environment for Java technology applications to run on small devices.

MIDP 1.0 actually builds on another specification, the Connected, Limited Device Configuration (CLDC). CLDC 1.0 is defined by JSR 30. CLDC defines the behavior of the Java Virtual Machine (JVM) that is used on mobile devices and provides some basic APIs. MIDP adds APIs for applications and user interfaces.

The complete set of software on a mobile device is often called a *stack*. The very first MIDP phones had the Java technology stack shown in Figure 1.1.

While MIDP 1.0 phones were being sold to the public, the MIDP 2.0 specification was already underway. It addressed shortcomings in MIDP 1.0 and added new features for gaming, enhanced user interface, and secure networking.

MIDP 2.0 is widely deployed on mobile phones today.

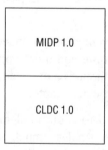

Figure 1.1   Initial MIDP stack

The reason MIDP is so popular with device manufacturers and wireless network operators *(carriers)* is the JVM. Native applications execute instructions directly on a device's processor. Badly behaved native applications can crash the entire device. A badly behaved Java technology–based application (Java application) will, at worst, crash the JVM, leaving the rest of the device still running smoothly. Device manufacturers and carriers like this design because it gives their users a degree of safety in running third-party software.

1.3 The First Umbrella: JTWI

Other JSRs, called *optional APIs,* were also being created at the same time that MIDP was growing up. The first optional APIs to be completed were for text messaging (JSR 120, Wireless Messaging API, or WMA) and multimedia support (JSR 135, Mobile Media API, or MMAPI). Since then, many more have been added: support for Bluetooth networking, Global Positioning System (GPS) hardware, 3D graphics, and enhanced multimedia are just a few.

The abundance of optional APIs became a challenge. As an application developer, how could you figure out which APIs you expected to be available on a device?

The first answer to this question was a specification called Java Technology for the Wireless Industry (JTWI, JSR 185). JTWI is an *umbrella* specification. It incorporates MIDP 2.0, CLDC 1.1 (or 1.0), WMA, and MMAPI. Support for MIDP, CLDC, and WMA is required, but MMAPI is optional (see Figure 1.2).

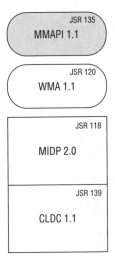

Figure 1.2   JTWI stack

Beyond merely assembling its component specifications, JTWI defines other requirements for implementations, such as minimums for memory, minimums for multithreading, and the behavior of APIs. The goal is to reduce ambiguity and provide application developers with a robust, predictable platform.

1.4 A Bigger Umbrella: MSA

JTWI provides a well-defined application environment. Many new APIs have been completed since JTWI was defined. JSR 248, the Mobile Service Architecture (MSA), is a newer umbrella specification, again based on MIDP 2.0. MSA is backwards compatible with JTWI but expands it considerably.

MSA defines two umbrellas. One is MSA, the other is the MSA *subset*. The subset is designed for devices that don't have the hardware power to support the full MSA stack (shown in Figure 1.3).

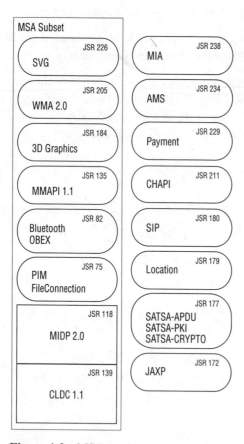

Figure 1.3   MSA stack

If you don't recognize some APIs in the diagram, don't worry. The next section is a quick fly-through of the APIs that are part of MSA. The rest of the book describes the APIs in detail.

APIs are either *mandatory* or *conditionally mandatory* in the MSA specification. APIs that require specific hardware, such as Bluetooth networking or GPS, are conditionally mandatory. The JSR 179 Location API, for instance, is conditionally mandatory because not all devices will have hardware that determines the device's location.

Some JSRs contain more than one API definition. JSR 177, for example, defines four APIs. In the MSA specification, one is not required at all (SATSA-JCRMI), two are conditionally mandatory depending on the smart card hardware available (SATSA-APDU and SATSA-PKI), and one is mandatory (SATSA-CRYPTO).

1.5   Understanding MSA APIs

Although Figure 1.3 is a big hairy pile of acronyms and numbers, it's easier to understand the whole picture when the APIs are grouped together by topic. Remember, you are just getting the broad outlines of MSA here. The rest of the book covers the APIs in detail.

1.5.1   Basic MIDP Platform

The fundamental application platform is based on CLDC and MIDP. CLDC provides a small JVM and fundamental APIs. MIDP adds APIs for user interface, application model, persistent storage, and HTTP and HTTPS networking.

MIDP also includes a *push registry* so that applications can be launched in response to incoming network activity.

1.5.2   Advanced Networking

JSR 120, WMA 1.1, enables applications to send and receive text messages using Short Message Service (SMS) or Cell Broadcast Service (CBS). The next version, JSR 205 or WMA 2.0, allows sending and receiving images and other media via Multimedia Message Service (MMS).

Devices that have Bluetooth hardware will implement the JSR 82 Bluetooth API. Devices with appropriate Bluetooth or infrared hardware can also implement the JSR 82 OBEX API.

MSA also includes JSR 180 Session Initiation Protocol (SIP) API, which is a standard way to set up communication sessions.

1.5.3 Multimedia

JSR 135, MMAPI, provides capabilities for playback and capture of media. The actual formats and protocols that are supported are determined by the capabilities of the device. A small subset of MMAPI for playing audio files is included as part of MIDP.

JSR 234, Advanced Multimedia Supplements (AMS), extends MMAPI with better support for cameras and new features for audio effects and 3D audio.

1.5.4 Advanced Graphics

MIDP 1.0 provides excellent capabilities for building user interfaces using predefined types as well as custom drawing. MIDP 2.0 adds more, including a game API.

MSA builds on MIDP's graphics capabilities with two advanced graphics APIs. The first is JSR 184, the Mobile 3D Graphics (M3G) API for J2ME. Applications can use M3G to build 3D scenes on the fly or load them from files.

JSR 226, the Scalable 2D Vector Graphics API, allows applications to play industry-standard scalable vector graphics (SVG) content.

1.5.5 Security and Transactions

MIDP 2.0 requires support for HTTPS connections, which is sufficient security for many applications. In addition, MSA includes APIs for communicating with a smart card and making payments.

JSR 177, Security and Trust Services APIs, defines four APIs. Three are part of MSA. SATSA-APDU and SATSA-PKI are useful for applications that want to use a smart card to do work or perform cryptographic operations. They provide an additional level of security for especially sensitive data. Both SATSA-APDU and SATSA-PKI are conditionally mandatory depending on the available hardware. SATSA-CRYPTO is a general-purpose cryptographic API and is a mandatory component of MSA.

Applications that allow users to make payments can use the JSR 229 Payment API. For example, a game that allows users to buy new levels or lives could use the Payment API.

1.5.6 Location

The JSR 179 Location API provides applications access to a device's physical location. Obviously, this works (and the Location API is available) only if the device has some way of determining its own location. Most of the time, the method is GPS.

1.5.7 Advanced Application Invocation

MIDP 2.0 provides a push registry for launching MIDlets in response to incoming network activity. MSA provides another way to launch applications, the JSR 211 Content Handler API (CHAPI). In essence, CHAPI maps content types to applications. If the device receives a movie file, for example, an application can be configured to launch and view the content.

1.5.8 Advanced Application Services

Finally, MSA provides three APIs to round out a highly capable application environment.

JSR 75 provides two important APIs. The Personal Information Management (PIM) API allows applications to read information stored in a device's phone book, calendar, and contact list. The FileConnection API gives applications the capability to read and write files stored on a device.

JSR 172 defines APIs for Web Services. MSA requires just one, the Java API for XML Parsing (JAXP).

Finally, the JSR 238 Mobile Internationalization API (MIA) defines a resource file structure and supporting API to make it easy to create multilingual applications that can be distributed to a global audience.

1.6 Looking beyond MSA 1.0

Although MIDP is the centerpiece of small device Java Technology, the landscape is constantly shifting. Stacks based on the Connected Device Configuration (CDC) are more appropriate for devices that are slightly larger than mobile phones, like Personal Digital Assistants (PDAs) and car navigation systems. CDC stacks are maturing more slowly than their CLDC counterparts, but their time is coming soon. CDC looks and acts more like desktop Java technology than CLDC does, so more sophisticated applications can be deployed on CDC stacks.

As if that weren't confusing enough, it's also likely that CDC stacks will include a MIDP implementation built on top of CDC.

The CDC counterpart to MSA is JSR 249, Advanced Mobile Service Architecture.

Another wrinkle to consider is JSR 271, MIDP 3.0, which won't be finished until well after MSA 1.0. You can track the progress of both JSR 249 and JSR 271 at the JCP Web site.

1.7 What about JavaFX Mobile?

Just before I finished writing this book, Sun Microsystems announced the JavaFX product line. JavaFX has two components with little overlap:

- JavaFX Script is a new programming language for quickly creating applications. JavaFX Script tools will make it easy for graphic designers and other non-geeky people to create applications for Java ME devices.
- JavaFX Mobile is a software stack for mobile phones. It is based on CDC and, in general, is slightly "larger" than CLDC/MIDP in terms of processor power and memory size. The exact specifications of JavaFX Mobile are evolving now, but JavaFX Mobile will be able to run MIDlet suites as well as CDC applications.

Much of what you learn in this book will be useful in the future world of JavaFX Mobile. More information on JavaFX Mobile is available here:

> http://www.sun.com/software/javafx/mobile/

1.8 Summary

MIDP is the core of Java technology mobile applications. Umbrella specifications group MIDP with other APIs to form a full-featured application environment. The first grouping was JTWI. The next, MSA, is the subject of this book. MSA includes APIs for text and multimedia messaging, multimedia, 3D graphics, XML parsing, advanced networking, and much more.

2

Tools

BUILDING MIDP applications is surprisingly easy. This chapter describes several development alternatives and explains some of the magic that these tools provide.

2.1 Sun Java Wireless Toolkit for CLDC: A Toaster Oven

The Sun Java Wireless Toolkit for CLDC, which used to be the J2ME Wireless Toolkit, is simple and powerful. If you already understand the Java programming language and are comfortable with a text editor, the toolkit is a great place to learn about MIDP.

The Sun Java Wireless Toolkit for CLDC includes three main components:

- *KToolbar* allows you to manage and build projects.
- The *emulator* is a simulated mobile phone. It enables you to test applications without having to use a real device.
- A collection of *utilities and tools* provides support for many MIDlet features and optional packages.

The Sun Java Wireless Toolkit for CLDC is similar to a toaster oven because it has a simple interface and a surprising amount of ability.

The toolkit keeps pace with the rapidly evolving Java ME landscape. The toolkit and its emulator support the Mobile Service Architecture (MSA) specification, providing a highly capable development environment well ahead of actual devices.

But how, you might be wondering, can the emulator send SMS messages? How can it support the Location API? What about Bluetooth? One of the wonders of the toolkit emulator is that it simulates any environment it cannot directly support. Network connections, of course, can be supported using network connections of the underlying desktop computer. For Short Message Service (SMS) and Multimedia Message Service (MMS), the toolkit provides a simulation environment such that different instances of the emulator can exchange messages. A messaging console utility can also exchange messages with running emulators (see Figure 2.1). Other utilities include settings to determine the emulator's simulated location (to support the Location API), a simulated Bluetooth environment, simulated smart card slots that connect with desktop smart card emulators, and more.

The Sun Java Wireless Toolkit also provides tools to monitor running applications. These include a memory monitor that shows every object and its size, a network monitor that displays all network traffic in or out of the emulator, and a method profiler that shows how much time your application spends in each of its methods.

Figure 2.1   Sun Java Wireless Toolkit emulator

For comprehensive information on the features and capabilities of the Sun Java Wireless Toolkit, read through the *Users Guide* in the documentation.

As of this writing, the current version is 2.5.1. The toolkit is freely available here:

http://java.sun.com/products/sjwtoolkit/

Before installing the toolkit, you will need the Java 2 Platform, Standard Edition Development Kit (JDK), version 1.5.0 or later, and Apple's QuickTime Player. Both are freely available.

2.2 NetBeans Mobility Pack: A Gourmet Kitchen

If you really like the muscle of an integrated development environment (IDE), the NetBeans Mobility Pack delivers a professional and powerful development experience.

NetBeans is an open-source IDE for the Java programming language. The Mobility Pack adds components to NetBeans that are necessary for MIDP development. It incorporates the Sun Java Wireless Toolkit emulator and utilities. Like a gourmet kitchen, NetBeans Mobility Pack allows you to create anything that the toolkit can create, but you get a much wider and more powerful selection of tools, like melon ballers and mini whisks.

You can download NetBeans Mobility Pack here:

http://www.netbeans.org/products/mobility/

One jazzy feature in NetBeans Mobility Pack is a visual editor with which you can create screens and screen flows for your application (see Figure 2.2). In addition, NetBeans offers the usual IDE features, such as a source code editor with lots of bells and whistles, refactoring tools, a debugger, access to version control systems, and much more.

2.3 Eclipse, Too

If you've fallen in love with Eclipse, you can use EclipseME to create MIDlet suites. EclipseME handles some details of connecting device emulators to the Eclipse development environment. It's available here:

http://eclipseme.org/

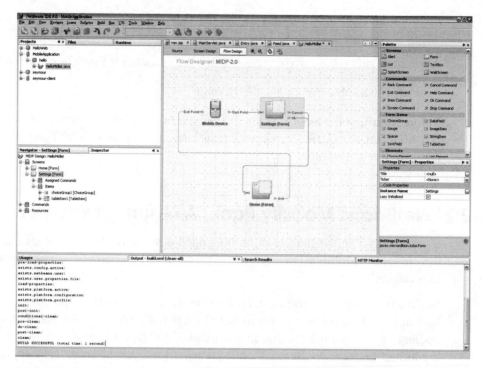

Figure 2.2   Visually editing screen flow in NetBeans Mobility Pack

2.4 Inside a MIDlet Suite

Both the Sun Java Wireless Toolkit and NetBeans Mobility Pack handle the
details of building and packaging MIDlet suites. If you use one of these tools,
you won't generally need to understand how things work under the hood. However, you should at least understand the basic structure of a MIDlet suite, and it's
a good idea to understand how the suite is built.

The MIDlet suite itself is a Java Archive (JAR) file. It contains the classes that
make up the application as well as any supporting resource files, such as images
and sounds (see Figure 2.3). The JAR file manifest contains attributes that fully
describe the MIDlet suite. You can read the MIDP specification to find out the
names and appropriate values for the attributes, but most of the time it's easier to
let your build tool worry about manifest attributes.

A separate file, the MIDlet descriptor (or JAD file), is a small text file that
describes the contents of a MIDlet suite (see Figure 2.4). It contains many of the
same attributes as the MIDlet suite descriptor. The purpose of the descriptor is to

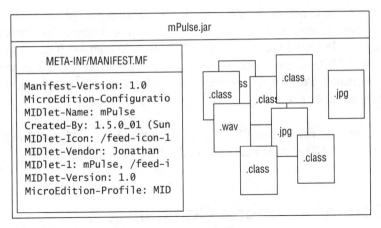

Figure 2.3 Example MIDlet suite JAR file structure

```
MIDlet-1: mPulse, /feed-icon-16x16.png, mPulseMIDlet
MIDlet-Icon: /feed-icon-16x16.png
MIDlet-Jar-Size: 12851
MIDlet-Jar-URL: mPulse.jar
MIDlet-Name: mPulse
MIDlet-Vendor: Jonathan
MIDlet-Version: 1.0
MicroEdition-Configuration: CLDC-1.0
MicroEdition-Profile: MIDP-2.0
```

Figure 2.4 Example MIDlet suite descriptor

allow a device to download and examine the descriptor before making a decision to download the whole MIDlet suite. The descriptor shows the size of the MIDlet suite, its required APIs, and other information that is useful to a device and a user in deciding whether or not to download and install a MIDlet suite.

2.5 Building a MIDlet Suite

Your build tool can create a MIDlet suite JAR file in three steps:

1. Compile the Java programming language source files to produce class files. This is accomplished using the javac compiler. A special flag, -bootclasspath, tells the compiler that the classes will run in a MIDP/ CLDC environment rather than a desktop Java platform.

2. *Preverify* the compiled Java classes. In the desktop Java platform, every class loaded into the virtual machine is verified to confirm it is correctly formed and won't do anything bad, like writing in memory it doesn't own. In a MIDP/CLDC environment, to save space, the bytecode verifier is less sophisticated. Preverifying prepares class files for the less sophisticated bytecode verifier.

3. Package preverified class files and resource files into a JAR file. Include the correct MIDlet suite attributes in the JAR file manifest.

2.6 The Command Line: A Campfire

Developers choose tools based on their experience and personalities. Some developers prefer the gritty power of the command line and a tool like Ant (http://ant.apache.org/). At a command line, you can accomplish the steps described in the previous section as follows:

1. If you have the Sun Java Wireless Toolkit installed in \WTK25, then you can compile a source file called YaYaMIDlet.java as follows. (With a newer version of javac, you might need to specify -target 1.2 to produce the right version of bytecode.)

```
javac -bootclasspath
        \WTK25\lib\cldcapi10.jar;\WTK25\lib\midpapi20.jar
    YaYaMIDlet.java
```

2. With the Sun Java Wireless Toolkit, you can preverify the class file from the last step like this:

```
\WTK25\bin\preverify
    -classpath
        \WTK25\lib\cldcapi10.jar;\WTK25\lib\midpapi20.jar
    -d .
    YaYaMIDlet
```

3. Packaging is done using the jar tool, which is part of the desktop Java platform development kit. You can create a MIDlet suite JAR from the class in the previous example like this, assuming the MIDlet suite attributes are in a plain text file called extra.mf:

```
jar cvmf extra.mf YaYa.jar YaYaMIDlet.class
```

4. Custom Ant tasks for building MIDP applications are freely available, and in fact, NetBeans uses its own set of custom Ant tasks to build applications. Here are two other possibilities:

http://antenna.sourceforge.net/
http://www.j2mepolish.org/

2.7 Preprocessors

One of the challenges of writing MIDlet applications is the wide variety of MIDP devices upon which your application will run. Different screen sizes, capabilities, and implementation bugs mean that it's difficult to make one set of source code that runs flawlessly on all devices.

A common answer to this challenge is to create a variety of application bundles targeted at a variety of devices or device types. You might, for example, build one bundle for Nokia Series 40 devices and another for certain types of Motorola devices.

In many cases, this is simply an issue for bundling your application. You might want to bundle art image files of different sizes depending on the target device screen size, for example. In addition, you can bundle different application properties to communicate device-specific values to your application.

In some cases, however, you might find yourself wanting to write code for specific devices. In this case, you need something like a C preprocessor, something that enables conditional compilation.

One example of this approach is J2ME Polish, created by Robert Virkus.

http://j2mepolish.org/

J2ME Polish provides a preprocessor, a database of device capabilities, and conditional resource bundling. It is based around the open-source build tool Ant.

Another possibility is Dennis Sosnoski's JEnable:

http://www.sosnoski.com/opensrc/jenable/

2.8 Obfuscators

An *obfuscator* optimizes a set of class files. Originally, the purpose of an obfuscator was to make it harder to reconstruct source code from class files *(decompiling)*, but obfuscators are also great at removing unused code and reducing the overall size of a MIDlet suite.

An obfuscator is crucial in applications that use third-party APIs. Without an obfuscator, the classes from the third-party API are bundled with your own application classes. Your MIDlet suite JAR file's size is increased directly by the size of the third-party API.

When you apply an obfuscator to your MIDlet suite JAR file, the obfuscator analyzes the class files, finds out exactly which classes and methods you are using, and discards everything else. In addition, it renames classes, member variables, and methods from human-readable names to much smaller machine-generated names.

Obfuscators have some limitations. In particular, they might throw out classes that are only accessed using `Class.forName()`. However, this usage is unusual in MIDP applications. Also, an obfuscator doesn't play nicely with a debugger. Leave the obfuscator out of the build while you are developing and debugging. Use the obfuscator when you are packaging a finished application.

ProGuard is an excellent obfuscator and is also free:

>   http://proguard.sourceforge.net/

2.9 Emulators

An emulator is a simulated device that runs on a desktop computer. Emulators are extremely helpful because they enable you to write source code, build, and run on one desktop computer.

Once you get your application running smoothly on an emulator, you should test it on a range of emulators. After that, you can start testing on real devices.

Emulators vary widely in their capabilities and accuracy. The Sun Java Wireless Toolkit emulator supports a zillion APIs, but it does not represent any real device. It's excellent for most of your development work.

Device manufacturers offer emulators that mimic the screen sizes, controls, and behavior of real devices. Most emulators can be integrated with the Sun Wireless Java Toolkit and NetBeans Mobility Pack. Table 2.1 presents some starting points.

2.10 Device Testing

Someday you will need to test your application on real devices, on real networks. This is a slow and humbling experience. Although you might have made your application run flawlessly on desktop emulators, real devices have the usual assortment of unexpected behavior.

Table 2.1 Where to Download Emulators

Web Site	URL
MOTODEV	http://developer.motorola.com/
Forum Nokia	http://forum.nokia.com/
BenQMobile	https://market.benqmobile.com/portal/main.aspx?LangID=0&pid=1
Sony Ericsson Developer World	http://developer.sonyericsson.com/
Sprint Application Developer Program	http://developer.sprint.com/

Some devices also allow for on-device debugging, with debugging information carried over a serial cable connected to your development computer. If you expect to target a specific device or a small number of devices, and those devices support it, on-device debugging could be a useful tool in developing your application.

2.11 Summary

MIDP development tools are readily available, and you can't beat the price. These tools know how to assemble MIDlet suites, allowing you to concentrate on writing source code. If you really want to, you can create MIDlet suites using a command line and some kind of automation, usually Ant. Device emulators are available to help in testing your application on a desktop computer. While budgeting your project, don't forget to include time and money for testing on real devices and real networks.

3

Quick Start

To make sure you get off to a flying start, this chapter describes a few simple parts of MIDP so that you can get something running right away. You'll also have a basic scaffolding upon which to build your later knowledge. Don't worry if it doesn't all make sense right away. Everything in this chapter is covered in more detail later in the book.

Fire up your development tool of choice and type as you go along. By the end of this chapter you will have your first running MIDlet.

3.1 Make Something That Runs

Phones and other MIDP devices know how to run MIDlets. A MIDlet is an application. To make your own MIDlet, you need to define a class that extends `javax.microedition.midlet.MIDlet`.

`MIDlet` has three methods that must be defined in subclasses:

- `startApp()` is called to initialize the MIDlet or to resume a paused MIDlet.
- `pauseApp()` is called whenever the system feels it should pause your application, perhaps in response to an incoming phone call.
- `destroyApp()` is called when it's time to clean up your application.

These three methods are *callback* methods because you don't get to call them yourself. The system calls them whenever it feels the urge.

For example, if I want to run a MIDlet on my Motorola RAZR V3, I have to go to a GAME.APP menu, which lists all the MIDlet suites installed on my phone. I choose the MIDlet suite I want to run, and if there is only one MIDlet in it, my V3 will create a new instance of the MIDlet class and call its startApp() method. If someone calls me while I'm running the application, my V3 will invoke the MIDlet's pauseApp() method so I can answer the telephone call. After my conversation is over, my V3 calls startApp() again to resume the application. When I choose to exit the application, my V3 calls the MIDlet's destroyApp() method.

On other devices (including emulators), the process for launching an application is likely to be different, but the basic life cycle of a MIDlet is the same.

Your first step is to create a new project in your build tool. In the Sun Java Wireless Toolkit, first launch KToolbar, then click on **New Project....** Fill in KickButt for the project name and KickButtMIDlet for the class name. Click **OK** on the next screen. Then create a source code file, {toolkit}\apps\KickButt\src\ KickButtMIDlet.java.

The next step is to write a MIDlet. Here is a simple one to get you started:

```
import javax.microedition.midlet.MIDlet;

public class KickButtMIDlet extends MIDlet {
    public void startApp() {}
    public void pauseApp() {}
    public void destroyApp(boolean unconditional) {}
}
```

You can compile and run it if you wish, but you cannot see anything happening. It is an exceptionally boring MIDlet. I suggest you wait until the next section when you'll get to see something on the screen.

Don't worry about that boolean argument in the destroyApp() method. You can read all about it when you get to Chapter 5, "The MIDlet Habitat."

3.2 Put Something on the Screen

MIDP includes a few ready-made screen classes in the javax.microedition. lcdui package. The one you'll use first is Form. To create one, specify a title.

To put the TextBox on the screen, use the Display class, which represents the screen of the device. Here is how it works, with the new stuff shown in bold:

```
import javax.microedition.lcdui.*;
import javax.microedition.midlet.MIDlet;

public class KickButtMIDlet extends MIDlet {
  public void startApp() {
    Form f = new Form("Kick Butt with MIDP!");
    Display.getDisplay(this).setCurrent(f);
  }

  public void pauseApp() {}
  public void destroyApp(boolean unconditional) {}
}
```

This one is worth building and running. It doesn't do much, but at least you get to see something on the screen. It should look like Figure 3.1.

3.3 Give the User Something to Do

The next step is to let your user make something happen. To this end, MIDP uses a clever mechanism called a *command*. You create a command by specifying the label you want to appear on the screen. The device or emulator gets to figure out

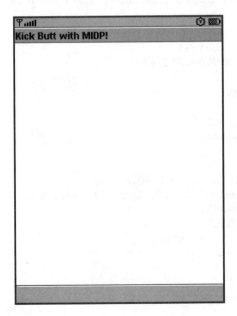

Figure 3.1 Your very first MIDlet

how to show it on the screen and how the user can invoke the command. Your application just has to respond to it.

This mechanism works well because MIDP devices are likely to have different ways for users to make things happen. Many mobile phones have soft buttons, unlabeled buttons that perform different actions depending on what is shown on the screen. Another device might have a click wheel or some more exotic type of input. Using commands ensures that your application can run correctly on a variety of devices.

Commands are fully explained in Chapter 7, "Basic User Interface."

To respond to a command, you must provide a CommandListener. The listener has a single method, commandAction(), which is called whenever a command is invoked.

In the KickButt example, the MIDlet itself will be a CommandListener. The Command is created and added to the TextBox inside the startApp() method. The call to setCommandListener() tells the system that the MIDlet (this) should be told about any command action that happens on the TextBox.

In commandAction(), the MIDlet checks to see if the command in question is the exit command it created earlier. It should be, because there are no other commands in the application. If so, the application is shut down. Later you'll use this same kind of logic with more commands.

```java
import javax.microedition.lcdui.*;
import javax.microedition.midlet.MIDlet;

public class KickButtMIDlet
    extends MIDlet
    implements CommandListener {
    private Command mExitCommand;

    public void startApp() {
        Form f = new Form("Kick Butt with MIDP!");
        mExitCommand = new Command("Exit", Command.EXIT, 0);
        f.addCommand(mExitCommand);
        f.setCommandListener(this);
        Display.getDisplay(this).setCurrent(f);
    }

    public void pauseApp() {}
    public void destroyApp(boolean unconditional) {}
```

```
public void commandAction(Command c, Displayable d) {
  if (c == mExitCommand) {
    destroyApp(true);
    notifyDestroyed();
  }
}
}
```

Try this one on for size (Figure 3.2). In the Sun Java Wireless Toolkit emulator, commands are mapped to soft buttons. Press the soft button below the **Exit** text on the screen to shut down the application.

3.4 Get the Source Code Online

The source code for this book is online. I'm not going to tell you to type all the example code in yourself, but I do encourage you to read it carefully. It's just as important to your understanding as reading along in the text.

The source code for this book is online at the book's Web site:

http://kickbutt.jonathanknudsen.com/download.html

Figure 3.2   Now with a command

3.5 Summary

In this chapter, you built your first MIDlet. You got acquainted with whatever development environment you're using, and you wrote an application that shows text on the screen and lets the user exit the application. Supported by these little wings, you can now fly into a sky full of the MSA APIs, starting with the basics and progressing through user interface, graphics, storage, networking, multimedia, and others.

At this point, you can pick and choose which topics you wish to read, although reading the rest of the book in order will give you an excellent grasp of the full MSA platform. If you're going to skip some chapters, I suggest that at a minimum you read about MIDlets, the basic user interface classes, record stores, and basic networking. After that, the sky is the limit.

4

Core APIs

THIS is the least exciting chapter of this book, but you should read it anyhow. Remember that great achievements are made up of many smaller achievements. To raise a child, you must learn how to change dirty diapers. To build a Great Pyramid, you must move a lot of rocks.

To kick butt with your MIDP applications, you have to understand the core APIs, which are similar but *not the same* as the corresponding APIs in the desktop Java platform.

- Fundamental classes in `java.lang` define strings, primitive type wrappers, and important classes like `Object` and `Thread`.
- The stream classes in `java.io` allow you to send and receive information. Stream classes are used mainly for networking and file access.
- The utilities in `java.util` include basic collections, classes for handling dates and times, and a random number generator.

Don't assume that you know all this stuff, even if you're experienced with Java technology on the desktop or in a server environment. The constraints of small devices dictate that *these* APIs are more compact and less rich than their desktop counterparts.

 Note: For all you geezers that can remember JDK 1.0 (circa 1996), the core APIs for MIDP/CLDC are very similar to the corresponding JDK 1.0 APIs. Nevertheless, they are not identical. Read on to find out exactly what you can and cannot do with the core APIs.

Note: MIDP, CLDC, and other mobile device Java technologies are grouped together as the Java Platform, Micro Edition (Java ME). Desktop Java technology is the Java Platform, Standard Edition (Java SE).

4.1   JVM Features You Might Miss

MIDP is based on Connected, Limited Device Configuration (CLDC), which is both a virtual machine specification and a set of core APIs. The virtual machine used in CLDC devices is more compact and has fewer features than its desktop cousin.

For reasons that are shrouded in the mists of legend, the CLDC virtual machine is known as the K Virtual Machine, or KVM. Some say the K refers to the kilobyte scale of CLDC devices, while others contend that K is short for Kaui, a project code name from the early days of MIDP.

Regardless of naming, KVM is missing some features compared to the Java SE platform:

- *No native methods.* The Java SE platform provides a way for Java applications to invoke native code. CLDC does not include any such mechanism.
- *No object finalizers.* When an object is harvested by the garbage collector in the Java SE platform, its `finalize()` method is called. In CLDC, `Object` has no `finalize()` method.
- *No reflection.* The Java SE platform allows applications to examine classes and invoke methods dynamically. CLDC does not include this feature.
- *No classloaders.* This is more of a relief than a hindrance. The CLDC implementation has a classloader, of course, but it's not accessible to applications. You cannot define other classloaders in your application.
- *Partial bytecode verifier.* As discussed in Chapter 2, class files are preverified at build time. A second stage of verification is run when classes are loaded on the device.

4.2   Strings, Primitive Types, and System Methods

`java.lang.String` represents character strings, just as in the Java SE platform. The MIDP/CLDC `String` does not have all the bells and whistles that are in the Java SE platform, but in other respects it behaves just as you would expect. For example, the MIDP/CLDC `String` does not have methods relating to `Locales`, `CharSequences`, or regular expressions.

Memory is often scarce in a MIDP/CLDC device, so you should be careful about string handling in your application. The MSA specification requires a 1MB heap, which is generous, but it's not the same unlimited feeling you get on the desktop. That heap memory might be shared with other running applications. Furthermore, if you rapidly create and discard many objects, the garbage collector might affect the performance of your application.

Although it's convenient to assemble strings using the + operator, it is not the most efficient method. Consider using a `StringBuffer` instead, which creates a new `String` object only when you call `toString()`.

MSA incorporates CLDC 1.1, which has all the same primitive types you'll find in Java SE. If you want to write applications on older CLDC 1.0 devices, you'll have to do without `float` and `double`. That's all I'm going to say on that subject, because this book is about MSA.

Just as in the Java SE platform, class wrappers for primitive types are present in the `java.lang` package. For example, `java.lang.Long` is a wrapper class for the primitive type `long`.

Finally, `java.lang.System` and `java.lang.Runtime` include methods that apply to the whole system. You can find out the total heap size, the free heap memory, and the current time. You can run the garbage collector manually. The method you are more likely to use is `System.getProperty()`, which retrieves the value of a system property.

4.3 Threads

In most respects, threads work just as they do in the Java SE platform. To do some work in another thread, create a `Thread` object and call `start()`. Your old friend `Runnable` is still around too. Not surprisingly, the `java.util.concurrent` package is not available.

Like memory, however, processing power can be scarce on a MIDP/CLDC device. Threads, in particular, can be a scarce commodity. The MSA specification requires that an application must be allowed to create ten threads. Just because you *can* doesn't mean you *should*. In general, try to use the fewest resources possible so that your application will run as smoothly as possible.

Many of the methods you will write in your applications are callbacks, which means that the thread is owned by the system, not your application. For example, when the device calls your MIDlet's `startApp()` method, the thread that executes `startApp()` is a system thread. The rule about system threads and callback methods is to be clean and brief. It's a lot like using a toaster in a cafeteria. You shouldn't melt cheese into the heating elements, and you shouldn't take all day because other people want to toast their bagels too.

If you must perform lengthy processing in response to a user action, put it in a separate application thread. Network connections definitely fall into this category, but plenty of other operations are slow enough to merit their own threads. Mobile devices are much less powerful than desktop computers, so even operations that seem to run quickly on a desktop emulator might be relatively slow on a real device.

4.4 Using Streams for Input and Output

In MIDP/CLDC, streams are defined in `java.io`, just as in the Java SE platform. To save space, the palette of streams in MIDP/CLDC is reduced to essentials. In particular, MIDP/CLDC does not contain more elaborate or exotic streams like `PushbackReader`, `PipedWriter`, and `LineNumberOutputStream`.

Despite the abbreviated `java.io` package, streams are fundamental to any type of input or output in MIDP/CLDC applications. Streams are used for reading and writing data over HTTP, IP, Bluetooth, and other types of network connections. Streams are used to exchange data with local file systems when they are available. Streams are crucial to the Generic Connection Framework, which is fully described in Chapter 18.

When working with `InputStream` or any of its subclasses, be wary of the `available()` method. Many programmers assume that it returns the number of bytes remaining in a file or network transmission, but in truth it returns the number of bytes that can be read without blocking. Most of the time, you have no use for this number.

Another common error with `InputStream` is assuming that the `read()` method will fully populate an array that is passed to it as long as there is enough data left in the stream. In reality, the implementation can read as much or as little data as it pleases. Always check the return value of `read()` to see how many bytes were actually pulled from the stream.

4.4.1 Be Clean

A final word of caution is to make sure you clean up after yourself. Like memory and threads, streams can also be a scarce resource on mobile devices, especially if they are related to network connections. Whatever streams you've opened, make sure you close them. Use `finally` to make sure streams get closed. This isn't good enough:

```
try {
  InputStream in = openNetworkStream();
  // Read data from in.
  in.close();
}
catch (IOException ioe) {
  // Handle exception here.
  // The stream doesn't get closed!
}
```

If any kind of exception is thrown while you are reading data, `in` will never be closed because your application will jump into the exception handler. A more robust solution follows. It's more trouble, but it'll work better and save you some heartburn.

```
try {
  InputStream in = openNetworkStream();
  try {
    // Read data from in.
  }
  finally {
    in.close();
  }
} catch (IOException ioe) {
  // Handle exception here.
}
```

You can make it a little less messy by bumping exception handling up to the containing method.

4.4.2 Reading Input Data Completely

One common problem in MIDP/CLDC applications is reading all the data from a stream when you don't know how much there will be. This often happens when you are retrieving data from a network connection.

A simple approach would be to allocate a big array and read directly into it. However, because memory is scarce, it makes more sense to allocate smaller chunks of memory as necessary.

Here is a method that reads all available data from an `InputStream` and returns the result as a properly sized byte array:

```
public byte[] readAll(InputStream in) throws IOException {
  ByteArrayOutputStream out = new ByteArrayOutputStream();
  byte[] buffer = new byte[1024];
  for (int n; (n = in.read(buffer)) > 0; )
    out.write(buffer, 0, n);
  return out.toByteArray();
}
```

4.5 Dates, Collections, and Random Numbers

As in the Java SE platform, `java.util` contains an assortment of useful utility classes. However, the toolbox is a lot smaller in MIDP/CLDC.

Dates are represented by `java.util.Date`, which is really just a thin wrapper for a `long` value representing the number of milliseconds since January 1, 1970. The `long` value is a standard way of representing instants in time and is exactly the same as in the Java SE platform.

A `long` or `Date` identifies a moment in time in a way that makes sense to a machine, but humans understand calendars and times specific to a time zone. The `Calendar` and `TimeZone` classes make it possible to convert between `Dates` and calendar fields that make sense to humans. In general, these classes are very similar to the Java SE platform, but a lot of the extra API weight (and convenience) has been shed in the interests of compactness.

Before you get too embroiled in `Calendar`, think about the needs of your application. If you just want to show a representation of a `Date` on the screen, or allow a user to enter a `Date` somehow, read about the `DateField` class in Chapter 8, "More User Interface." It might be just what you need.

The `java.util` package also contains rudimentary collections, although they are a pale shadow of the Collections API that is part of the Java SE platform. MIDP/CLDC includes `Vector` and `Stack` for keeping lists of objects and `HashTable` for mapping keys to objects. The `Enumeration` interface completes the party as a way to iterate through lists.

None of the collections are multithread safe. If you plan on accessing a collection from more than one thread, you must take steps to avoid trouble.

Finally, `java.util.Random` is a simple pseudorandom number generator. Create a `Random` and call one of its `next` methods to retrieve a pseudorandom number.

4.6 Summary

In this chapter, you learned about the core APIs of MIDP/CLDC. Classes in `java.lang`, `java.io`, and `java.util` provide stream handling, object collections, and other important functionality. These APIs are similar to the Java SE platform, but they are reduced in size and complexity to fit neatly on small devices.

Section II

The Lives of MIDlets

5

The MIDlet
Habitat

YOU know a little bit about MIDlets already. In this chapter, you'll learn the details of how MIDlets live and die and how devices prevent bad MIDlets from performing evil deeds.

5.1 The MIDlet Life Cycle

The entire life of a MIDlet is controlled by application management software (AMS), a nebulous term that refers to whatever it is on the device that takes care of MIDlets.

When the user asks to run a MIDlet, it is the AMS that creates an instance of the MIDlet and calls its startApp() method. When it's time for the application to exit, the AMS takes care of cleaning up. The AMS handles installing and removing MIDlet suites as well as advanced functions like the push registry and content handling, both of which are described in Chapter 6, "Starting MIDlets Automatically."

5.1.1 AMS, the MIDlet Puppeteer

MIDlets have three states: *active*, *paused*, and *destroyed*. Figure 5.1 illustrates how the AMS moves a MIDlet between states.

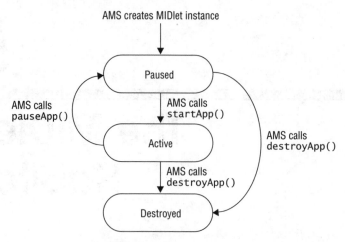

Figure 5.1   The MIDlet life cycle

The AMS can pause or destroy a MIDlet at any time, for any reason, so you should be scrupulous about cleaning up:

- When your MIDlet is paused, shut down any media players and network connections. Release as much memory and as many threads as possible.
- When your MIDlet is destroyed, shut down everything. Close network connections, shut down threads and timers, and close media players.

Also note that startApp() can be called multiple times over the lifetime of the MIDlet. Make sure you are not performing the same initialization code over and over. For example, consider the MIDlet from Chapter 3, "Quick Start." If the MIDlet is paused and restarted, the TextBox and Command will be re-created. A more correct implementation looks like this:

```
import javax.microedition.lcdui.*;
import javax.microedition.midlet.MIDlet;

public class KickButtMIDlet
    extends MIDlet
    implements CommandListener {
  private Form mForm;
  private Command mExitCommand;

  public void startApp() {
    if (mForm == null) {
      mForm = new Form("Kick Butt with MIDP!");
      mExitCommand = new Command("Exit", Command.EXIT, 0);
```

```
        mForm.addCommand(mExitCommand);
        mForm.setCommandListener(this);
      }
      Display.getDisplay(this).setCurrent(mForm);
    }

    public void pauseApp() {}
    public void destroyApp(boolean unconditional) {}

    public void commandAction(Command c, Displayable d) {
      if (c == mExitCommand) {
        destroyApp(true);
        notifyDestroyed();
      }
    }
  }
}
```

5.1.2 What about That `unconditional` Argument?

When the AMS calls `destroyApp()`, it passes a `boolean` argument. If this argument is `true`, it means the MIDlet is going to be shut down, period. If the argument is `false`, the MIDlet has a chance at rescucitation. In that case, if the MIDlet throws a `MIDletStateChangeException`, then the MIDlet should stay in its current state, either active or paused.

5.1.3 MIDlets Can Control Their Destinies

A MIDlet can move itself between states:

- An active MIDlet that wishes to enter the paused state can call `notifyPaused()`. In this case, the AMS does not call `pauseApp()`, so you should perform whatever cleaning up is necessary before calling `notifyPaused()`. In most cases, simply call `pauseApp()` before calling `notifyPaused()`.

- An active or paused MIDlet can send itself into the destroyed state by calling `notifyDestroyed()`. The AMS will *not* call `destroyApp()`, so you need to clean up first. In the previous example, when the MIDlet exits, it calls `destroyApp(true)` first, for cleanup, then `notifyDestroyed()`, to let the AMS know that the MIDlet is now in the destroyed state.

- A paused MIDlet can attempt to wake itself up by calling `resumeRequest()`.

How can a paused MIDlet do anything? It's possible that a paused MIDlet can still have running threads, which could call `resumeRequest()` or `notifyDestroyed()`. However, the concept of a paused MIDlet varies from platform to platform. The emulator in the Sun Java Wireless Toolkit leaves threads running while a MIDlet is paused. My Motorola V3 does not.

If your goal is to run your MIDlet at a specific time, use `registerAlarm()` in `PushRegistry`, which is described in Chapter 6.

5.2 Using the Browser and Making Calls

Many modern mobile phones have a browser. You can ask the device to show a page in the browser using `MIDlet`'s `platformRequest()` method. Just pass in the URL of the page.

You can also pass the URL of a MIDlet suite descriptor, in which case the device should attempt to install the MIDlet suite. You can even pass the URL of an updated version of the running MIDlet suite. In this case, the running MIDlet suite will be shut down before the new version is installed.

A `tel:` string passed to `platformRequest()` asks the device to make a voice call. This string should conform to RFC 3966 (available at http://www.ietf.org/rfc/rfc3966.txt). For example, `platformRequest("tel:+18008247777")` requests that the device call the telephone number (800) 824-7777 in the United States.

The device will ask the user for permission to open the browser, install a MIDlet suite, or make a voice call.

`platformRequest()` will do its best to honor the request. Devices with limited resources can choose to shut down the current MIDlet before launching the browser, installing a MIDlet suite, or making a voice call. If this is the case, `platformRequest()` will return `true`. Otherwise it returns `false`. Note that the return value of `platformRequest()` does not indicate whether the device was successful in honoring the call to `platformRequest()`.

5.3 Application Properties

Back in Chapter 2, "Tools," you learned about the structure of a MIDlet suite and the MIDlet suite descriptor. The manifest of the MIDlet suite JAR file and the MIDlet suite descriptor both contain attributes that describe the MIDlet suite itself.

In addition to these attributes, you are free to define your own attributes, which are *application properties*. Defining your own attributes is extremely useful, because it allows you to define important information in the MIDlet descriptor without hard-coding it into your application. For example, in a MIDlet that retrieves an image from the network, you could define an application property that holds the URL of the image. If the location of the image changes, you can change the attribute in the descriptor without changing anything in your code. No rebuilding is necessary.

Inside a MIDlet, use the `getAppProperty()` method to retrieve the value of an application property. Just supply the name of the property and the method will return its value.

Your development tool provides a way to edit application properties, which will be automatically built into the MIDlet suite descriptor and the manifest of the MIDlet suite JAR file. In the Sun Java Wireless Toolkit, for example, click on the **Settings...** button in KToolbar, then select the **User Defined** item. Add new application properties. In NetBeans Mobility Pack, right-click on your project, then choose **Properties**. In the properties window, choose the **Attributes** item in the left list. Click on **Add** to create application properties.

5.4 Protection Domains and Signed MIDlet Suites

MIDP applications have a security model that is designed to prevent bad MIDlets from spending users' money or stealing their information. The basis of this model is *protection domains*. A protection domain determines what operations are permitted in a MIDlet. Every MIDlet suite that is installed on a device goes into some protection domain.

A protection domain has rules that determine what happens when a MIDlet tries to perform a *sensitive* operation, like connecting to the network (which could cost money) or reading a file (which could be a privacy concern). Whenever a MIDlet attempts a sensitive operation, the device consults the protection domain to see if the operation is allowed, denied, or if the user will be prompted for permission.

Unfortunately, restricted APIs can vary between implementations. For example, capturing an image is restricted on some devices but not on others. Playing audio or video is restricted on some handsets but not others.

MIDlet suites are assigned to protection domains at installation time. If a MIDlet suite is cryptographically signed, it will be placed in a protection domain that corresponds to the root of the signer's keys. Unsigned MIDlet suites are placed in a different protection domain. In general, signed MIDlet suites are considered more trustworthy because their source can be determined.

The definition of protection domains is flexible in the MIDP and MSA specifications, which leaves device manufacturers and wireless carriers some latitude in implementing the security model. In general, you might expect to find a few protection domains on a device:

- The *unidentified third-party* or *untrusted* domain holds all unsigned MIDlet suites. It may deny permissions or prompt the user for every attempted sensitive operation.

- A *manufacturer* or *operator* domain contains MIDlet suites that have been signed using keys derived from the manufacturer or operator. Usually, this means that the manufacturer or operator will submit the application to some kind of testing or certification before agreeing to cryptographically sign the MIDlet suite. Because of the testing or certification, this protection domain is likely to allow MIDlets the most freedom in performing sensitive operations.

- The *identified third-party* domain contains MIDlet suites that are cryptographically signed with keys obtained from well-known certificate authorities, like VeriSign or Thawte. In general, MIDlet suites in this protection domain have less freedom than MIDlet suites in the manufacturer or operator domain, because no testing or certification has occurred. However, this mechanism does allow devices to run third-party software with some amount of confidence and fewer user prompts than would be encountered in the unidentified third-party domain.

There really isn't any magic about a signed MIDlet suite. The signature and its associated certificate chain are added as attributes to the MIDlet suite descriptor and the manifest of the MIDlet suite JAR file.

You can use your MIDlet development tool to cryptographically sign a MIDlet suite, using either test keys created on your desktop or real keys obtained from a certificate authority.

In the Sun Java Wireless Toolkit, choose **Project > Sign** from the menu to get started. Consult the *Users Guide* for full details. In NetBeans Mobility Pack, right-click on your project and choose **Properties**. Then select the **Signing** item from the left list. Again, consult the documentation for full details.

5.5 Permissions

Now that you understand the broad outlines of the MIDlet security model, this section describes how the rubber meets the road.

Every sensitive operation has a corresponding named permission. For example, the permission to make an HTTP network connection is called `javax.micro-edition.io.Connector.http`. A protection domain is a list of permissions, some of which are allowed and some of which might be allowed if the user says so. Any permission that is not listed in the protection domain is denied.

When a MIDlet attempts a sensitive operation, the device consults the containing protection domain to figure out what to do. If the corresponding permission is not in the protection domain, the operation will not be performed and a `SecurityException` is thrown in the MIDlet. If the permission requires the user's approval, the device takes care of showing an appropriate prompt to ask for permission. Depending on the user's answer, the operation will proceed or a `SecurityException` will be thrown. If the permission is granted outright in the protection domain, the operation proceeds directly.

In your own code, then, you should expect sensitive operations to throw `SecurityExceptions` and try to handle them gracefully.

Suppose your application must use a sensitive operation to function. It is a waste of time to install such an application into a protection domain that denies the sensitive operation. Fortunately, the solution to this problem is simple: attributes in the MIDlet suite descriptor can show which permissions are required by a MIDlet suite and which ones would be nice to have.

In the Sun Java Wireless Toolkit, you can specify required and nice-to-have permissions by clicking on **Settings...**, then choosing **Permissions** from the left list. The **MIDlet-Permissions** box is a list of all permissions your MIDlet suite requires, while **MIDlet-Permissions-Opt** is the permissions that your MIDlet suite would like to have but doesn't need.

In NetBeans Mobility Pack, right-click on your project and choose **Properties**. Then select **API Permissions** from the left list. Add whatever permissions you wish and use the checkboxes to determine whether they are required or nice-to-have.

When your MIDlet suite is packaged, the permissions you've chosen are written into the descriptor. At installation time, a device can examine these permissions and compare them with the permissions in the protection domain where it will put the MIDlet suite. If the MIDlet suite requires permissions that are not present in the protection domain, the device can stop the installation or give the user the chance to stop the installation.

You can explicitly check for a permission in your MIDlet by using `check-Permission()` in the `MIDlet` class. Pass in the name of a permission, and you'll get back 0 if the permission is denied, 1 if the permission is allowed, and −1 if the device can't figure out the answer, most likely because the user will be prompted to allow or deny the permission.

5.6 The Bottom Line on MIDlet Signing

Signing MIDlets is a tricky and time-consuming business. Like device testing, signing will only succeed if you devote time and energy to it. Some money is also involved, as you will need to buy one or more code-signing certificates in order to get the job done.

Given the cost of code signing, your first consideration should be whether you need to sign your application at all. The whole purpose of signing is to enable your application to use sensitive APIs. Often, your immediate need is to eliminate user-facing security prompts so that your application is easier and smoother to use.

In some cases, it is easier to write your application a bit differently to avoid signing. For example, if you have modest needs for persistent storage, use the record store API (Chapter 14, "Storage and Resources") instead of the FileConnection API (Chapter 15, "Reading and Writing Files"). The record store API needs no special security clearance, while the FileConnection API will catapult you into the world of signing.

If your application depends on a feature that requires signing, make sure you get started early in your product cycle. The behavior of a MIDlet changes when it is signed, often in subtle ways. It's important that your development and testing efforts work with the signed application so you can accurately observe its behavior.

Determining what kind of certificate you need is also a challenge. The kind you need depends on where you expect to deploy your application—specifically, which root certificates are installed on a device and how they are mapped to protection domains. This is highly variable between devices from different manufacturers on different networks. You might need to get a signing certificate from a manufacturer or a carrier. Sometimes a general-purpose certificate from a certificate authority like Verisign or Thawte is sufficient. Your first source for this kind of information should be the community of MIDP developers who are facing the same kinds of problems. Here is one useful discussion about finding appropriate signing certificates:

http://archives.java.sun.com/cgi-bin/wa?A2=ind0601&L= kvm-interest&F=&S=&P=7105

5.7 Summary

This chapter described the life of a MIDlet. A MIDlet has a distinct life cycle consisting of paused, active, and destroyed states. The life cycle is controlled by the device, although MIDlets themselves can also move from one state to another. The `platformRequest()` method allows MIDlets to show a page in the device's browser, install a MIDlet suite, or make a voice call. MIDlets can retrieve application properties defined in the MIDlet suite descriptor. MIDlet suites live in a protection domain that determines whether sensitive operations can be performed. Each sensitive operation has a corresponding permission. MIDlet suites can specify which permissions they require and which they would like to have with MIDlet suite descriptor attributes.

Starting MIDlets Automatically

ONE way a MIDlet comes to life is when a person chooses to run it. In this chapter, you'll find out other ways that a MIDlet can be launched.

- Incoming network connections can start a MIDlet. For example, a Short Message Service (SMS) message arriving on a certain port or an incoming socket connection could launch a MIDlet.

- MIDlets can request to be started at a specific time.

- MIDlets can respond to specific types of content. For example, an audio player MIDlet can be set to handle one or more audio file types. Other applications can ask the device to launch a MIDlet to handle a certain type of content.

6.1 Responding to Network Connections

MIDP defines a *push registry* so that incoming network connections can launch specific MIDlets. The push registry simply maps network connection strings to MIDlet class names. When a network connection comes to the device, a matching entry in the push registry will cause the corresponding MIDlet to be launched.

Three pieces of information are needed to register a MIDlet in the push registry:

- A *connection string* represents an incoming network connection. You'll learn all about connection strings in Chapter 18, but you'll see some examples in this chapter. A connection string that represents incoming SMS messages on port 50,000 is `sms://:50000`.
- A class name describes the MIDlet that should be launched to handle the network connection.
- The last item is a string representing allowed senders. You can use wildcards in this string, so if you are interested in all incoming network connections from any address, use `*`.

There are two ways to create an entry in the push registry. *Dynamic* registration occurs while the MIDlet is running. *Static* registration occurs when the MIDlet suite is installed.

6.1.1 Dynamic Registration

The push registry is represented by a single class, `javax.microedition.io.PushRegistry`, which has only static methods. To add an entry, just call `registerConnection()`. For instance, here is how to register `PushyMIDlet` to respond to incoming SMS network connections on port 50,000 from any sender:

```
PushRegistry.registerConnection(
    "sms://:50000", "PushyMIDlet", "*");
```

This is powerful stuff. If this method succeeds, any incoming SMS message on port 50,000 will cause `PushyMIDlet` to be launched.

To clear an existing push registry entry, just supply the connection string to `unregisterConnection()`. The previous connection could be cleared like this:

```
PushRegistry.unregisterConnection("sms://:50000");
```

6.1.2 Static Registration

Information about push registry entries can be embedded in the MIDlet suite's descriptor. Your build tool will handle the details.

In the Sun Java Wireless Toolkit, click on **Settings...**, then choose **Push Registry** from the list on the left. Click **Add** to create a new entry. Enter a connection string, a MIDlet class name, and the allowed senders, and press **OK** to add the entry. You can examine the descriptor with a text editor to see the information that was added.

In NetBeans Mobility Pack, right-click on your project and choose **Properties**. Click on **Push Registry** in the left column and push **Add...**. Choose a MIDlet class name, specify the allowed senders, fill in the connection string, and press **OK** to add the entry.

When your MIDlet suite is about to be installed, the device finds the push registry entry in the descriptor. It can check to see if the specified connection is available. If it is available, the push registry will be updated as the MIDlet suite is installed.

Static entries in the push registry are automatically cleared when the MIDlet suite is removed from the device.

6.1.3 Finding Incoming Connections

To find out what incoming connections are mapped to your MIDlet suite, call PushRegistry's listConnections() method. Pass false to listConnections() to get a list of every connection. Pass true to get a list of connections that have input available.

The connection strings returned by listConnections() tell only part of the story. They are the registered incoming connections for the entire MIDlet suite. If you want to find out the specific MIDlet class name and allowed senders, pass the connection string to getMIDlet() and getFilter() respectively.

6.1.4 A Push Registry Example

PushyMIDlet shows how to register and unregister with the push registry. It also retrieves the currently registered connections and any connections with waiting data:

```
import javax.microedition.io.*;
import javax.microedition.lcdui.*;
import javax.microedition.midlet.MIDlet;

import javax.wireless.messaging.*;

public class PushyMIDlet
    extends MIDlet
    implements CommandListener {
  protected static final String kConnection = "sms://:50000";

  private Display mDisplay;

  private Form mForm;
  private Command mExitCommand;
```

continued

```
    private Command mRegisterCommand, mUnregisterCommand;

public void startApp() {
  if (mForm == null) {
    mForm = new Form("PushyMIDlet");
    mExitCommand = new Command("Exit", Command.EXIT, 0);
    mRegisterCommand = new Command("Register",
        Command.SCREEN, 0);
    mUnregisterCommand = new Command("Unregister",
        Command.SCREEN, 0);
    mForm.addCommand(mExitCommand);
    mForm.addCommand(mRegisterCommand);
    mForm.addCommand(mUnregisterCommand);

    mForm.setCommandListener(this);

    mDisplay = Display.getDisplay(this);
  }
  mDisplay.setCurrent(mForm);

  try {
    String[] connections;
    connections = PushRegistry.listConnections(false);
    if (connections.length > 0) {
      mForm.append("Registered connections:");
      for (int i = 0; i < connections.length; i++)
        mForm.append(connections[i]);
    }

    connections = PushRegistry.listConnections(true);
    if (connections.length > 0) {
      // We know there should be only one.
      mForm.append("Connections waiting:");
      for (int i = 0; i < connections.length; i++)
        mForm.append("  " + connections[i]);
    }

  }
  catch (Exception e) {
    mForm.append(e.toString());
  }
}

public void pauseApp() {}
public void destroyApp(boolean unconditional) {}

public void commandAction(Command c, Displayable d) {
  if (c == mExitCommand) {
    destroyApp(true);
    notifyDestroyed();
```

```
      }
    else if (c == mRegisterCommand) {
      RegisterRunnable rr = new RegisterRunnable(mForm);
      Thread t = new Thread(rr);
      t.start();
    }
    else if (c == mUnregisterCommand) {
      UnregisterRunnable ur = new UnregisterRunnable(mForm);
      Thread t = new Thread(ur);
      t.start();
    }
  }
}

class RegisterRunnable implements Runnable {
  private Form mForm;

  public RegisterRunnable(Form f) { mForm = f; }

  public void run() {
    try {
      PushRegistry.registerConnection(
          PushyMIDlet.kConnection, "PushyMIDlet", "*");
      mForm.append("Registered!");
    }
    catch (Exception e) {
      mForm.append(e.toString());
    }
  }
}

class UnregisterRunnable implements Runnable {
  private Form mForm;

  public UnregisterRunnable(Form f) { mForm = f; }

  public void run() {
    try {
      PushRegistry.unregisterConnection(
          PushyMIDlet.kConnection);
      mForm.append("Unregistered!");
    }
    catch (Exception e) {
      mForm.append(e.toString());
    }
  }
}
```

To fully appreciate this example on an emulator, you need to simulate installing the MIDlet suite over the air (OTA), just as you would on a real device. The whole point of the example is to show how an incoming network connection can start a MIDlet that isn't already running. In the Sun Java Wireless Toolkit, choose **Project > Run via OTA** from the KToolbar menu. Follow the prompts to install and run the MIDlet suite. Check the *Users Guide* if you are not sure what to do. NetBeans Mobility Pack uses the same emulator, so the installation and running will be similar. To activate OTA mode, right-click on your project, choose **Properties**, click on **Running** in the left pane, and choose **Execute through OTA**.

Run PushyMIDlet and choose **Register** to get set up in the push registry (see Figure 6.1).

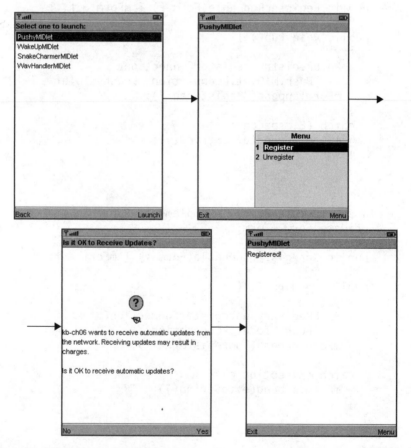

Figure 6.1   Running PushyMIDlet

Now exit `PushyMIDlet`, which returns the emulator to its list of installed applications. A real device will return to its idle screen. To test the push registry, you must send an SMS message on port 50,000 to the device or emulator.

In the Sun Java Wireless Toolkit, you can use the WMA Console to simulate sending a message to the running emulator (Figure 6.2).

If you download the source code for the book, the `kb-ch06` suite also includes `SendMIDlet`, which prompts you for a destination number and a message and sends the message on port 50,000.

When the emulator receives the incoming SMS, it asks for permission to run `PushyMIDlet`. If you grant permission, you'll see a message about a waiting network connection (Figure 6.3).

Now that you understand how to run the example, take some time to understand the source code.

The first part of the constructor takes care of setting up the main form, which includes commands for registering, unregistering, and exiting. The second part of the constructor calls `PushRegistry.listConnections()` twice. The first time is to retrieve all registered connections. The second time is to retrieve connections that have waiting data. When you send a message to an idle emulator or device, `PushyMIDlet` should wake up and realize that data is waiting at `sms://:50000`.

Other than that, it's a mostly straightforward example. When you choose the **Register** or **Unregister** commands, the actual calls are put in their own threads,

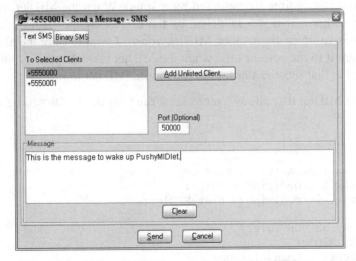

Figure 6.2 Using the WMA console to send an SMS message

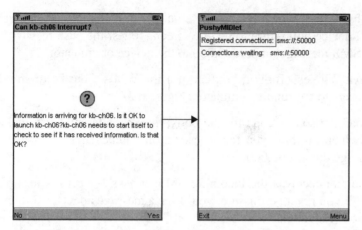

Figure 6.3   PushyMIDlet awakens!

using `RegisterRunnable` and `UnregisterRunnable` respectively. As I mentioned, it's a good idea to isolate networking or push registry code in an application thread rather than using the system thread that calls `commandAction()`. The Sun Java Wireless Toolkit emulator will get stalled if push registry work is performed in a system thread.

6.2   Running a MIDlet at a Specific Time

Use `registerAlarm()` in `PushRegistry` to request that a MIDlet be run at a specific time. Just pass a time (represented by a `long`). When the MIDlet runs, there is no way to know if it was launched by the user or by the push registry alarm. If you are writing an alarm clock MIDlet, you will need to store the alarm time and compare it to the current time when the MIDlet runs. Another strategy is have one MIDlet that sets the alarm time for another MIDlet to run.

Here is a simple MIDlet that allows you to set a time for the MIDlet to be run again.

```
import java.util.*;

import javax.microedition.io.*;
import javax.microedition.lcdui.*;
import javax.microedition.midlet.MIDlet;

public class WakeUpMIDlet
    extends MIDlet
    implements CommandListener {
  private Display mDisplay;
```

```java
  private Form mForm;
  private DateField mDateField;
  private Command mExitCommand, mSetCommand;

  public void startApp() {
    if (mForm == null) {
      mForm = new Form("WakeUpMIDlet");
      mDateField = new DateField("Alarm", DateField.DATE_TIME);
      mForm.append(mDateField);
      mExitCommand = new Command("Exit", Command.EXIT, 0);
      mSetCommand = new Command("Set", Command.SCREEN, 0);
      mForm.addCommand(mExitCommand);
      mForm.addCommand(mSetCommand);
      mForm.setCommandListener(this);

      mDisplay = Display.getDisplay(this);
    }
    mDisplay.setCurrent(mForm);
  }

  public void pauseApp() {}

  public void destroyApp(boolean unconditional) {}

  public void commandAction(Command c, Displayable d) {
    if (c == mExitCommand) {
      destroyApp(true);
      notifyDestroyed();
    }
    else if (c == mSetCommand) {
      Date alarmDate = mDateField.getDate();
      if (alarmDate == null)
        return;
      long alarm = alarmDate.getTime();
      Thread t = new Thread(new AlarmRunnable(mForm, alarm));
      t.start();
    }
  }
}

class AlarmRunnable implements Runnable {
  private Form mForm;
  private long mAlarm;

  public AlarmRunnable(Form form, long alarm) {
    mForm = form;
    mAlarm = alarm;
  }
```

continued

```
    public void run() {
      try {
        PushRegistry.registerAlarm("WakeUpMIDlet", mAlarm);
        mForm.append("Set!");
      }
      catch (Exception e) { mForm.append(e.toString()); }
    }
  }
```

You will have to run `WakeUpMIDlet` in OTA mode in order to see things working on the emulator.

`WakeUpMIDlet` uses a `DateField` to allow you to set the alarm time. When you've set a time, choose the **Set** command to register the alarm with the push registry. Now exit the MIDlet and wait for your alarm time. The device will usually ask the user for permission to start up `WakeUpMIDlet`. When it starts up, you'll just see the `Form` with the `DateField` again.

6.3   Responding to Content

Devices can receive and store many different types of content, including images, sounds, applications, and application-specific data like game levels. The JSR 211 Content Handler API (CHAPI) maps content to MIDlets. CHAPI is required by the MSA specficiation.

Content is mapped to MIDlets using the content type. A MIDlet that knows what to do with a certain type of content is a *handler*. Applications can request a handler for content that they do not recognize.

Handlers have associated *actions*, which are a high-level exposure of the kinds of operations the handler can perform with the content. To the rest of the world, a content handler is a magic box that knows what to do with some kind of content and gives the calling application some buttons to push. For example, a content handler that plays audio files could provide one action to play the content and one action to save the content on the local file system.

CHAPI is not restricted to MIDlets. Content handlers can be other types of applications, such as the Xlets of the Connected Device Configuration (CDC) stack or even native applications. Likewise, native applications on a device (a browser, for instance) are free to use CHAPI to find handlers for unrecognized content types. The device's implementation determines the depth of native integration.

Although CHAPI has lots of potential, it is unclear how powerful real-world implementations will be. Lots of power is available if the device's browser, messaging client, and e-mail client are all integrated with the CHAPI registry. In that case, a game application could act as a content handler and receive new game levels or add-ins via SMS or e-mail messages. Users could click on all sorts of interesting content in their browsers and have it displayed or consumed by content handler MIDlets. Unfortunately, neither the CHAPI specification nor the MSA specification makes any requirements on CHAPI's integration with the rest of the device. In the absence of such teeth, CHAPI's main value is allowing MIDlets to cooperate with each other.

In this chapter, I describe how your MIDlets can use CHAPI to run a content handler and how you can write a content handler MIDlet yourself.

6.3.1 Invoking a Content Handler

Your application can invoke a content handler without having to know much about the handler itself. The centerpiece of CHAPI is the `javax.microedition.content.Registry` class, which is conceptually similar to `PushRegistry`.

To run a content handler, first create an `Invocation` that represents the content you want handled, then pass it to one of `Registry`'s `invoke()` methods.

Here is a complete example that attempts to run a handler for an audio file on the Internet:

```
import javax.microedition.lcdui.*;
import javax.microedition.midlet.MIDlet;

import javax.microedition.content.*;

public class SnakeCharmerMIDlet
    extends MIDlet
    implements CommandListener, Runnable {
  private Display mDisplay;

  private Form mForm;
  private Command mExitCommand;

  private Command mGoCommand;

  public void startApp() {
    if (mForm == null) {
      mForm = new Form("SnakeCharmerMIDlet");
      mExitCommand = new Command("Exit", Command.EXIT, 0);
      mGoCommand = new Command("Go", Command.SCREEN, 0);
```

continued

```
        mForm.addCommand(mExitCommand);
        mForm.addCommand(mGoCommand);

        mForm.setCommandListener(this);

        mDisplay = Display.getDisplay(this);
    }
      mDisplay.setCurrent(mForm);
    }

    public void pauseApp() {}
    public void destroyApp(boolean unconditional) {}

    public void commandAction(Command c, Displayable d) {
        if (c == mExitCommand) {
            destroyApp(true);
            notifyDestroyed();
        }
        else if (c == mGoCommand) {
            Thread t = new Thread(this);
            t.start();
        }
    }

    public void run() {
        try {
            String url =
                "http://kickbutt.jonathanknudsen.com/audio/Glass.wav";
            Invocation invocation = new Invocation(url);
            Registry registry =
                Registry.getRegistry("SnakeCharmerMIDlet");
            boolean mustExit = registry.invoke(invocation);
            if (mustExit == true) {
                destroyApp(true);
                notifyDestroyed();
            }
        }
        catch (Exception e) {
            mForm.append(e.toString());
        }
    }
}
```

Everything up until run() has to do with the user interface of the MIDlet and should look familiar. In run(), SnakeCharmerMIDlet creates an Invocation based on the URL of an audio file. Then it retrieves an instance of the Registry by passing in its own class name. To find and invoke an appropriate handler, the MIDlet calls the `Registry`'s `invoke()` method.

On some devices (including the Sun Java Wireless Toolkit emulator), only one MIDlet can be running at a time. If `invoke()` returns `true`, it means that the current running application should shut itself down. The application management software (AMS) will take care of starting up the content handler and passing the `Invocation` to it. When the handler has finished and shut down, the AMS restarts the original application.

There are more complicated ways to create an `Invocation`. You can be more specific about the type of content, or you can even specify which content handler you wish to use. If the content handler supports more than one action, you can specify which action to use.

By itself, `SnakeCharmerMIDlet` isn't much fun (Figure 6.4). You can try it if you wish, but without an appropriate content handler, all you'll get is an exception from `invoke()`. The next section contains the content handler, and the following section describes how to make everything run.

6.3.2 Writing a Content Handler MIDlet

A content handler MIDlet resembles the basic structure of a push registry MIDlet. It usually runs a separate thread that listens for incoming content, and it checks for waiting content when initializing.

Figure 6.4   It's not much fun without the content handler.

Here is a content handler MIDlet that knows how to play a WAV audio file. You'll find all about audio in Chapter 23, but for now just take the two lines that play the file on faith.

```java
import java.io.*;

import javax.microedition.io.*;
import javax.microedition.lcdui.*;
import javax.microedition.midlet.MIDlet;
import javax.microedition.media.*;

import javax.microedition.content.*;

public class WavHandlerMIDlet
    extends MIDlet
    implements CommandListener {
  private Display mDisplay;

  private Form mForm;
  private Command mExitCommand;

  private Command mRegisterCommand, mUnregisterCommand;

  public void startApp() {
    if (mForm == null) {
      mForm = new Form("WavHandlerMIDlet");
      mExitCommand = new Command("Exit", Command.EXIT, 0);
      mRegisterCommand = new Command("Register",
          Command.SCREEN, 0);
      mUnregisterCommand = new Command("Unregister",
          Command.SCREEN, 0);
      mForm.addCommand(mExitCommand);
      mForm.addCommand(mRegisterCommand);
      mForm.addCommand(mUnregisterCommand);

      mForm.setCommandListener(this);

      mDisplay = Display.getDisplay(this);

      InvocationRunnable ir = new InvocationRunnable(mForm);
      Thread t = new Thread(ir);
      t.start();
    }
    mDisplay.setCurrent(mForm);
  }

  public void pauseApp() {}
  public void destroyApp(boolean unconditional) {}
```

```
    public void commandAction(Command c, Displayable d) {
      if (c == mExitCommand) {
        destroyApp(true);
        notifyDestroyed();
      }
      else if (c == mRegisterCommand) {
        RegisterContentRunnable rr =
            new RegisterContentRunnable(mForm);
        Thread t = new Thread(rr);
        t.start();
      }
      else if (c == mUnregisterCommand) {
        UnregisterContentRunnable ur =
            new UnregisterContentRunnable(mForm);
        Thread t = new Thread(ur);
        t.start();
      }
    }
}

class RegisterContentRunnable implements Runnable {
  private Form mForm;

  public RegisterContentRunnable(Form f) { mForm = f; }

  public void run() {
    try {
      String handlerName = "WavHandlerMIDlet";
      String[] types = { "audio/x-wav" };
      String[] suffixes = { ".wav" };
      String[] actions = { "open" };
      String[] actionNames = { "Play" };
      String locale =
          System.getProperty("microedition.locale");
      if (locale == null) locale = "en-US";
      ActionNameMap anm =
          new ActionNameMap(actions, actionNames, locale);
      ActionNameMap[] actionnames = { anm };
      String id = "WavHandlerMIDlet";
      String[] access = null;

      Registry registry = Registry.getRegistry(handlerName);
      registry.register(handlerName, types, suffixes,
          actions, actionnames, id, access);
      InvocationRunnable ir = new InvocationRunnable(mForm);
      Thread t = new Thread(ir);
      t.start();
      mForm.append("Registered.");
```

continued

```
      }
      catch (Exception e) {
        mForm.append(e.toString());
      }
    }
  }
}

class UnregisterContentRunnable implements Runnable {
  private Form mForm;

  public UnregisterContentRunnable(Form f) { mForm = f; }

  public void run() {
    try {
      String handlerName = "WavHandlerMIDlet";
      Registry registry = Registry.getRegistry(handlerName);
      boolean success = registry.unregister(handlerName);
      mForm.append("unregister() returned " + success);
    }
    catch (Exception e) {
      mForm.append(e.toString());
    }
  }
}

class InvocationRunnable implements Runnable {
  private Form mForm;

  private boolean mTrucking;

  public InvocationRunnable(Form f) {
    mForm = f;
    mTrucking = true;
  }

  public void run() {
    try {
      ContentHandlerServer chs =
          Registry.getServer("WavHandlerMIDlet");
      while (mTrucking) {
        Invocation invocation = chs.getRequest(true);
        mForm.append("Incoming content!");
        InputConnection ic =
            (InputConnection)invocation.open(false);
        InputStream in = ic.openInputStream();
        Player player = Manager.createPlayer(in, "audio/x-wav");
        player.start();
      }
```

```
          }
      catch (ContentHandlerException che) {
        if (che.getErrorCode() != che.NO_REGISTERED_HANDLER)
          mForm.append(che.toString());
      }
      catch (Exception e) {
        mForm.append(e.toString());
      }
    }
  }
```

WavHandlerMIDlet includes three separate Runnable implementations for regis-tering the content handler, unregistering the content handler, and waiting for incoming content.

You need quite a bit of information to register a content handler:

- The most important item is the class name of the content handler.

- A string array contains the content types supported by the content handler. These should be MIME types. In our example, the content handler sup-ports the audio/x-wav type.

- A string array of suffixes is a fallback for situations in which MIME types are not available. When reading data from a file, for example, the device might have to locate a content handler based on the filename suffix.

- The content handler's actions, and appropriate display strings, are passed as an array of ActionNameMaps. Actions are strings that are specific to your application, but *action names* are suitable for display to the user. Each ActionNameMap contains action names in a specific language. In the WavHandlerMIDlet example, a single ActionNameMap for United States English is used to map the open action to the Play action name.

- You can assign an ID to your content handler, which is useful if you want to invoke a specific content handler from another application.

- Finally, if you wish to limit access to the content handler, pass a string array of IDs that are allowed access. Passing null for this argument allows any application to use the content handler.

Unregistering is much easier. Just pass the class name to Registry's unregister() method. If the return value is true, the content handler was successfully unregistered.

In WavHandlerMIDlet, the InvocationRunnable class handles incoming con-tent. The basic idea is simple. Get a ContentHandlerServer and keep asking it for incoming `Invocations`. The `ContentHandlerServer` is returned from the `Registry` when you call `getServer()` with the class name of the content handler.

You can retrieve the next incoming invocation with `getRequest()`. Pass `true` to wait for an incoming request. If you pass `false`, `getRequest()` returns right away, but the result might be `null`.

Once you've got an incoming `Invocation`, you can retrieve the actual content by calling `open()` on the `Invocation`. The content is returned as a `Connection` or some subtype, which is fully covered in Chapter 18. The sound data is retrieved using this object.

6.3.3 Putting It All Together

Assuming you have `SnakeCharmerMIDlet` and `WavHandlerMIDlet` ready to go, here is how you can test them out.

First, try running `SnakeCharmerMIDlet` to verify that an appropriate content handler cannot be found. You'll have to run the MIDlet in OTA mode. Once you've installed the MIDlet suite, run `SnakeCharmerMIDlet` and choose the **Go** command. You should see an exception message that says "no registered handler." This makes sense.

Next, run `WavHandlerMIDlet` and choose the **Register** command. You will see a message on the screen that says "Registered" (Figure 6.5).

Figure 6.5   Now the content handler is registered.

Now exit WavHandlerMIDlet and go back to SnakeCharmerMIDlet. This time when you choose **Go**, SnakeCharmerMIDlet exits to allow WavHandlerMIDlet to launch and play the sound. When you manually leave WavHandlerMIDlet, SnakeCharmerMIDlet is automatically started again (Figure 6.6).

6.3.4 Static Content Handler Registration

WavHandlerMIDlet shows how to register a content handler at runtime, but you can also arrange to have content handlers registered at installation time. This is also similar to how the push registry works. Special attributes in the MIDlet suite descriptor specify which content handlers should be registered when the MIDlet suite is installed.

Your development tool formats the attributes for you. In the Sun Java Wireless Toolkit, click on **Settings...** in KToolbar, then choose **Content Handlers** from the list on the left. Click **Add** to add a new content handler. You can specify all the same information that gets passed to Registry's register() method, like content types and filename suffixes. The **Actions** tab gives you a chance to enter the actions and action names for as many locales as you wish.

In NetBeans Mobility Pack, you will have to add the attributes manually. By the time you read this, things might have changed, but right now, the content handler

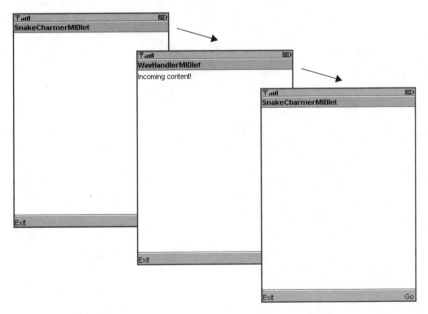

Figure 6.6   WavHandlerMIDlet obligingly handles content for SnakeCharmerMIDlet.

attributes appear in the list as custom items. To see how this works, use Net-Beans to import the CHAPIDemo project from wherever the Mobility Pack is installed. Then right-click on the imported project and select **Attributes** in the left pane.

6.4 Summary

This chapter describes how MIDlets can be run automatically. The push registry can launch MIDlets to respond to specific types of incoming network connections. MIDlets can register at runtime using the PushRegistry API or at installation time based on MIDlet suite descriptor attributes. MIDlets can also be launched at specific times. The Content Handler API makes it possible for MIDlets to launch other applications to display or manipulate specific kinds of data. Content handlers can be registered through the Registry API or at installation time based on descriptor attributes.

Section III

User Interface

7

Basic User Interface

BUILDING a user interface in MIDP is entirely different from desktop or server application development. The MIDP user interface APIs, known as LCDUI, were designed for the unique constraints of a small environment:

- Screen sizes vary among devices. The screens you get with MIDP adjust smoothly to any screen size.
- Input methods vary among devices. LCDUI offers the abstraction of *commands*, which can adapt to the specific controls of a device.

This chapter and Chapter 8, "More User Interface," discuss the screens that LCDUI supplies and their supporting baggage. If you want more control or are trying to do something fancy, you can do all the drawing yourself using Canvas or GameCanvas, which are covered in Chapter 9, "Creating Custom Screens," and Chapter 11, "Using the Game API," respectively. Another approach is to build an SVG Tiny user interface for your application. See Chapter 12, "Scalable Vector Graphics," for information about using the JSR 226 SVG API to interact with the user.

LCDUI offers four ready-made screens, all descendants of javax.microedition. lcdui.Displayable:

- TextBox has a title and a text area that fills the whole screen.
- Alert is suitable for showing short messages to the user. In addition to text, it can show an icon and make an appropriate sound.

- List shows a list of items that can have associated icons. List can be used as a menu.

- Form can contain a combination of items, like checkboxes, text fields, images, and others.

This chapter introduces the fundamentals of LCDUI and its two simplest screens, TextBox and Alert. It also describes commands in full detail. The next chapter explores the more complex and useful screens, List and Form.

7.1 How to Show Screens

The device's display is represented by an instance of javax.microedition. lcdui.Display. You've already seen this class. To use it, pass your MIDlet object to the static getDisplay() method. Usually, you do this in the MIDlet's constructor or startApp(), something like this:

```
Display d = Display.getDisplay(this);
```

To show one of the four screen types, use one of Display's setCurrent() methods. You've seen this kind of thing already:

```
Form f = new Form("Sign in");
d.setCurrent(f);
```

This snippet is how it works for TextBox, List, and Form. You just create the screen and put it up.

Alert is different. Alert is supposed to show a message to the user, but it is a temporary notice on the way to another screen. To show an Alert, you have to also tell Display about the next screen by using a different form of setCurrent():

```
Alert a = new Alert("Empty alert");
d.setCurrent(a, f);
```

This code tells Display to show the Alert a first. When the Alert is finished, the Form f will become the current screen.

Keep in mind that setCurrent() does not immediately change what the user sees. It merely queues a request to the device to change the current screen next time it gets a chance. Suppose you call setCurrent() during the startApp() method of your application. The screen update might not happen until startApp() returns and relinquishes control of the system thread.

Even when you show screens on the display, you will not get to cover the *whole* display. Usually, devices reserve a status bar of themselves, something that shows battery life, signal strength, and other information. Even the emulator in your development tool will show this behavior. If you really want the whole display, use `setFullScreenMode()` in `Canvas` (see Chapter 9).

7.2 TextBox, the Runt of the Litter

`TextBox` is one of those things that sounds good on paper but isn't of much practical use, like some of those kitchen tools that are collecting dust in the back corners of your cabinets. Did you really think you would ever want to make your own beef jerky?

`TextBox` uses the entire screen to display text or allow the user to input text. This capability might have made sense a few years ago when many mobile phones had tiny displays, but nowadays displays are quite a bit larger. While it's possible you could use `TextBox` to display a lot of text (instructions, perhaps), you'd be better off using a `Form` instead, because you'll have more control over the text and be able to include images. On the flip side, you could use `TextBox` to allow the user to input a lot of text, but that's a bad idea too. Inputting text is painful on mobile devices. If your application calls for extensive text input on a mobile device, you should modify your application design. For text input, use a `TextField` in a `Form` instead. You'll find out all about these classes in the next chapter.

`TextBox` has a title and a large text area that usually takes up the rest of the screen. The actual appearance of `TextBox` is determined by the device.

Create a `TextBox` by specifying the title, the text, the maximum length, and constraints. The constraints are defined by constants in the `TextField` class, which is part of the `Form` family and are described in the next chapter. The constraints are as follows:

- `TextField.ANY` allows any type of input.
- `TextField.DECIMAL` allows numbers with decimal points.
- `TextField.EMAILADDR` limits input to valid characters in an e-mail address.
- `TextField.NUMERIC` is for numbers without decimal points.
- `TextField.PHONENUMBER` allows telephone numbers.
- `TextField.URL` is for entering URLs.

As if that weren't enough, you can make a constraint more specific by adding a *modifier* to it. Here are the modifiers:

- INITIAL_CAPS_SENTENCE makes the first letter a capital letter.
- INITIAL_CAPS_WORD makes the first letter of each word a capital letter.
- NON_PREDICTIVE is used to suppress whatever fancy text input guessing your device might be doing. Many phones let you tap away on the numeric keyboard and make educated guesses about the words you might be trying to form. Using the NON_PREDICTIVE modifier should turn off this behavior.
- PASSWORD usually shows characters as asterisks so that anyone looking over your shoulder won't be able to see your password. Sometimes password fields show you the last character that you're typing so you can make sure it's correct.
- SENSITIVE is for information that shouldn't be stored in a predictive input dictionary or cached in any other way.
- UNEDITABLE is for text that cannot be edited.

The constraints and modifiers are really only *suggestions* to the implementation. It's a lot like when you ask the plumber to take his muddy boots off before walking across your carpet. You can ask, but it doesn't mean anything is going to happen. The Sun Java Wireless Toolkit emulator is good about honoring constraints and modifiers, but my Motorola V3 doesn't seem to understand INITIAL_CAPS_WORD or NON_PREDICTIVE.

Some combinations do not work. If you try to create a TextBox with the constraint NUMERIC and initial text "Aardvark," the TextBox constructor throws IllegalArgumentException.

7.3 Input Modes

The constraints apply to the content of the TextBox, but you can also request an *input mode* to assist your users. You don't actually request the input mode, you just ask the device to make it easy to enter a certain set of characters. The device should select whatever input mode it has that corresponds.

You can request a Unicode character block or an input subset. The names are defined in the Java SE classes java.lang.Character.UnicodeBlock and java.awt.im.InputSubset respectively. Finally, MIDP defines the subsets MIDP_UPPERCASE_LATIN and MIDP_LOWERCASE_LATIN for the entry of uppercase and lowercase Latin letters. To request an appropriate input mode, pass the string name of the corresponding constant to TextBox's `setInitialInputMode()` method.

The following example requests an input mode appropriate for entering Hebrew characters:

```
// TextBox tb = ...
tb.setInitialInputMode("UCB_HEBREW");
```

7.4 Using Alerts for Notifications

Alerts are good for displaying a message to the user. They have four attributes that control how they are presented:

- The *title* and *text* have the same meaning as `TextBox`, although the presentation is likely to be a little different.
- You can supply an *image* to be displayed in the `Alert`. Pass `null` to `Alert`'s constructor to show no image.
- An *alert type* is a hint. If you tell the device that the `Alert` you want to show is an informational alert, the device might try to display it using a standard image and might even play a sound.

The alert types are defined as static constants in `AlertType` and have the self-explanatory names `ALARM`, `CONFIRMATION`, `ERROR`, `INFO`, and `WARNING`.

Alerts have a *timeout* that determines how long the alert is shown on the display before the next screen is shown. The timeout has a default value, which is returned from `getDefaultTimeout()`. You can set a new timeout value (in milliseconds) with `setTimeout()`. If you prefer that your users have to explicitly dismiss an alert, you call `setTimeout(Alert.FOREVER)`. The system will provide some way to dismiss the alert (probably a **Done** or **OK** command).

You can add commands to an alert, just as you can to any other screen, but the rules about commands and command listeners are a little funky. Check the `Alert` API documentation for details. If you find yourself wanting to add commands to an alert, consider using a different type of screen.

Each device has some freedom in deciding how to show an alert. Some have icon images and sounds for the alert types. Some show the image you've supplied and some do not. The arguments you are passing to the `Alert` constructor are requests, not orders, although you can be sure that the title and message text will show up on the display.

7.5   A Very Quick Introduction to Images

You won't learn the whole story about images until Chapter 9, but for now just know that you can load an image from a resource file using this kind of code:

```
try {
  Image i = Image.createImage("/Minerva-t.png");
}
catch (IOException ioe) {
  // Handle the exception.
}
catch (Exception e) {
  // Handle other types of exceptions.
}
```

This code *does not* load an image from a file system. It looks for the resource file Minerva-t.png inside the MIDlet suite JAR file. If you place resource files in the right place in your development project, your development tool will package them into the MIDlet suite JAR file. In the Sun Java Wireless Toolkit, the correct place for resource files is the res directory of your project.

It's a good idea to catch Exception in addition to IOException. Errors in the image bits might cause IllegalArgumentExceptions. It's much better for you to catch these and handle them properly than to have your application fail unexpectedly in the field.

Depending on the device, an alert might have a preferred size for images, such that if you supply an image of the right size, it will display particularly well. You can ask Display for this size by passing Display.ALERT to getBestImageWidth() and getBestImageHeight().

7.6   Putting It Together

This example shows how to use TextBox and Alert.

```
import javax.microedition.lcdui.*;
import javax.microedition.midlet.MIDlet;

public class UIOneMIDlet
    extends MIDlet
    implements CommandListener {
  private Display mDisplay;

  private TextBox mTextBox;
```

```
    private Command mExitCommand, mAlertCommand;

    public void startApp() {
      if (mTextBox == null) {
        mTextBox = new TextBox("Kick Butt with MIDP!",
            "Choose 'Show alert' to see an Alert.",
            128, TextField.UNEDITABLE);
        mExitCommand = new Command("Exit", Command.EXIT, 0);
        mAlertCommand = new Command("Show alert",
            Command.SCREEN, 0);
        mTextBox.addCommand(mExitCommand);
        mTextBox.addCommand(mAlertCommand);
        mTextBox.setCommandListener(this);
        mDisplay = Display.getDisplay(this);
      }
      mDisplay.setCurrent(mTextBox);
    }

    public void pauseApp() {}

    public void destroyApp(boolean unconditional) {}

    public void commandAction(Command c, Displayable d) {
      if (c == mExitCommand) {
        destroyApp(true);
        notifyDestroyed();
      }
      else if (c == mAlertCommand) {
        Image i = null;
        try { i = Image.createImage("/Minerva-t.png"); }
        catch (java.io.IOException ioe) {}
        catch (Exception e) {}
        Alert a = new Alert("This is the title.",
            "This is the message.",
            i, AlertType.INFO);
        a.setTimeout(5000); // Five seconds.
        mDisplay.setCurrent(a, mTextBox);
      }
    }
  }
```

On the Sun Java Wireless Toolkit emulator, the alert looks like Figure 7.1.

As you can see, it is very easy to create and display an alert. Play around with the parameters in Alert's constructor to see the effects. In the Sun Java Wireless Toolkit emulator, AlertType.ALARM and AlertType.CONFIRMATION have associated sounds. Also try the FOREVER timeout to see how it behaves.

Figure 7.1 An alert in the toolkit emulator

7.7 Good for the Old Ticker

All of MIDP's screens can display a *ticker*, which is text that scrolls across the screen, just like that famous sign in Times Square in New York City. For example,

```
Display d = Display.getDisplay(this);
Form f = new Form("Kick Butt with MIDP!");
f.setTicker(new Ticker("I had two birds / " +
        "But I needed three / " +
        "To take me away / " +
        "From the A & P. "));
d.setCurrent(f);
```

In the Sun Java Wireless Toolkit emulator, it looks like the example in Figure 7.2.

7.8 The Whole Story on Commands

You already learned a little about commands in Chapter 3, "Quick Start." Now you'll get the whole story.

A command represents an action that a user can perform in your application. The device decides how the command is shown to the user, and the device figures out how the user invokes the command. Your application provides a listener object that is notified when a command is invoked.

Figure 7.2 A ticker

Commands have a short label, a long label, a type, and a priority. The device decides which label to show. One possibility is that the short label is displayed on the screen next to a soft button and the long label is displayed in a menu of commands. The long label is used only if it is available; it's possible to create a Command with only a short label.

The command type helps the device figure out how to show the command. Command types are defined by constants in Command. The types for common commands are BACK, CANCEL, EXIT, HELP, OK, and STOP. Application-specific commands use the type SCREEN. Finally, the type ITEM is used for commands that are applied to Form items, but you won't learn about that until the next chapter.

A device is allowed to use a label other than the one you've specified, depending on the command type. For example, if you create a command using new Command("Ooga booga", Command.EXIT, 0), the device could decide to use a label of "Exit" or "Quit" instead of the one you supplied, resulting in a more consistent user experience.

If there are more commands than space on the screen, some of the commands might be hidden in a menu. The Sun Java Wireless Toolkit emulator has space for two commands, one for each of its soft buttons. If you add more commands to a screen, one soft button still invokes a command, while the other soft button brings up a menu of all the others. Figure 7.3 shows a screen with four commands, with the menu of additional commands showing.

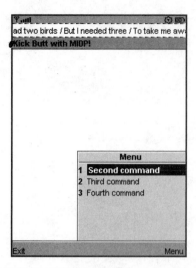

Figure 7.3 Commands that won't fit are stuck in a menu.

The command priority tells the device how important a command is relative to the other commands in a screen. Lower priorities are more important. Assuming you cared more about letting users spend money than viewing a license agreement, you might create command priorities like this:

```
Command exitCommand = new Command("Exit", Command.EXIT, 8);
Command nextCommand = new Command("Next item",
    "Show the next item", Command.SCREEN, 2);
Command addCommand = new Command("Add to cart",
    "Add this item to your shopping cart",
    Command.SCREEN, 2);
Command licenseCommand = new Command("View license",
    Command.SCREEN, 700);
```

Each screen has one command listener that is notified when a command is invoked. The command listener can be any object, but it is often convenient to make the MIDlet a command listener. The CommandListener interface has one method:

```
public void commandAction(Command c, Displayable d)
```

The Displayable is the screen whose command has just been invoked. You can register a single listener with multiple screens, in which case it is useful to know to which screen's command you are responding. The Command parameter is, of course, the command that the user has invoked.

Remember that the system thread that calls your commandAction() method does not belong to you. Be quick about your work in commandAction(), or create your own thread if you must do something that takes a long time.

7.9 Command Placement

The placement of commands is, in some cases, inscrutable. Even the simplest use of commands sometimes leads to an uneven user experience across a variety of devices.

One surprising example is a List (from the next chapter) that has a single command, **OK** (Figure 7.4). My Motorola V3 and Sun's emulator behave as you would expect, although it's probably just lucky that the **OK** command is on the right side in both of them.

Now try this on a Nokia Series 40 handset (Figure 7.5). Nokia adds its own **Mark** or **Unmark** command to this type of list, mapped to the center select button. The left and right soft buttons are both available, but for some reason the **OK** command gets stuck inside an **Options** menu. When you choose **Options**, you're taken to another screen with the **OK** command, a **Select** command, and a **Back** command. Yuck!

If you need to provide a user experience with more consistency across platforms, you'll have to build your own solution using Canvas, which is described in Chapter 9.

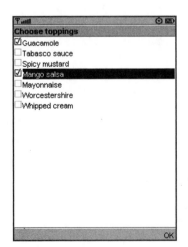

Figure 7.4 No surprises here.

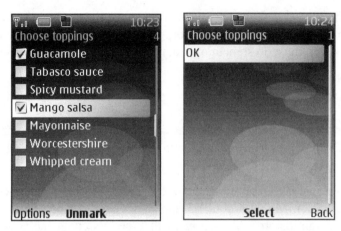

Figure 7.5   The **OK** command is hidden in an **Options** menu.

7.10 Summary

In this chapter, you got an introduction to MIDP's user interface APIs. You learned about the simplest screens, TextBox and Alert, and how to show them on a device's display. All Displayables can show a ticker, which is scrolling text. The user performs actions in an application by using commands. The device determines how commands look and how the user invokes them. A command listener object, which is often a MIDlet, responds to commands.

8

More User Interface

THE real stars of LCDUI are `List` and `Form`. Both classes provide practical interactive displays that are well-suited to small screens. `List` is just what it sounds like, a simple presentation of text and image items that adapts well to any screen size. `Forms` can hold a variety of items, everything from text input fields and images to date and time editors. The constraints of a small display mean that complex forms are awkward, but simple forms are very useful.

8.1 Lists

A `List` shows as many items as it can fit on the display. An item has a text label and can also have an associated image.

Lists come in three varieties, which are represented by constants in the `List` class:

- `EXCLUSIVE` lists allow only one selection. The items in an `EXCLUSIVE` list are commonly shown as radio buttons.
- `MULTIPLE` lists allow more than one item to be selected. A common representation is checkboxes.
- An `IMPLICIT` list is a special case of `EXCLUSIVE`. It looks just like a menu, but the event handling is different.

The three types of lists appear in the Sun Java Wireless Toolkit emulator as shown in Figure 8.1.

To create a list, supply a title and a list type to the constructor. You can also supply a string array and an `Image` array representing the items, if you have them available.

```
List entreeList = new List("Select an entree", List.EXCLUSIVE);
```

To add items to the end of a list, pass the label and the image to `append()`. If you don't have an image, pass `null`, but the label must not be `null`.

```
entreeList.append("Grilled chicken", null);
```

Other methods to manage items are straightforward. The list items are numbered, beginning with 0. To add an item at a specific position, use `insert()`. You can remove items with `delete()` and `deleteAll()`. To retrieve the label or image for an item, pass the item index to `getString()` and `getImage()` respectively.

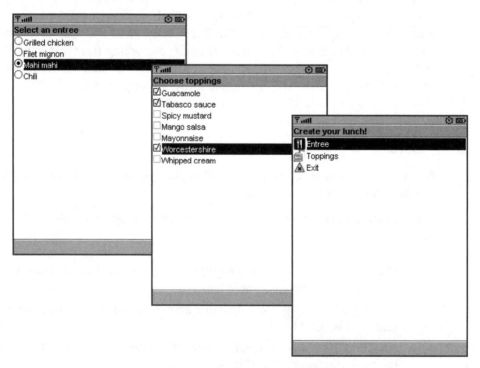

Figure 8.1   List types: EXCLUSIVE, MULTIPLE, and IMPLICIT

To ensure that your lists look as nice as possible, you should try to use images with appropriate sizes. At runtime, you can ask `Display` for the best size of list item images, as shown here:

```
Display d = Display.getDisplay(this);
int biw = d.getBestImageWidth(Display.LIST_ELEMENT);
int bih = d.getBestImageHeight(Display.LIST_ELEMENT);
```

This size is likely to vary among devices. One way to create a portable application is to find out the best image sizes for all or most of the devices you wish to support. Package images in these sizes with your MIDlet suite and select the most appropriate images at runtime.

8.2 List Selections

The method for finding the current selection in a list varies depending on the type of list. `EXLUSIVE` and `IMPLICIT` lists work the same with respect to selection because only one item can be selected at a time. You can retrieve the zero-based index of the currently selected item by calling `getSelectedIndex()`. If the list has just been initialized, it is possible that there is no selection at all, in which case `getSelectedIndex()` will return 1. Make sure your application is prepared for this possibility.

`MULTIPLE` lists work differently. To find out which items are selected and which are not, pass a `boolean` array to `getSelectedFlags()`. The array should have `size()` elements. Selected items will have a corresponding `true` value in the array.

To change the selection from the application, use `setSelectedIndex()` or `setSelectedFlags()`, depending on the list type.

8.3 Handling List Events

Except for the `IMPLICIT` type, lists work like any other screen. This is great news because it means you already know what to do. You can add commands and set a command listener. Your users will browse through a list, make one or more selections, and then choose one of the commands you have added, probably **OK** or **Cancel** or **Back**.

`IMPLICIT` lists work a little differently, but they still work within the Command and `CommandListener` structure. When you make a selection, an event is fired immediately to the registered `CommandListener`. The `Command` that is fired is a special one, `List.SELECT_COMMAND`. You can test for it in `commandAction()` in your listener.

You do not get any notifications as the user browses lists and checks or unchecks items. MIDP's `List` is not that specific. If you want more fine-grained control, you need to create your own user interfaces, as described in Chapter 9, "Creating Custom Screens," and Chapter 10, "Custom Items."

8.4 Three Lists in One Example

To give you some idea what's possible with `List`, take a look at the following example, which simulates a lunch menu. You can choose exactly one entree (an `EXCLUSIVE` list) and as many toppings as you wish (a `MULTIPLE` list). A main menu (an `IMPLICIT` list) controls the whole thing. There are some images for the main menu as well, so you can see how that looks.

```
import javax.microedition.lcdui.*;
import javax.microedition.midlet.MIDlet;

public class UITwoMIDlet
    extends MIDlet
    implements CommandListener {
  private static final String kEntree = "Entree";
  private static final String kToppings = "Toppings";
  private static final String kExit = "Exit";

  private Display mDisplay;

  private List mMainList, mEntreeList, mToppingsList;

  private Command mOKCommand;

  public void startApp() {
    if (mMainList == null) {
      mMainList = new List("Create your lunch!", List.IMPLICIT);
      Image entreeImage = null;
      Image toppingsImage = null;
      Image exitImage = null;
      try {
        entreeImage = Image.createImage("/entrees.png");
        toppingsImage = Image.createImage("/toppings.png");
        exitImage = Image.createImage("/exit.png");
      }
      catch (java.io.IOException ioe) {}
      catch (Exception e) {}
```

```
    mMainList.append(kEntree, entreeImage);
    mMainList.append(kToppings, toppingsImage);
    mMainList.append(kExit, exitImage);
    mMainList.setCommandListener(this);

    mOKCommand = new Command("OK", Command.OK, 0);

    mEntreeList =
        new List("Select an entree", List.EXCLUSIVE);
    mEntreeList.append("Grilled chicken", null);
    mEntreeList.append("Filet mignon", null);
    mEntreeList.append("Mahi mahi", null);
    mEntreeList.append("Chili", null);
    mEntreeList.addCommand(mOKCommand);
    mEntreeList.setCommandListener(this);

    mToppingsList =
        new List("Choose toppings", List.MULTIPLE);
    mToppingsList.append("Guacamole", null);
    mToppingsList.append("Tabasco sauce", null);
    mToppingsList.append("Spicy mustard", null);
    mToppingsList.append("Mango salsa", null);
    mToppingsList.append("Mayonnaise", null);
    mToppingsList.append("Worcestershire", null);
    mToppingsList.append("Whipped cream", null);
    mToppingsList.addCommand(mOKCommand);
    mToppingsList.setCommandListener(this);

    mDisplay = Display.getDisplay(this);
  }
  mDisplay.setCurrent(mMainList);
}

public void pauseApp() {}

public void destroyApp(boolean unconditional) {}

public void commandAction(Command c, Displayable d) {
  if (c == List.SELECT_COMMAND && d == mMainList) {
    int actionIndex = mMainList.getSelectedIndex();
    if (actionIndex < 0) return;
    String action = mMainList.getString(actionIndex);
    if (action.equals(kExit)) {
      destroyApp(true);
      notifyDestroyed();
    }
```

continued

```
        else if (action.equals(kEntree)) {
          mDisplay.setCurrent(mEntreeList);
        }
        else if (action.equals(kToppings)) {
          mDisplay.setCurrent(mToppingsList);
        }
      }
      else if (c == mOKCommand) {
        mDisplay.setCurrent(mMainList);
      }
    }
  }
```

Take special note of the event handling in commandAction(). To catch events from the IMPLICIT list, test for List.SELECT_COMMAND. Depending on the value of the selection, the application shows the entree list, the toppings list, or exits.

If the **OK** command is invoked on either the entree list or the toppings list, the main menu is shown again.

8.5 Advanced List Control

Two methods provide advanced control over the appearance of a List. The first, setFont(), allows applications to request a particular font for a specific item in the List. You'll learn all about fonts in Chapter 9.

The second method is setFitPolicy(). You can specify TEXT_WRAP_ON, TEXT_WRAP_OFF, or TEXT_WRAP_DEFAULT. The fit policy is used for items whose labels are too long to fit on a single line.

According to the specification, TEXT_WRAP_ON means that long list items are shown on multiple lines. TEXT_WRAP_OFF means that long lines will be truncated so each list item is one text line. TEXT_WRAP_DEFAULT means the default value for the platform. Sun's emulator and my Nokia 6030 are polite enough to show ellipsis (...) at the end of list items that won't fit on a single line, but my Motorola RAZR V3 simply chops off the line at the end of the last word that will fit.

8.6 Using Forms

Forms are like Swiss army knives: they are versatile and useful, but if you make them too big, they get heavy and pull your pants down.

Forms are similar in some respects to windows or dialog boxes in desktop programming. You can add *items* (think *widgets* or *components*) to create a customized user interface. LCDUI is full of useful items, all descendants of the Item class:

- StringItem shows a text string with an optional label.
- TextField is editable text with a label.
- ImageItem shows an image with an optional label.
- ChoiceGroup is kind of like a miniature List. The EXCLUSIVE and MULTIPLE flavors are the same as before, while a new type, POPUP, is a variation on EXCLUSIVE. Most devices will show a POPUP ChoiceGroup as a combo box.
- Gauge is used to indicate progress or allow input. It is something like a slider in the desktop world, although of course appearances vary among devices.
- Spacer is an invisible item that you can use to control the layout of other items on the form.
- DateField, which you met briefly in Chapter 6, represents a point in time.
- If you can't find an item that suits your needs, you can create your own by subclassing CustomItem. Read all about it in Chapter 10.

Before you even have to worry about items, though, Form offers some shortcuts to make it easy to add text and image items. Just pass a string or an image to append(), like this:

```
Form f = new Form("Dream");
try {
  Image mlkImage = Image.createImage("/mlk-small.png");
  mForm.append(mlkImage);
}
catch (java.io.IOException ioe) {}
catch (Exception e) {}
mForm.append("I have a dream...");
```

On the Sun Java Wireless Toolkit emulator, with an **Exit** command, the result looks like Figure 8.2.

Users navigate through forms one item at a time. In the screenshot in Figure 8.2, the image is the active item, indicated by the frame drawn around it. Usually, navigation from one item to the next is accomplished using the arrow keys, although of course the exact mechanism is left to the device.

Figure 8.2   A simple Form

When all the items in a form won't fit on the screen, the device allows scrolling up and down as users navigate through the items.

8.7   Working with Items

Most items are easy to create, so I won't spend a lot of time on them here. StringItem and ImageItem are best illustrated by example.

```
// Form f = ...
// Image mlkImage = ...
ImageItem ii = new ImageItem("MLK", mlkImage,
    ImageItem.LAYOUT_DEFAULT, "Martin Luther King Jr.");
f.append(ii);
StringItem si = new StringItem("Speech:", "I have a dream...");
f.append(si);
```

The ImageItem constructor takes a label, an image, a *layout directive*, which is described in the next section, and alternate text, which is shown if the image cannot be displayed for any reason.

StringItem and ImageItem also support an appearance mode, which means you can request the device to display the string or image as a hyperlink or a button. See the Item documentation for more information.

Most of the behavior of TextBox comes from TextField, so you are already familiar with input constraints and input modes. Specify a label, the text, a maximum size, and constraints to create a TextField.

```
// Form f = ...
TextField tf = new TextField("Name:", "Victor Hugo",
        512, TextField.ANY);
f.append(tf);
```

You can retrieve the current value of a TextField with getString().

ChoiceGroup looks a lot like List because both classes implement the Choice interface. Here is one example using the POPUP type. The null parameters are for images.

```
ChoiceGroup cg = new ChoiceGroup("Color:",
    ChoiceGroup.POPUP);
cg.append("Blue", null);
cg.append("Red", null);
cg.append("Purple", null);
cg.append("Yellow", null);
f.append(cg);
```

A DateField is an item that represents a point in time. DateField can show a day, a time of day, or both. Create one by specifying a title and the type of display you want. The types are DATE, TIME, and DATE_TIME.

A point in time is represented by a long wrapped in a Date. You can set or retrieve this value using setDate() and getDate().

8.8 Gauges

Gauges are trickier than you might think.

Gauges that allow user input are *interactive*. They are a lot like sliders in the desktop world. Your application usually sets a maximum value and the current value. After that, the user can modify the setting. The Gauge constructor accepts a title, a flag that is true for interactive gauges, a maximum value, and a current value. Here is an interactive gauge that has a maximum value of 5 and a current value of 3:

```
Gauge gauge = new Gauge("Interactive", true, 5, 3);
```

Noninteractive gauges are generally useful for showing progress in something that takes a long time, like a network connection or a long computation. You can specify a maximum value and update the current value from your application, or you can use one of two special flavors of noninteractive gauges.

Continuous noninteractive gauges show some kind of animation that indicates the application is working on something. This is nice because you don't need to create a new thread in your application and your users get to see something blinking or moving that makes them feel like something is actually happening. Create a continuous gauge by passing INDEFINITE for the maximum value and CONTINUOUS_RUNNING for the current value:

```
Gauge cgauge = new Gauge("Non-I continuous", false,
    Gauge.INDEFINITE, Gauge.CONTINUOUS_RUNNING);
```

Incremental noninteractive gauges work almost the same way, but your application has to poke them every once in a while to get them to move. Create one this way:

```
Gauge igauge = new Gauge("Non-I incremental", false,
    Gauge.INDEFINITE, Gauge.INCREMENTAL_UPDATING);
```

To make the incremental noninteractive gauge move, set its value to INCREMENTAL_UPDATING.

```
ig.setValue(Gauge.INCREMENTAL_UPDATING);
```

Finally, you can also set noninteractive indefinite gauges to appear idle by setting the value to either CONTINUOUS_IDLE or INCREMENTAL_IDLE.

The appearance of gauges depends on the device, as usual. The Sun Java Wireless Toolkit emulator uses simple animations for nonincremental indefinite gauges. Other devices use animations that resemble desktop progress bars. See Figure 8.3.

8.9 Controlling Item Layout

Forms will normally lay out items the way you read text. For devices that display English text, the layout runs left to right in rows from top to bottom. Devices that display other languages, like Arabic or Hebrew, can lay out items from right to left and top to bottom. You can exert some control over the layout using *layout directives*.

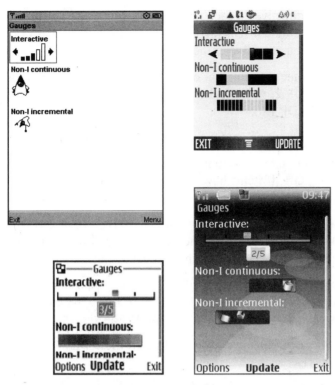

Figure 8.3   Clockwise from top left: gauges on Sun's toolkit, Motorola RAZR V3, Nokia Series 40 3rd edition, and Nokia Series 40

Although I describe the techniques briefly in this section, I don't spend a lot of time tweaking form layouts, for the following reasons:

- Even if you get a form layout perfect on one device, it's going to be significantly different on a different-sized screen.

- Devices are likely to interpret your form layout directives in subtly different ways, which could produce unexpected results on different devices.

- If you have a form with a lot of content that needs organizing, you should probably rethink your application design rather than try to make the form look better. Remember, you should use a mobile phone to present a *small* amount of information and receive a *small* amount of input. If you're trying to cram some desktop application into a MIDlet, it's time to return to square one.

You can set the layout directive on each item. As the device lays out the items in a form, it keeps track of the *current* layout directive. If an item doesn't change anything, it gets the layout directive of the previous item.

A layout directive is some combination of the constants in the Item class. The first one to use is LAYOUT_2, which indicates that you are using the layout rules from MIDP 2.0 (not MIDP 1.0).

To indicate the default layout policy for the form, use LAYOUT_DEFAULT.

Rows of items in a form share a horizontal layout, one of LAYOUT_LEFT, LAYOUT_CENTER, or LAYOUT_RIGHT. If items have a different horizontal layout, they will be placed on separate lines.

Within a line, items can have a vertical layout, either LAYOUT_TOP, LAYOUT_VCENTER, or LAYOUT_BOTTOM. The total height of the line is dictated by the tallest item. Shorter items will be placed according to the vertical layout.

You can request that items be expanded to fill the available space horizontally with LAYOUT_EXPAND or vertically with LAYOUT_VEXPAND. Likewise, to request that items be made as small as possible, use LAYOUT_SHRINK and LAYOUT_VSHRINK.

Finally, you can control line breaking with LAYOUT_NEWLINE_BEFORE and LAYOUT_NEWLINE_AFTER.

For an exhaustive discussion of form layout, consult the documentation for the Form class.

One additional trick for controlling form layout is the Spacer class, also a descendant of Item. It is invisible but has a minimum size so that you can put a certain amount of space between items in the form. Create a Spacer by specifying the minimum width and height.

8.10 Please Drink Form Responsibly

Don't be corrupted by the power of forms. Good user design is simple and intuitive. Add more than three or four items to a form and use it on a 128×128 screen, and you'll realize you've created something that's neither simple nor intuitive.

Simplify ruthlessly and question everything. Are the knobs and buttons you're putting on your form necessary? What do your users care about? Can you offer options and configuration using a desktop browser interface instead of a mobile interface? Will item layout trickery make your form more usable? Are you using commands effectively? Can your grandma use this thing? Your son? Your buddy Bo?

The following example is not simple or intuitive, but it will give you a good idea of how to create items and add them to a form.

I've used some magic in getColorImage() to create color swatches for the ChoiceGroup, but otherwise everything should be straightforward. You'll learn all about images and colors in the next chapter.

```
import java.util.*;

import javax.microedition.lcdui.*;
import javax.microedition.midlet.MIDlet;

public class UITwoFormMIDlet
    extends MIDlet
    implements CommandListener {
  private Display mDisplay;

  private Form mForm;

  private Command mExitCommand;

  public void startApp() {
    if (mForm == null) {
      mDisplay = Display.getDisplay(this);

      mForm = new Form("Dream");

      /*
      try {
        Image mlkImage = Image.createImage("/mlk-small.png");
        mForm.append(mlkImage);
      }
      catch (java.io.IOException ioe) {}
      catch (Exception e) {}
      */

      /*
      mForm.append("I have a dream...");
      */

      try {
        Image mlkImage = Image.createImage("/mlk-small.png");
        ImageItem ii = new ImageItem("MLK", mlkImage,
            Item.LAYOUT_2, "Martin Luther King Jr.");
        mForm.append(ii);
      }
      catch (java.io.IOException ioe) {}
      catch (Exception e) {}
```

continued

```
        StringItem si = new StringItem("Speech:",
            "I have a dream...");
        mForm.append(si);

        TextField tf = new TextField("Name:", "Victor Hugo",
            512, TextField.ANY);
        mForm.append(tf);

        int iw = mDisplay.getBestImageWidth(
            Display.CHOICE_GROUP_ELEMENT);
        int ih = mDisplay.getBestImageHeight(
            Display.CHOICE_GROUP_ELEMENT);
        Image blueImage = getColorImage(0x0000ff, iw, ih);
        Image redImage = getColorImage(0xff0000, iw, ih);
        Image purpleImage = getColorImage(0xff00ff, iw, ih);
        Image yellowImage = getColorImage(0xffff00, iw, ih);

        ChoiceGroup cg = new ChoiceGroup("Color:",
            ChoiceGroup.POPUP);
        cg.append("Blue", blueImage);
        cg.append("Red", redImage);
        cg.append("Purple", purpleImage);
        cg.append("Yellow", yellowImage);
        mForm.append(cg);

        long now = System.currentTimeMillis();
        DateField df = new DateField("Now:", DateField.DATE_TIME);
        df.setDate(new Date(now));
        mForm.append(df);

        Gauge g = new Gauge("Interactive", true, 5, 3);
        mForm.append(g);

        Gauge cgauge = new Gauge("Non-I continuous", false,
            Gauge.INDEFINITE, Gauge.CONTINUOUS_RUNNING);
        mForm.append(cgauge);

        mExitCommand = new Command("Exit", Command.EXIT, 0);
        mForm.addCommand(mExitCommand);
        mForm.setCommandListener(this);
    }
    mDisplay.setCurrent(mForm);
}

public void pauseApp() {}

public void destroyApp(boolean unconditional) {}
```

```
public void commandAction(Command c, Displayable d) {
  if (c == mExitCommand) {
    destroyApp(true);
    notifyDestroyed();
  }
}

private Image getColorImage(int c, int w, int h) {
  Image ci = Image.createImage(w, h);
  Graphics ig = ci.getGraphics();
  ig.setColor(c);
  ig.fillRoundRect(0, 0, w, h, w / 2, h / 2);
  return ci;
}
}
```

8.11 Item Change Events and Item Commands

Items fire off change events when their contents are changed. For example, a
ChoiceGroup will fire an event when the currently selected item changes. You can
receive these notifications by passing a listener to setItemStateListener() on
the containing Form.

ItemStateListener is an interface with one method:

```
public void itemStateChanged(Item item)
```

You know which item is changed, but you don't know how it changed or which
Form it belongs to. One possible use for ItemStateListener is form validation.
Every time you get an itemStateChanged() call, examine the data on the Form.
If it is valid, you can add an **OK** command to the form.

The last important wrinkle with respect to forms is *item commands*. Item commands are just like regular screen commands except they are specific to an item
in a form. You add them directly to an Item with addCommand(). The device
should only show the item command when that item is active.

The event handling for item commands is separate from the command handling
for screens. Create an ItemCommandListener and pass it to the item's setItem-
CommandListener() method to receive notifications. ItemCommandListener has
a single method, commandAction(), which receives a reference to the Command
that was invoked and the Item owning the Command.

Here is an example that shows an interactive gauge. As you change the value of the gauge, an ItemStateListener retrieves the current value and shows it in a StringItem. The StringItem has its command, which clears the text.

```java
import javax.microedition.lcdui.*;
import javax.microedition.midlet.*;

public class ItemMIDlet
    extends MIDlet
    implements CommandListener,
               ItemCommandListener,
               ItemStateListener {
  private Form mForm;
  private Gauge mGauge;
  private StringItem mStatus;
  private Command mExitCommand, mClearCommand;

  public void startApp() {
    if (mForm == null) {
      mForm = new Form("Item Events and Commands");

      mGauge = new Gauge("Change me!", true, 8, 4);
      mForm.append(mGauge);

      mStatus = new StringItem("Status:", "");
      mClearCommand = new Command("Clear", Command.ITEM, 0);
      mStatus.addCommand(mClearCommand);
      mStatus.setItemCommandListener(this);
      mForm.append(mStatus);

      mExitCommand = new Command("Exit", Command.EXIT, 0);
      mForm.addCommand(mExitCommand);
      mForm.setCommandListener(this);
      mForm.setItemStateListener(this);
    }
    Display.getDisplay(this).setCurrent(mForm);
  }

  public void pauseApp() {}

  public void destroyApp(boolean unconditional) {}

  // CommandListener method.

  public void commandAction(Command c, Displayable s) {
    if (c == mExitCommand) {
```

```
      destroyApp(true);
      notifyDestroyed();
    }
  }

  // ItemCommandListener method.

  public void commandAction(Command c, Item item) {
    if (c == mClearCommand && item == mStatus)
      mStatus.setText("");
  }

  // ItemStateListener method.

  public void itemStateChanged(Item item) {
    if (item == mGauge)
      mStatus.setText("gauge = " + mGauge.getValue());
  }
}
```

Figure 8.4 shows it on Sun's emulator, the Nokia Series 40 3rd edition emulator, and a Motorola RAZR V3. Notice again how commands don't necessarily show up in the same places on different devices.

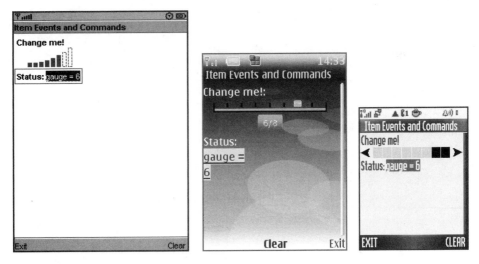

Figure 8.4 Item events and commands

8.12 Summary

This chapter describes List and Form, two useful screens. Lists can allow multiple selections, a single selection, or can act like a menu. Each list item can have an associated image. Forms are collections of items. Items can display or allow editing of strings, images, lists, points in time, and gauges. The layout of items on a form can be controlled with layout directives. Your application can be notified when item values change. Furthermore, items can have their own Commands, which are shown only when the item is active. You now know everything there is to know about prepackaged screen classes. The next three chapters describe how you can do your own drawing.

Section IV

Graphics

9

Creating Custom Screens

IF the plain old LCDUI screens are not sufficiently jazzy or flexible for your application, you can create your own screen using a *canvas*. It's more work, but it's more fun. You can control almost all of the drawing on the display and you get fine-grained event information as well.

The Canvas class is a lot like the other screens, a descendent of the Displayable class. This means that it can have commands, a title, and a ticker.

You can't just create a canvas directly, as you can with other screens. Canvas is an abstract class, with a single abstract method, paint(). You must write a subclass of Canvas and define a paint() method that draws whatever you want. Then you can create an instance of your canvas and show it on the device.

9.1 Getting Information about the Display

A successful canvas adapts to different devices smoothly. To adapt, your canvas must understand its milieu. If you want to draw a border around the whole display, you need to know the size of the display.

Getting the canvas size is easy. Just use the getWidth() and getHeight() methods. Sizes returned are in pixels. In general, a canvas will not occupy the entire device display, because the device usually reserves some screen real estate to show network signal strength, battery power, and other information. You can request the entire display space using setFullScreenMode(true), but ultimately the device decides exactly how much of the display you get. If the size of your canvas changes for any reason, the device calls sizeChanged() in your Canvas subclass.

Displays are either color or grayscale. You can find out what type of display a device possesses by calling isColor() in Display. For grayscale displays, numColors() (also in Display) returns the number of gray levels. For color displays, numColors() returns the total number of distinct colors that can be used.

Alpha compositing is a technique by which colors can be blended with the colors that are already on the display. Alpha levels are also called *transparency*. MIDP devices can support alpha compositing for images if they wish. You can find out if your device supports alpha compositing by calling numAlphaLevels() in Display. The minimum return value is 2, which indicates no blending (one value is fully transparent, the other is fully opaque).

Double buffering is a technique for reducing flicker in animations. Call isDoubleBuffered() in Canvas to find out if the device implements double buffering. Most (if not all) devices nowadays are double buffered.

9.2 How Painting Works

The paint() method is called whenever the device decides the display needs to be updated. The device passes a Graphics object that represents the device's display. Your application calls methods in Graphics to show shapes, text, and images on the display.

If you want to update the display, call repaint() in Canvas. The device will eventually call your paint() method again, but it won't happen immediately. For animations, then, you can start a separate thread that updates the application's state and then calls repaint().

A refinement of Canvas, GameCanvas, provides more control over repainting. You'll learn about it in Chapter 11, "Using the Game API."

9.3 Making Colors

Regardless of the color support of the underlying display, colors in MIDlets are always represented as a packed integer. Eight bits of red, green, and blue occupy the low 24 bits of the integer.

```
int red = 0xff0000;
int green = 0x00ff00;
int blue = 0x0000ff;
int gray = 0x777777;
```

The upper eight bits are unused, except in the special case of alpha compositing with images.

To set the current drawing color, use setColor() in Graphics.

Most devices have a set of colors that are used for menus and other screens. Display provides a method, getColor(), that you can use to retrieve the device's preferred color scheme. Pass one of the following constants to retrieve the corresponding color:

- COLOR_BACKGROUND
- COLOR_FOREGROUND
- COLOR_BORDER
- COLOR_HIGHLIGHTED_BACKGROUND
- COLOR_HIGHLIGHTED_FOREGROUND
- COLOR_HIGHLIGHTED_BORDER

Although it's nice that you can ask the device for its preferred color scheme, don't believe everything it tells you. There is no guarantee that you'll get meaningful colors. The Nokia 6270 emulator returns the same color (white) for both COLOR_BACKGROUND and COLOR_FOREGROUND. This is fine for drawing white cows in a blizzard, but not practical otherwise.

Here is a simple canvas that clears itself and draws a rectangle using the device's preferred colors. If the background and foreground colors are the same, it sets the background color to be the opposite of the foreground.

```
import javax.microedition.lcdui.*;

public class BoxCanvas
    extends Canvas {
  private final Display mDisplay;

  public BoxCanvas(Display d) {
    mDisplay = d;
  }

  public void paint(Graphics g) {
    int w = getWidth();
    int h = getHeight();

    int bg = mDisplay.getColor(Display.COLOR_BACKGROUND);
    int fg = mDisplay.getColor(Display.COLOR_FOREGROUND);
    if (bg == fg) bg = ~fg;
```

continued

```
        g.setColor(bg);
        g.fillRect(0, 0, w - 1, h - 1);

        g.setColor(fg);
        g.fillRect(w / 4, h / 4, w / 2, h / 2);
    }
}
```

You'll learn about fillRect() in the next section.

To show the canvas on the display, you need to create a simple MIDlet. In the rest of this chapter, I'll assume you can write your own MIDlet, but here is one to get you started:

```
import javax.microedition.lcdui.*;
import javax.microedition.midlet.MIDlet;

public class BoxMIDlet
    extends MIDlet
    implements CommandListener {
  private Canvas mCanvas;
  private Command mOKCommand;

  public void startApp() {
    Display display = Display.getDisplay(this);

    if (mCanvas == null) {
      mCanvas = new BoxCanvas(display);
      mOKCommand = new Command("OK", Command.OK, 0);
      mCanvas.addCommand(mOKCommand);
      mCanvas.setCommandListener(this);
    }
    display.setCurrent(mCanvas);
  }

  public void pauseApp() {}

  public void destroyApp(boolean unconditional) {}

  public void commandAction(Command c, Displayable d) {
    if (c == mOKCommand) {
      destroyApp(true);
      notifyDestroyed();
    }
  }
}
```

If you download the source code for the book, you'll find a single MIDlet, `Nine-MIDlet`, that is capable of displaying nearly all the `Canvas` examples in this chapter.

The output is not inspiring (Figure 9.1), but you have to crawl before you can walk.

9.4 Drawing Lines and Shapes

MIDP uses a coordinate system that places the origin at the upper left corner of the display. The x axis increases to the right, and the y axis increases downward.

You can move the origin of the coordinate system by passing the change in x and y to `Graphics`' `translate()` method. The current translation is returned from `getTranslateX()` and `getTranslateY()`.

Coordinates correspond to pixels on the display, but the points themselves are located *between* the pixels. This is important because it affects how shapes are drawn and filled.

For example, if you fill a rectangle whose corner is 2, 1 and whose width is 3 and height is 4, you'll get the result shown in Figure 9.2.

Figure 9.1 Your first canvas

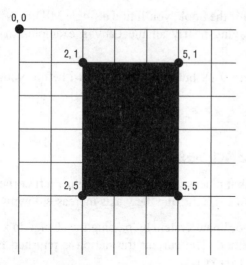

Figure 9.2 Filling a rectangle

If you want to draw the outline of a shape, the pixels that are directly down and to the right of the coordinates you specify are filled. So, for example, if you draw a rectangle with the same origin of 2, 1 and a width of 3 and a height of 4, it comes out as shown in Figure 9.3.

If you want to show a shape as well as its outline, the safest method is to first fill the shape, then draw the outline afterwards. This ensures that you'll see all of the

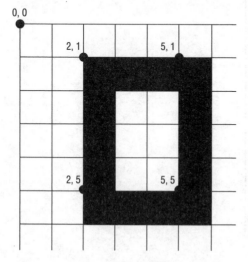

Figure 9.3 Drawing a rectangle

outline, even if the filled shape and its outline overlap. Even if you think you've got it all figured out, it's very possible that the filled shape and the outline will overlap either because of a miscalculation on your part or an incorrect implementation on a device. Just draw the outline last.

Graphics offers a straightforward set of methods for drawing and filling shapes. Drawing and filling are done using the current color.

```
public void drawLine(int x1, int y1, int x2, int y2)
public void drawRect(int x, int y, int width, int height)
public void fillRect(int x, int y, int width, int height)
public void fillTriangle(int x1, int y1, int x2, int y2,
    int x3, int y3)
```

For rectangles with rounded corners, specify a vertical and horizontal radius for the corners:

```
public void drawRoundRect(int x, int y, int width, int height,
    int arcWidth, int arcHeight)
public void fillRoundRect(int x, int y, int width, int height,
    int arcWidth, int arcHeight)
```

Finally, you can create arcs by specifying the bounding rectangle of an ellipse, a start angle, and a angle extent. Angles are measured in degrees, starting from zero pointing right and increasing counterclockwise.

```
public void drawArc(int x, int y, int width, int height,
    int startAngle, int arcAngle)
public void fillArc(int x, int y, int width, int height,
    int startAngle, int arcAngle)
```

One final feature of drawing lines and shape outlines is the *stroke style*. The Graphics object maintains a current stroke style that is used to draw lines. Call setStrokeStyle() with either SOLID or DOTTED to make a change.

The best way to learn this stuff is by trying it out, so here is a canvas class that shows off the shapes you can draw and fill.

```
import javax.microedition.lcdui.*;

public class ShapeCanvas
    extends Canvas {
  private final Display mDisplay;

  public ShapeCanvas(Display d) {
    mDisplay = d;
  }
```

continued

```
public void paint(Graphics g) {
  int w = getWidth();
  int h = getHeight();
  int bc = mDisplay.getColor(Display.COLOR_BACKGROUND);

  g.setColor(bc);
  g.fillRect(0, 0, w - 1, h - 1);

  int pad = w / 12;
  int cw = w / 2;
  int ch = h / 3;
  int aw = cw - pad * 2 - 1;
  int ah = ch - pad * 2 - 1;

  g.setColor(0xffff00);
  g.fillRect(cw + pad + 1, pad + 1, aw, ah);
  g.setColor(0x0000ff);
  g.drawLine(pad, ch - pad, cw - pad, pad);
  g.drawRect(cw + pad, pad, aw, ah);

  g.setColor(0xffff00);
  g.fillRoundRect(pad + 1, ch + pad + 1, aw, ah, pad, pad);
  g.setColor(0x0000ff);
  g.drawRoundRect(pad, ch + pad, aw, ah, pad, pad);

  g.setColor(0xffff00);
  g.fillArc(cw + pad, ch + pad, aw, ah, -20, 270);
  g.setColor(0x0000ff);
  g.drawArc(cw + pad, ch + pad, aw, ah, -20, 270);

  g.setColor(0xffff00);
  int x1 = pad, y1 = ch + ch + pad,
      x2 = cw - pad, y2 = ch + ch + ch / 2,
      x3 = cw / 2 - pad, y3 = ch + ch + ch - pad;
  g.fillTriangle(x1, y1, x2, y2, x3, y3);
  g.setColor(0x0000ff);
  g.drawLine(x1, y1, x2, y2);
  g.drawLine(x2, y2, x3, y3);
  g.drawLine(x3, y3, x1, y1);
  }
}
```

Figure 9.4 shows ShapeCanvas running on three different platforms. Notice how the Nokia 6135 emulator has black as a background color instead of white.

Note how ShapeCanvas adapts to different screen sizes. All the drawing in paint() is based on the canvas size.

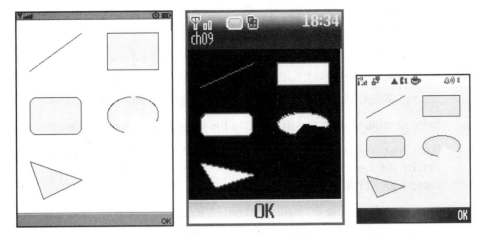

Figure 9.4   Sun's toolkit, Nokia 6136 emulator, and Motorola RAZR V3

9.5 Drawing Text

Drawing text in MIDP is pretty simple: just supply the text and tell the device where to put it. The method you'll probably use all the time is this one:

```
public void drawString(String str, int x, int y, int anchor)
```

The anchor argument tells the device how to place the text relative to the point x, y. It is a combination of a vertical value and a horizontal value. For text, the vertical values are TOP, BASELINE, and BOTTOM. The horizontal values are LEFT, HCENTER, and RIGHT. In English text, the *baseline* is the line upon which most letters lie, with descenders like the bottom of a *g* and the tail of a *y* dipping below the baseline. For example, this code places a string at the top center of a canvas:

```
public void paint(Graphics g) {
  int w = getWidth();

  g.drawString("Firenze", w / 2, 0,
      Graphics.HCENTER | Graphics.TOP);
}
```

Graphics also contains methods for drawing part of a string, an array of characters, or a single character, but most of time you will use drawString().

Text is drawn using the current color and the current *font*. The font determines the shape of the characters. Don't get your hopes up, though, because you don't get much of a choice. The `javax.microedition.lcdui.Font` class provides three font faces:

- `FACE_SYSTEM` is the font normally used by the device.
- `FACE_MONOSPACE` has characters that are all the same width.
- `FACE_PROPORTIONAL` has characters with variable widths.

Keep in mind that fonts will not look the same on different devices.

Each font comes in three sizes: `SIZE_SMALL`, `SIZE_MEDIUM`, and `SIZE_LARGE`. Finally, the font can be `STYLE_PLAIN`, `STYLE_BOLD`, `STYLE_ITALIC`, possibly combined with `STYLE_UNDERLINED`.

To retrieve a font, use the static `getFont()` method, passing the face, size, and style:

```
Font f = Font.getFont(Font.FACE_PROPORTIONAL,
    Font.SIZE_LARGE, Font.BOLD);
```

Font provides two other static methods for retrieving fonts in a more general way. The first is `getDefaultFont()`. The second is `getFont()`, which takes a single argument, either `FONT_INPUT_TEXT` or `FONT_STATIC_TEXT`. This method is most useful when you write a custom form item and want the text to match other form items. Chapter 10, "Custom Items," has information about custom form items.

Once you've retrieved a font that you like, pass the `Font` object to `setFont()` in `Graphics`. All subsequent text will be drawn using the current font.

To wrap things up, here is a small example that shows some text near the middle of the screen (see Figure 9.5).

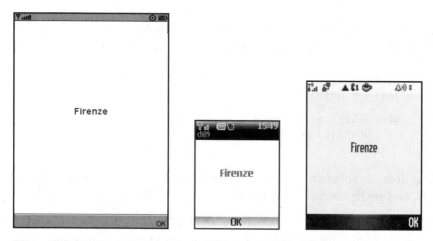

Figure 9.5   The same font can look different on different devices.

```
import javax.microedition.lcdui.*;

public class FirenzeCanvas
    extends Canvas {
  public void paint(Graphics g) {
    int w = getWidth();
    int h = getHeight();

    g.setColor(0xffffff);
    g.fillRect(0, 0, w - 1, h - 1);

    Font f = Font.getFont(Font.FACE_PROPORTIONAL,
        Font.STYLE_BOLD, Font.SIZE_LARGE);
    g.setFont(f);
    g.setColor(0x0077ff);
    g.drawString("Firenze", w / 2, h / 2,
        Graphics.HCENTER | Graphics.BOTTOM);
  }
}
```

9.6 Measuring Text

Drawing text is a little more complicated if you want to make it handle different display sizes and different device fonts gracefully. To adapt, your application needs a way to understand how large text will be on the screen.

Font offers methods that are handy for measuring text. The height of a single line of text is returned by getHeight(). This method is handy for rendering multiple lines of text and for centering text vertically.

Find the width of a particular string by passing it to stringWidth(). Other variations on this method are available if you need them: substringWidth(), charsWidth(), and charWidth().

Using these methods, you can perform fundamental operations like word wrapping. Here is a canvas that defines a generally useful wrap() method. Based on the current font, wrap() fits as much of each line as it can based on the available width. Lines are broken at spaces, if they are available. The height of the resulting text is returned.

The canvas in Figure 9.6 uses the wrapping implementation to draw a long string. A red frame is drawn around the entire text. If you use this method in your own code, you can also make use of getWrapHeight(), which calculates the height for a piece of text without drawing it. Also note that you can use the

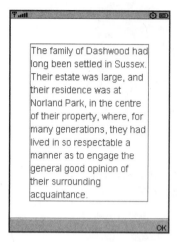

Figure 9.6   WrapCanvas demonstrates word wrapping.

same wrap() method for right-justified or centered text just by modifying the anchor value.

```
import javax.microedition.lcdui.*;

public class WrapCanvas
    extends Canvas {
  private Font mFont;
  private String mString =
      "The family of Dashwood had long been " +
      "settled in Sussex. Their estate was large, " +
      "and their residence was at Norland Park, in " +
      "the centre of their property, where, for " +
      "many generations, they had lived in so " +
      "respectable a manner as to engage the general " +
      "good opinion of their surrounding acquaintance.";

  public void paint(Graphics g) {
    int w = getWidth();
    int h = getHeight();

    g.setColor(0xffffff);
    g.fillRect(0, 0, w, h);

    int x = w / 8;
    int y = h / 8;
    int ww = w * 3 / 4;
    int anchor = Graphics.TOP | Graphics.LEFT;
```

```
  if (mFont == null) {
    int[] size = { Font.SIZE_LARGE, Font.SIZE_MEDIUM,
        Font.SIZE_SMALL };
    for (int i = 0; i < size.length; i++) {
      mFont = Font.getFont(Font.FACE_PROPORTIONAL,
          Font.STYLE_PLAIN, size[i]);
      g.setFont(mFont);
      int wh = getWrapHeight(g, mString, x, y, ww, anchor);
      if (wh < h - y) break;
    }
  }

  g.setFont(mFont);
  g.setColor(0x7700ff);
  int wh = wrap(g, mString, x, y, ww, anchor);

  g.setColor(0xff0000);
  g.drawRect(x - 1, y, ww, wh);
}

public int getWrapHeight(Graphics g, String s,
    int x, int y, int w, int anchor) {
  return wrapImplementation(g, s, x, y, w, anchor, false);
}

private int wrap(Graphics g, String s,
    int x, int y, int w, int anchor) {
  return wrapImplementation(g, s, x, y, w, anchor, true);
}

private int wrapImplementation(Graphics g, String s,
    int x, int y, int w, int anchor, boolean draw) {
  Font f = g.getFont();
  int oldy = y;

  boolean trucking = true;
  int i = 0;
  int length = 0;
  int space = -1;

  while (trucking) {
    boolean write = false;

    if (i >= s.length()) trucking = false;
    else if (s.charAt(i) == ' ') i++;
    else {
      int pw = f.substringWidth(s, i, length);
```

continued

```
        if (pw > w) {
          if (space > 0) length = space;
          else length--;
          write = true;
        }
        else if (i + length >= s.length()) {
          write = true;
          trucking = false;
        }
        else {
          if (s.charAt(i + length) == ' ') space = length;
          length++;
        }
      }

      if (write) {
        if (draw) g.drawSubstring(s, i, length, x, y, anchor);
        i += length;
        y += f.getHeight();
        length = 0;
        space = -1;
      }
    }

    return y - oldy;
  }
}
```

9.7 Creating Images

Although it's possible to create custom screens using text and shapes, you'll probably want to use images for the best possible visual impact. It's easy enough to adapt shapes and text to differing screen sizes, but the rendering is aliased (jaggy), and you're at the mercy of the device's fonts.

The problem with images is that they have a fixed size, which means adapting to different device display sizes is a challenge. One technique is to assemble screens from an assortment of images. For example, a title bar could be created from a left end, a right end, and an image could be tiled (repeated) to form the middle. The problem is similar to designing adaptable graphic borders for Web pages.

MSA dictates that devices must be able to load PNG and JPEG images. Other image formats might be supported, but that support is the device's prerogative.

If you were paying attention back in Chapter 7, "Basic User Interface," you already know how to load an image from a file in the MIDlet suite JAR:

```
try {
  Image i = Image.createImage("/Minerva-t.png");
}
catch (IOException ioe) {
  // Handle the exception.
}
catch (Exception e) {
  // Handle other types of exceptions.
}
```

Two other variants on `createImage()` allow you to load an image from a byte array or an input stream.

Images are either *mutable* or *immutable*. You can draw on *mutable* images, as you'll see in a moment. The `createImage()` methods described so far return immutable images.

Two additional `createImage()` methods create immutable images from another image or part of another image.

```
public static Image createImage(Image source)
public static Image createImage(Image image,
    int x, int y, int width, int height, int transform)
```

In the second version, x, y, width, and height describe the region of the source image you want to use to create the returned image. In addition, you can flip the region or rotate it by specifying a `transform` value from the `javax.micro-edition.lcdui.game.Sprite` class (which you'll read about later):

- `TRANS_NONE` does nothing.
- `TRANS_ROT90`, `TRANS_ROT180`, and `TRANS_ROT270` rotate the source image region clockwise by the specified number of degrees. This is opposite from the angle direction used in `drawArc()` and `fillArc()`.
- `TRANS_MIRROR` flips the source image region horizontally.
- `TRANS_MIRROR_ROT90`, `TRANS_MIRROR_ROT180`, and `TRANS_MIRROR_ROT270` flip the image and subsequently rotate it.

This version of `createImage()` is handy for creating lots of images to be used at runtime from a single larger resource image. Using a single resource image helps keep the overall size of the MIDlet suite JAR low. Also, the ability to flip and rotate image regions means that you can use one set of source images to create a wide variety of useful images in your application. In the next section, I'll show you some source code that slices up and transforms an image of three cars, as shown in Figure 9.7.

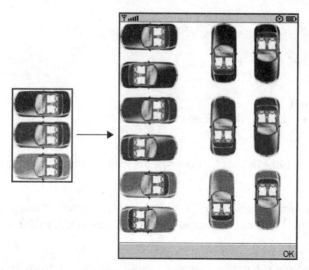

Figure 9.7   Use one source image to create lots of images at runtime.

9.8 Drawing Images

Drawing images is a lot like drawing text. All you have to supply is the image and an anchor point.

The anchor points work nearly the same as for drawing text, except the BASELINE anchor point won't work with images. Instead, you can use VCENTER to specify that the image should be vertically centered with respect to the anchor point.

If the device supports alpha compositing, images that contain alpha information will be blended with existing drawing on the canvas.

Here is the complete source code for CarCanvas, which shows how to split up and transform the car image. All the image transformation craziness happens in loadImages().

```
import javax.microedition.lcdui.*;
import javax.microedition.lcdui.game.Sprite;

public class CarCanvas
    extends Canvas {
  private Image[] mImages;

  public CarCanvas() { loadImages(); }
```

```
public void paint(Graphics g) {
  int w = getWidth();
  int h = getHeight();

  g.setColor(0xcccccc);
  g.fillRect(0, 0, w, h);

  int pad = w / 12;
  int cw = w / 2;
  int ch = h / 3;

  if (mImages == null) {
    g.setColor(0x000000);
    g.drawString("Couldn't load images", w / 2, h / 2,
        Graphics.HCENTER | Graphics.BOTTOM);
    return;
  }

  for (int i = 0; i < 3; i++) {
    // Left image.
    g.drawImage(mImages[i * 4 + 0],
        0, ch * i, Graphics.TOP | Graphics.LEFT);
    // Right image.
    g.drawImage(mImages[i * 4 + 2],
        0, ch * i + ch / 2, Graphics.TOP | Graphics.LEFT);
    // Up image.
    g.drawImage(mImages[i * 4 + 1],
        cw, ch * i, Graphics.TOP | Graphics.LEFT);
    // Down image.
    g.drawImage(mImages[i * 4 + 3],
        cw + cw / 2, ch * i, Graphics.TOP | Graphics.LEFT);
  }
}

private void loadImages() {
  try {
    // Load the large image.
    Image big = Image.createImage("/tricolor-cars-s.png");
    int bigw = big.getWidth();
    int bigh = big.getHeight();

    // Split it into three car images.
    Image[] cars = new Image[3];
    for (int i = 0; i < 3; i++) {
      cars[i] = Image.createImage(big, 0, bigh * i / 3,
          bigw, bigh / 3, Sprite.TRANS_NONE);
    }
```

continued

```
        // Create the transformations.
        mImages = new Image[12];
        for (int i = 0; i < 12; i += 4) {
          Image base = cars[i / 4];
          int bw = base.getWidth();
          int bh = base.getHeight();
          mImages[i     ] = base;
          mImages[i + 1] = Image.createImage(base, 0, 0,
              bw, bh, Sprite.TRANS_ROT90);
          mImages[i + 2] = Image.createImage(base, 0, 0,
              bw, bh, Sprite.TRANS_ROT180);
          mImages[i + 3] = Image.createImage(base, 0, 0,
              bw, bh, Sprite.TRANS_ROT270);
        }
      }
      catch (java.io.IOException ioe) {}
    }
  }
```

9.9 Keeping Resources Small

One of the challenges of creating MIDP applications is keeping the overall size small. This is necessary because MIDP devices have limited storage space and processing power. Also, because current wireless networks are relatively slow, keeping the MIDlet suite small means faster downloading times.

One way to keep a MIDlet suite small is by minimizing the space taken up by image resources.

- Instead of many image files, combine a set of images into one file and split it up at runtime. You'll save on the overhead of the graphic file format.
- Minimize the number of images you need by using the Sprite transformations described previously. If you have a spaceship that spins around through twelve different positions, you can supply only three positions and generate the rest by rotating by 90, 180, or 270 degrees.
- Minimize the number of colors in the image.
- Make sure your desktop image software isn't saving some kind of preview or icon image into the image file.

For example, I once had a sequence of twelve images for a spinning animation (AnimationGauge in the next chapter). As separate files, the twelve images were 8,093 bytes. Combined into one file, they were 4,691 bytes. When I used just three frames instead of twelve, the resulting file was just 2,253 bytes.

9.10 Drawing on Images

All the images you've learned about are immutable. Mutable images are cool because you can draw directly on them. Here is how it works:

1. Create a mutable image by passing a width and height to yet another version of the static method `createImage()` in `Image`.
2. Retrieve a `Graphics` object from the image with `getGraphics()`.
3. Draw on the image using the `Graphics` object.

Here is an example that demonstrates how you can use this technique. It creates and uses a smallish tile image for a brushed metal title bar, much like you've seen in iTunes. It's a classy look for very low cost. The tile image is created in `getTitleTileImage()`. The size of the image is based on the height of the title bar, which in turn is based on the height of the current font.

```
import javax.microedition.lcdui.*;

public class TitleTileCanvas extends Canvas {
  private Image mTitleTileImage;

  public void paint(Graphics g) {
    int w = getWidth();
    int h = getHeight();

    g.setColor(0xaa0033);
    g.fillRect(0, 0, w, h);

    int rh = g.getFont().getHeight() + 6;
    Image tti = getTitleTileImage(rh);
    for (int x = 0; x <= w; x += tti.getWidth())
      g.drawImage(tti, x, 0, Graphics.TOP | Graphics.LEFT);

    g.setColor(0x000000);
    g.drawString("Here is a title!", w / 2, 3,
        Graphics.TOP | Graphics.HCENTER);
  }

  public Image getTitleTileImage(int rowHeight) {
    if (mTitleTileImage == null ||
        mTitleTileImage.getHeight() != rowHeight) {
      int w = rowHeight;
      mTitleTileImage = Image.createImage(w, rowHeight);
      Graphics ig = mTitleTileImage.getGraphics();
```

continued

```
      for (int y = 0; y < rowHeight; y++) {
        ig.setGrayScale(255 - 128 * y / rowHeight);
        ig.drawLine(0, y, w, y);
      }
    }
    return mTitleTileImage;
  }

}
```

Figure 9.8 shows how that lovely title bar looks when it's running:

You might be tempted to load images from resource files and try to draw on them, but that won't work directly. Images that are created from files are immutable, so when you try to call getGraphics() to draw on them, an exception is thrown.

The workaround is to create a mutable image and draw the immutable image on it. Here is a method that does that:

```
private Image createMutable(Image im) {
  Image m = Image.createImage(im.getWidth(), im.getHeight());
  Graphics ig = m.getGraphics();
  ig.drawImage(im, 0, 0, Graphics.LEFT | Graphics.TOP);
  return m;
}
```

Figure 9.8   The title bar is composed of a dynamically generated tile image.

9.11 Getting Your Fingers on the Bits

For all you control freaks out there, MIDP offers the ability to directly examine and manipulate the color of individual pixels in an image.

You can retrieve the data for an image with Image's getRGB() method:

```
public void getRGB(int[] rgbData,
    int offset, int scanlength,
    int x, int y, int width, int height)
```

x, y, width, and height describe the portion of the image you are retrieving. The offset and scanlength arguments can be used to place the image data at a certain location in the integer array or to interleave it with other data. scanlength indicates the number of array entries between the data for each image row. Most of the time, you'll just pass 0 for the offset and use the image width as the scanlength. Here is an example that retrieves an image's data into an array that is just big enough to contain it.

```
private int[] getTightRGB(Image image) {
  int w = image.getWidth();
  int h = image.getHeight();

  int[] data = new int[w * h];
  image.getRGB(data, 0, w, 0, 0, w, h);
  return data;
}
```

Once you've got image data, you can display it by calling this method in Graphics:

```
public void drawRGB(int[] rgbData,
    int offset, int scanlength,
    int x, int y, int width, int height,
    boolean processAlpha)
```

The processAlpha flag tells Graphics whether your integer array contains alpha data in addition to red, green, and blue. If you pass true for processAlpha, then the high-order 8 bits of each integer will be interpreted as an alpha value. Note that whatever you do with alpha values, the device might or might not support alpha blending. Call Display's numAlphaLevels() to find out what the device supports.

Instead of drawing the RGB integer array directly, you can create a new image from the integer array using this method in `Image`:

```
public static Image createRGBImage(int[] rgb,
    int width, int height, boolean processAlpha)
```

Here's an example that loads an image from a resource, obtains its data with `getRGB()`, then adds some random noise to each pixel. Notice how the `frizz()` method preserves alpha information, if there is any, so the call to `drawRGB()` includes a `processAlpha` value of `true`.

```
import java.util.Random;

import javax.microedition.lcdui.*;

public class RGBCanvas
    extends Canvas {
  private Image mImage;
  private int[] mData;

  public RGBCanvas() { loadImage(); }

  public void paint(Graphics g) {
    int w = getWidth();
    int h = getHeight();

    g.setColor(0xffffff);
    g.fillRect(0, 0, w, h);

    if (mImage == null) {
      g.setColor(0x000000);
      g.drawString("Couldn't load image", w / 2, h / 2,
          Graphics.HCENTER | Graphics.BOTTOM);
      return;
    }

    int iw = mImage.getWidth();
    int ih = mImage.getHeight();
    int x = w * 3 / 4 - iw / 2;
    int y = (h - ih) / 2;

    g.drawImage(mImage, x - w / 2, y,
        Graphics.LEFT | Graphics.TOP);
    g.drawRGB(mData, 0, iw, x, y, iw, ih, true);
  }
```

```
private void loadImage() {
  try {
    mImage = Image.createImage("/king.png");
    mData = getTightRGB(mImage);
    frizz();
  }
  catch (java.io.IOException ioe) {}
}

private int[] getTightRGB(Image image) {
  int w = image.getWidth();
  int h = image.getHeight();

  int[] data = new int[w * h];
  image.getRGB(data, 0, w, 0, 0, w, h);
  return data;
}

private void frizz() {
  Random random = new Random();
  for (int i = 0; i < mData.length; i++) {
    int c = mData[i];
    int a = c & 0xff000000;
    int r = (c & 0x00ff0000) >> 16;
    int g = (c & 0x0000ff00) >>  8;
    int b = c & 0x000000ff;

    int f = (random.nextInt() % 64) - 32;
    r = Math.max(0x00, Math.min(0xff, r + f));
    g = Math.max(0x00, Math.min(0xff, g + f));
    b = Math.max(0x00, Math.min(0xff, b + f));

    c = a |
        ((r << 16) & 0x00ff0000) |
        ((g << 8) & 0x0000ff00) |
        b;

    mData[i] = c;
  }
}
}
```

In paint(), the original image and the processed integer array are displayed next to each other, as in Figure 9.9.

Figure 9.9   Processing an image by manipulating its integer array

9.12 Clipping

One last technique related to Graphics is *clipping*. Clipping limits all drawing on the display to a specific region. It's as if you placed a stencil over the display and then drew on top of it.

Graphics supports only rectangular clipping regions. Pass the rectangle's corner, width, and height to setClip() to set the current clipping region. A related method, clipRect(), sets the clipping region to the intersection of the current clipping region and the rectangle passed to clipRect().

9.13 Event Handling

Canvas subclasses are notified about key presses, pointer activity, and whether the canvas is being shown. Your application can respond to these notifications by overriding corresponding methods.

Key presses are passed to keyPressed() and keyReleased(). The value that is passed to these methods is a *key code*. Devices are likely to have their own sets of key codes, except for a few standard ones defined by constants in Canvas: KEY_NUM0 through KEY_NUM9, KEY_STAR, and KEY_POUND.

You can ask the device for a human-readable name of a key by passing the key code to `getKeyName()`. This capability is useful if you want to display the controls for an application in a help screen.

A key that is held down might generate *repeat events*. Ask your canvas about this by calling `hasRepeatEvents()`. If the canvas supports repeat events, the repeating key code will be passed to `keyRepeated()`.

To make applications as portable as possible, `Canvas` offers an abstraction of key codes called *game actions*. Convert a key code to a game action with `getGame-Action()`. The game action constants are UP, DOWN, LEFT, RIGHT, FIRE, GAME_A, GAME_B, GAME_C, and GAME_D. It's possible that more than one key can map to the same game action. On my Motorola RAZR, for example, the arrow keys map to UP, DOWN, LEFT, and RIGHT, but the 2, 8, 4, and 6 keys do as well.

Here is a `Canvas` subclass that should help you make some sense of key codes and game actions. It waits for incoming key events and prints information about them on the display. Remember, key codes are likely to vary among devices, so your event handling should be based on game actions or the standard key codes.

```
import javax.microedition.lcdui.*;

public class KeyCanvas
    extends Canvas {
  private String mMessage = "Press any key!";
  private int mKeyCode;

  public void paint(Graphics g) {
    int w = getWidth();
    int h = getHeight();

    g.setColor(0xffffff);
    g.fillRect(0, 0, w, h);

    int fh = g.getFont().getHeight();
    int y = h / 2 - fh * 2;

    int kc = mKeyCode;

    g.setColor(0x000000);
    g.drawString(mMessage, w / 2, y,
        Graphics.HCENTER | Graphics.BOTTOM);
    y += fh;
    if (kc != 0) {
      String kn = getKeyName(kc);
      if (kn == null) kn = "";
```

continued

```
        int ga = getGameAction(kc);
        String gn = getGameActionName(ga);
        g.drawString("Key code: " + kc, w / 2, y,
            Graphics.HCENTER | Graphics.BOTTOM);
        y += fh;
        g.drawString("Key name: " + kn, w / 2, y,
            Graphics.HCENTER | Graphics.BOTTOM);
        y += fh;
        g.drawString("Game action: " + gn, w / 2, y,
            Graphics.HCENTER | Graphics.BOTTOM);
    }
}

protected void keyPressed(int keyCode) {
    mMessage = "keyPressed()";
    mKeyCode = keyCode;
    repaint();
}

protected void keyReleased(int keyCode) {
    mMessage = "keyReleased()";
    mKeyCode = keyCode;
    repaint();
}

protected void keyRepeated(int keyCode) {
    mMessage = "keyRepeated()";
    mKeyCode = keyCode;
    repaint();
}

private String getGameActionName(int gameAction) {
    String name = "";
    switch (gameAction) {
        case UP: name = "UP"; break;
        case DOWN: name = "DOWN"; break;
        case LEFT: name = "LEFT"; break;
        case RIGHT: name = "RIGHT"; break;
        case FIRE: name = "FIRE"; break;
        case GAME_A: name = "GAME_A"; break;
        case GAME_B: name = "GAME_B"; break;
        case GAME_C: name = "GAME_C"; break;
        case GAME_D: name = "GAME_D"; break;
        default: break;
    }
    return name;
}
}
```

Some MIDP devices have touch screens. In the MIDP world, touch screens generate *pointer events*. Call hasPointerEvents() in your canvas to find out if these are supported. Call hasPointerMotionEvents() to see if dragging is supported. Pointer events are delivered to your application in the pointerPressed(), pointerReleased(), and pointerDragged() methods. The device passes the x and y coordinates of the event to the appropriate method.

Finally, a canvas receives notification when it is about to be shown or about to be removed from the display. The showNotify() method is called just before a canvas is shown, while hideNotify() is called just before something else is shown in place of the canvas. These are very important methods. They are great places to start and stop animation threads and sounds.

9.14 Controlling Command Placement

If the vagaries of command placement are causing you heartburn, you can use a full screen canvas and some ugly code to provide a more consistent user experience. Almost all MIDP devices have two soft keys located at the bottom left and bottom right of the screen. You can draw your own commands or menu labels at the bottom left and bottom right of a full-screen canvas. By responding directly to the soft keys (in your Canvas's key event methods), you can simulate commands but have more control over their placement.

Soft buttons have different key codes on different platforms, but in many cases you can determine the proper key codes at runtime. One way is to examine the existing mapping between key codes and game actions to see if it matches a known device or device class. Another possibility is to look at the system property microedition.platform.

Here is one example of a keyPressed() method that tests for the left and right soft buttons.

```
protected void keyPressed(int keyCode) {
    // Initialize keycode constants.
    int fnleft = -6;
    int fnright = -7;

    try {
        if (getGameAction(-6) == Canvas.DOWN) {
            // Motorola V3.
            fnleft = -21;
```

continued

```
            fnright = -22;
        }
    }
    catch (IllegalArgumentException ex) {}

    if (keyCode == fnleft) {
      // Left soft button pressed!
    }
    else if (keyCode == fnright) {
      // Right soft button pressed!
    }
}
```

It works correctly on Sun's emulator, Nokia Series 40 devices, and my Motorola V3 (Figure 9.10). You should be able to expand on this technique to support more devices. In the example code, look at SoftCanvas (and SoftMIDlet) to see how to draw and respond to your own soft button commands. Notice the consistent experience on different devices.

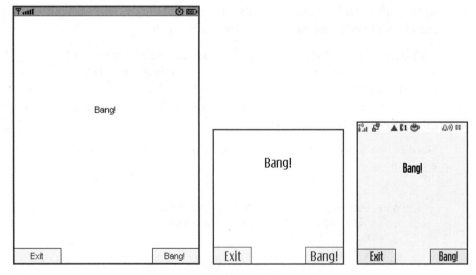

Figure 9.10 SoftCanvas behaves the same on different devices.

9.15 Summary

Canvas is the base class for all custom screens. Create a subclass to draw shapes, text, and images and respond to incoming events. Graphics is capable of drawing lines, rectangles, rounded rectangles, arcs, and triangles. A few different fonts are available, but they will appear different from device to device. Images can be loaded from resource files, created dynamically, and manipulated at the pixel level. Key events can be captured, and game actions provide a useful abstraction of different device key layouts. For a unique presentation and user experience, use a subclass of Canvas.

10

Custom Items

A middle ground lies between the easy path of canned LCDUI screens and the raw bravado of using `Canvas`. *Custom items* are your own items that can be placed into standard forms.

A custom item is very similar to a canvas, but it has some additional equipment to allow it to be part of a form. Create a custom item by subclassing `javax.microedition.lcdui.CustomItem`.

10.1 Custom Item Sizing

The size of a custom item is determined by the form. In your own implementation, you must specify a *minimum* and a *preferred* size for your custom item. The minimum is the smallest size your item can possibly be. The preferred size is the size at which your item will look its best and operate most smoothly.

The minimum and preferred sizes refer to the *content area* of the custom item, which is the part you are responsible for drawing. The entire area of a custom item includes a label and possibly a border, both of which are drawn by the device.

To communicate the minimum content size to the containing form, your `CustomItem` subclass must define two methods:

```
protected abstract int getMinContentWidth()
protected abstract int getMinContentHeight()
```

The methods for preferred size are passed a trial value from the form as it performs its layout. The form asks, "If I make you this height, what width would you like?" or "If I make you this width, what height would you like?"

```
protected abstract int getPrefContentWidth(int height)
protected abstract int getPrefContentHeight(int width)
```

A CustomItem's size can change as additional items are added to its containing form. As with Canvas, CustomItem includes a sizeChanged() method that is called when the item gets bigger or smaller.

10.2 Painting

As with Canvas, you must define a paint() method for your custom item. In addition to a Graphics object, CustomItem's paint() method is passed the width and height of the content area.

```
protected abstract void paint(Graphics g, int w, int h)
```

Like Canvas, CustomItem has a repaint() method you can use to request that the item be rendered again.

10.3 A Pretty Wait Indicator

You know enough now to write a simple custom item. Subclass CustomItem, implement the four size methods, implement paint(), and you're done. The following example displays a rotating indicator, useful for letting users know you're doing something that might take a while. You could more easily use a continuous noninteractive Gauge for this purpose, but writing your own custom item gives you more control over the appearance of the item on different devices.

This example, AnimationGauge, is created by supplying an image that contains one-quarter of the frames of a rotating animation. AnimationGauge transforms whatever frames you supply to rotate the animation through a full circle.

AnimationGauge creates a timer thread to drive the animation. The timeStep() method advances the animation by one frame.

```
import java.io.IOException;
import java.util.*;

import javax.microedition.lcdui.*;
import javax.microedition.lcdui.game.Sprite;
```

```
public class AnimationGauge
    extends CustomItem {
  private Image mImage;
  private int mIndex;
  private int mN; // Number of frames.
  private int mS; // Frame width and height.

  private Timer mTimer;

  public AnimationGauge(String filename) throws IOException {
    super("");
    mImage = Image.createImage(filename);
    mS = mImage.getHeight();

    mN = mImage.getWidth() / mS * 4;
  }

  public void showNotify() {
    mTimer = new Timer();
    TimerTask task = new TimerTask() {
      public void run() {
        timeStep();
      }
    };
    mTimer.schedule(task, 0, 100);
  }

  public void hideNotify() {
    if (mTimer != null) {
      mTimer.cancel();
      mTimer = null;
    }
  }

  public void paint(Graphics g, int w, int h) {
    int i = mIndex % (mN / 4);
    int x = i * mS;

    int ti = (mIndex - i) / (mN / 4);
    int tx = Sprite.TRANS_NONE;
    if (ti == 1) tx = Sprite.TRANS_ROT90;
    if (ti == 2) tx = Sprite.TRANS_ROT180;
    if (ti == 3) tx = Sprite.TRANS_ROT270;

    g.drawRegion(mImage, x, 0, mS, mS,
        tx, w / 2, h / 2,
        Graphics.HCENTER | Graphics.VCENTER);
  }
```

continued

```
public int getMinContentWidth() { return mS; }
public int getMinContentHeight() { return mS; }

public int getPrefContentWidth(int h) { return mS; }
public int getPrefContentHeight(int width) { return mS; }

public void timeStep() {
  mIndex = (mIndex + 1) % mN;
  repaint();
}
}
```

As with Canvas, the perfect place to start and stop animations is in the show-Notify() and hideNotify() methods. The paint() method simply chooses the appropriate frame and its transformation and draws one frame of the original image.

The minimum and preferred sizes of the AnimationGauge are calculated on the basis of the height of the image, which is the same as the height of one frame, and frames are square.

A suitable image is shown in Figure 10.1.

The image is 96 × 32 pixels. It contains three 32 × 32 frames of an animation. The three frames can be rotated in increments of 90 degrees to form a complete set.

The code to create the AnimationGauge is simple:

```
Form f = new Form("Pretty Wait Indicator");
AnimationGauge ag = new AnimationGauge("/p3.png");
f.append(ag);
```

Figure 10.2 shows the AnimationGauge as part of a form on Sun's emulator, the Nokia 6270 emulator, and the Motorola V3. The form also contains an image (the lizard) and another custom item, which you'll see in the next section.

The image I used here has a transparent background, so you can see how the Nokia 6270's spiffy background shows through. You can see that Motorola V3 does not support alpha blending. The image looks chunkier because the partially transpar-

Figure 10.1   Image frames for animation

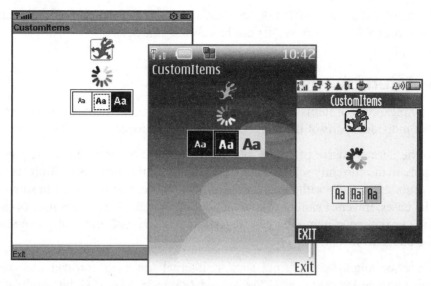

Figure 10.2 The AnimationGauge and FontChoice custom items

ent pixels around the edges of the lines are rendered fully opaque. Likewise, the lizard, which contains some partial transparency, looks chunkier on the Motorola.

 Note: The book's Web site also contains the source code for a Java SE utility, Progressor, that generates the images I used for AnimationGauge.

10.4 Handling Events in Custom Items

Event handling in custom items is just like event handling in canvases. The same callback methods are defined in CustomItem: keyPressed(), keyReleased(), pointerDragged(), and so forth.

Game actions are supported through the getGameAction() method, but don't forget that the game action constants are defined in Canvas, not CustomItem.

Your custom item receives events based on the capabilities of the device as well as the implementation of Form. Some key events might be swallowed by the form to be used in navigation. You can find out what kind of events your custom item might expect to receive by calling getInteractionModes(). This method returns some combination of KEY_PRESS, KEY_RELEASE, KEY_REPEAT, POINTER_DRAG,

POINTER_PRESS, and POINTER_RELEASE. Any set flag indicates that the corresponding callback event handler can be called by the device.

10.5 Internal Traversal

Complex custom items will probably support *internal traversal*, which means that individual parts of the item can have the input focus.

In the normal course of events, one item in a form has input focus. Key events apply to the currently selected item. You can move the input focus from one item to another (usually with the arrow keys), which is called *traversal*. In some special cases, traversal can move into and out of an item. A good example of this is the ChoiceGroup item. You can traverse into a ChoiceGroup and move among the elements it contains.

A device might or might not support internal traversal. You can find out by checking the TRAVERSE_HORIZONTAL and TRAVERSE_VERTICAL bits in the return value of getInteractionModes(). If you do want to implement internal traversal in your custom item, you'll have to override the traverse() method. It's exceptionally complicated. Check out the CustomItem documentation for the full story. I'll describe it briefly here.

```
protected boolean traverse(int dir,
    int viewportWidth, int viewportHeight,
    int[] visRect_inout)
```

The return value indicates whether traversal continues inside your item (true) or whether traversal leaves your item (false). The default implementation returns false every time, which means no internal traversal occurs.

To implement internal traversal, override traverse() and return true at appropriate times. The dir argument tells you how the user is attempting to traverse: typically, it is Canvas.UP, Canvas.DOWN, Canvas.LEFT, or Canvas.RIGHT.

The viewportWidth and viewportHeight arguments describe the viewable area of the containing form.

visRect_inout describes the currently visible rectangle of the item. Upon returning, you should modify it to contain the currently selected portion of the item. This enables the device to scroll the form to show that part of the item if it happens to be partially or fully off the screen.

traverse() is tricky. One of the trickiest things about traverse() is that it is called in two subtly different ways. It is first called when the user traverses from another item into your item. It is also called when the user traverses inside your item.

The device calls another method, `traverseOut()`, when traversal leaves your item. Typically, this happens when you return `false` from `traverse()`.

The following code skeleton shows how you can use a member variable, `mIsTraversing`, to keep track of internal traversal. Set it to `true` in `traverse()` and unset it in `traverseOut()`. You can also examine this variable in `paint()` to create a visual representation of focus.

```
private boolean mIsTraversing;

protected boolean traverse(int dir,
    int viewportWidth, int viewportHeight,
    int[] visRect_inout) {
boolean more = true;

  // Entering the item.
  if (mIsTraversing == false) {
    mIsTraversing = true;
    return mIsTraversing;
  }

  // Traversing internally.

  // Set more as appropriate.

  // set visRect_inout

  mIsTraversing = true;

  return more;
}

protected void traverseOut() {
  mIsTraversing = false;
}
```

The next section has a complete example that shows one way to work with `traverse()` and `traverseOut()`.

10.6 An Interactive Example

The following example is a custom item that allows the user to select a font size. Supply it with a font face and style, and it will display the small, medium, and large versions of the font. When the item has input focus, any key press will change the current size.

```
import javax.microedition.lcdui.*;

public class FontChoice
    extends CustomItem {
  private String mString = "Aa";
  private int mPad = 4;

  // Default plain colors.
  private int mBG  = 0x404040;
  private int mFG  = 0x808080;
  // Default selected colors.
  private int mBGS = 0xffafaf;
  private int mFGS = 0xff0000;

  private Font[] mFonts;

  private int mN; // Number of fonts.
  private int mS; // Cell side.

  private boolean mIsTraversing;
  private int mFocus;
  private int mSelection;

  public FontChoice() { this(null); }

  public FontChoice(Display d) {
    super("");

    mFocus = 0;
    mSelection = 0;

    if (d != null) {
      mBG = d.getColor(Display.COLOR_BACKGROUND);
      mFG = d.getColor(Display.COLOR_FOREGROUND);
      mBGS = d.getColor(Display.COLOR_HIGHLIGHTED_BACKGROUND);
      mFGS = d.getColor(Display.COLOR_HIGHLIGHTED_FOREGROUND);
    }

    // Hard code to three fonts in different sizes.
    mN = 3;
    int[] sizes = {
        Font.SIZE_SMALL,
        Font.SIZE_MEDIUM,
        Font.SIZE_LARGE };
    mFonts = new Font[mN];
```

```
    for (int i = 0; i < sizes.length; i++) {
      mFonts[i] = Font.getFont(
          Font.FACE_PROPORTIONAL,
          Font.STYLE_BOLD,
          sizes[i]);
    }

    // Calculate cell side.
    mS = mFonts[2].stringWidth(mString) + mPad * 2;
  }

  public Font getFont() { return mFonts[mSelection]; }

  public void paint(Graphics g, int w, int h) {
    for (int i = 0; i < mN; i++) {
      int bg = mBG;
      int fg = mFG;

      if (i == mSelection) {
        bg = mBGS;
        fg = mFGS;
      }

      if (fg == bg) bg = ~fg;

      int x = 1 + i * (mS + 1);
      int y = 1;

      // Draw the background.
      g.setColor(bg);
      g.fillRect(x, y, mS, mS);

      // Draw the string.
      Font f = mFonts[i];
      int fh = f.getHeight();
      g.setColor(fg);
      g.setFont(f);
      g.drawString(mString, x + mS / 2, mS / 2 + fh / 2,
          Graphics.HCENTER | Graphics.BOTTOM);

      // Draw the focus rectangle.
      if (mIsTraversing && i == mFocus) {
        int inset = mPad - 2;
        g.setStrokeStyle(Graphics.DOTTED);
        g.drawRect(x + inset, y + inset,
            mS - inset * 2 - 1, mS - inset * 2 - 1);
      }
```

continued

```
      // Draw the divider line.
      g.setStrokeStyle(Graphics.SOLID);
      g.setColor(mFG);
      g.drawLine(x + mS, 0, x + mS, mS + 1);
    }

    // Draw the outline.
    g.setColor(mFG);
    g.drawRect(0, 0, (mS + 1) * mN, mS + 1);
  }

  public int getMinContentWidth() {
    return getPrefContentWidth(0);
  }

  public int getMinContentHeight() {
    return getPrefContentHeight(0);
  }

  public int getPrefContentWidth(int height) {
    return 1 + (mS + 1) * mN;
  }

  public int getPrefContentHeight(int width) {
    return mS + 2;
  }

  protected void keyPressed(int keyCode) {
    if (getGameAction(keyCode) == Canvas.FIRE)
      mSelection = mFocus;
    repaint();
  }

  protected boolean traverse(int dir,
      int viewportWidth, int viewportHeight,
      int[] visRect_inout) {
    boolean more = true;

    // Entering the item.
    if (mIsTraversing == false) {
      mIsTraversing = true;
      repaint();
      return mIsTraversing;
    }

    // Traversing internally.
```

```
      switch (dir) {
        case Canvas.DOWN:
        case Canvas.RIGHT:
          mFocus++;
          if (mFocus >= mN) {
            more = false;
            mFocus--;
          }
          break;
        case Canvas.UP:
        case Canvas.LEFT:
          mFocus--;
          if (mFocus < 0) {
            more = false;
            mFocus++;
          }
          break;
        case CustomItem.NONE:
        default:
          break;
      }

      visRect_inout[0] = 1 + mFocus * (mS + 1);
      visRect_inout[1] = 1;
      visRect_inout[2] = mS;
      visRect_inout[3] = mS;

      mIsTraversing = true;

      repaint();

      return more;
    }

    protected void traverseOut() {
      mIsTraversing = false;
    }
  }
```

You've already seen this custom item in the previous screen shots. The
FontChoice example illustrates some of the slings and arrows of outrageous
MIDP implementations. Motorola's V3, for example, appears to provide exactly
the same font regardless of what size you request. Another oddity is that the
select (or fire) key on Sun's emulator and the Motorola V3 will change the currently selected font size, but the same key on the Nokia 6270 and 6136 emulators
(and my 6030 device) does not get passed to keyPressed().

10.7 Summary

If you want to create a specialized application user interface, CustomItems offer some advanced control without the heavy responsibility of creating canvases. In some respects, custom items behave just like canvases. Custom items have a minimum size and a preferred size, which your subclass must return from corresponding methods. Implement paint() to display the custom item, and implement event callbacks to respond to key presses and pointer events. More complex custom items might have internal traversal. You can implement internal traversal by overriding traverse() and, perhaps, traverseOut(). This chapter includes two examples to get you started on your own custom items.

11

Using the
Game API

ONE popular category of Java ME applications is games. Even when faster data networks make other types of applications more popular, games will always be an important part of the Java ME ecosystem.

MIDP has a Game API designed to help you create 2D action or board games. It has a souped-up canvas and supports building a screen using multiple layers. The entire API consists of five classes in the `javax.microedition.lcdui.game` package.

11.1 Tight Looping with GameCanvas

Suppose you write a typical game using `Canvas`. You do your own drawing in `paint()` and respond to key events in the event callback methods. You have a separate thread that updates the game's state and requests screen updates using `repaint()`. It looks something like this:

```
import java.util.*;

import javax.microedition.lcdui.*;

public class TypicalCanvas
    extends Canvas {
  private Timer mTimer;
```

continued

```java
    public void showNotify() {
      mTimer = new Timer();
      TimerTask task = new TimerTask() {
        public void run() {
          updateGameState();
          repaint();
        }
      };
      mTimer.schedule(task, 0, 20);
    }

    public void hideNotify() {
      if (mTimer != null) {
        mTimer.cancel();
        mTimer = null;
      }
    }

    private void updateGameState() {
      // Move things, check for collisions, etc.
    }

    public void paint(Graphics g) {
      // Draw the game.
    }

    public void keyPressed(int keyCode) {
      // Handle key events.
    }
  }
```

The main disadvantage of this structure is inappropriate threading. The main game loop is in the timer task, which is in an application thread, but paint() and the key event methods are both called from the device's thread. If your game loop is running faster than the device can process paint(), you might end up with missing frames and jerky motion. If the system is calling key event methods when your application thread is partway through updating the game state, users might see strange or inconsistent behavior.

GameCanvas addresses these problems by adding methods that allow you to place your entire game loop in a single thread.

With GameCanvas, you can ask the device if any keys are pressed without having to wait for the key event methods. In addition, you can tell the GameCanvas to redraw itself immediately. These methods collapse your game class into a simpler, neater form. In particular, notice how the key events and painting are now manipulated directly in the timer task's run() method.

```
import javax.microedition.lcdui.*;
import java.util.*;

import javax.microedition.lcdui.*;
import javax.microedition.lcdui.game.*;

public class TypicalGameCanvas
    extends GameCanvas {
  private Timer mTimer;

  public TypicalGameCanvas() { super(true); }

  public void showNotify() {
    mTimer = new Timer();
    final Graphics g = getGraphics();

    TimerTask task = new TimerTask() {
      public void run() {
        processKeys();
        updateGameState();
        render(g);
        flushGraphics();
      }
    };
    mTimer.schedule(task, 0, 20);
  }

  public void hideNotify() {
    if (mTimer != null) {
      mTimer.cancel();
      mTimer = null;
    }
  }

  private void processKeys() {
    int keys = getKeyStates();
    // Test for pressed keys.
  }

  private void updateGameState() {
    // Move things, check for collisions, etc.
  }

  public void render(Graphics g) {
    // Draw the game.
  }
}
```

Now that you understand the big picture, I'll describe the new methods in more detail.

For immediate drawing, first obtain a Graphics from getGraphics(). The object returned is for drawing into an off-screen buffer. Do as much drawing as you wish, then call flushGraphics() to put the buffer on the screen. flush-Graphics() will not return until the screen has been updated. This means you can do all of your drawing in your application thread without worrying about the device's threading. For more tuned updates, another version of flushGraphics() accepts a rectangle that describes the specific region you want to update.

To check for pressed keys, call getKeyStates(). You'll get an integer that is some bitwise combination of the following constants:

- DOWN_PRESSED
- FIRE_PRESSED
- GAME_A_PRESSED
- GAME_B_PRESSED
- GAME_C_PRESSED
- GAME_D_PRESSED
- LEFT_PRESSED
- RIGHT_PRESSED
- UP_PRESSED

These constants correspond to the game actions defined in Canvas.

The key states are *latched*, which means if somebody presses and releases a button in the time between your calls to getKeyStates(), the corresponding bit will stay set.

The GameCanvas constructor accepts a boolean argument, which indicates whether or not the normal key event methods should be called. When the argument is true, keyPressed(), keyRepeated(), and keyReleased() will not be called and getKeyStates() will be the only way of responding to key presses.

Here is a simple GameCanvas that displays an animated crosshairs. You can move it around, and when you press the fire key, the display shows "Bang!" at your current location.

```
import java.util.*;

import javax.microedition.lcdui.*;
import javax.microedition.lcdui.game.*;
```

```java
public class BangCanvas
    extends GameCanvas {
  private Timer mTimer;

  private int mX, mY, mDelta, mS;
  private int mBangX, mBangY;

  public BangCanvas() {
    super(true);

    mX = getWidth() / 2;
    mY = getHeight() / 2;
    mDelta = 0;
    mS = 12;
    mBangX = mBangY = -1;
  }

  public void showNotify() {
    mTimer = new Timer();
    final Graphics g = getGraphics();

    TimerTask task = new TimerTask() {
      public void run() {
        processKeys();
        updateGameState();
        render(g);
        flushGraphics();
      }
    };
    mTimer.schedule(task, 0, 20);
  }

  public void hideNotify() {
    if (mTimer != null) {
      mTimer.cancel();
      mTimer = null;
    }
  }

  private void processKeys() {
    int w = getWidth();
    int h = getHeight();
    int d = 5;

    int keys = getKeyStates();
    if ((keys & LEFT_PRESSED) != 0) mX = Math.max(mX - d, 0);
    if ((keys & RIGHT_PRESSED) != 0) mX = Math.min(mX + d, w);
```

continued

```
        if ((keys & UP_PRESSED) != 0) mY = Math.max(mY - d, 0);
        if ((keys & DOWN_PRESSED) != 0) mY = Math.min(mY + d, h);
        if ((keys & FIRE_PRESSED) != 0) {
          mBangX = mX;
          mBangY = mY;
        }
      }

      private void updateGameState() {
        mDelta = (mDelta + 1) % (mS * 2);
      }

      public void render(Graphics g) {
        g.setColor(0xffffff);
        g.fillRect(0, 0, getWidth(), getHeight());

        g.setColor(0x000000);
        g.drawLine(mX - mS, mY, mX + mS, mY);
        g.drawLine(mX, mY - mS, mX, mY + mS);

        int f = (mDelta < mS) ? mDelta : mS * 2 - mDelta;
        g.drawRect(mX - mS + f, mY - mS + f,
            (mS - f) * 2, (mS - f) * 2);

        if (mBangX >= 0 && mBangY >= 0) {
          int fh = g.getFont().getHeight();
          g.setColor(0xff0000);
          g.drawString("Bang!", mBangX, mBangY - fh / 2,
              Graphics.HCENTER | Graphics.TOP);
        }
      }
    }
  }
```

Figure 11.1 shows it on Sun's emulator. The example code from the book's Web site includes ElevenMIDlet, which runs all of the examples in this chapter.

11.2 Building Scenes with Layers

The rest of the Game API has to do with *layers*. A layer is a rectangular graphic element. It has a location and a size. Compose a complete scene by combining layers. The Game API offers two types of layers: *tiled layers* and *sprites*. A tiled layer is created by assembling small images into a larger picture. A sprite is an animated image created from a collection of frames.

TiledLayer and Sprite are both subclasses of Layer. Layers have a position, a size, and can be visible or invisible.

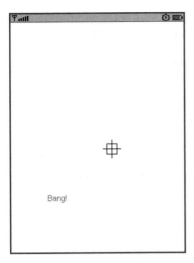

Figure 11.1 The BangCanvas example

A *layer manager* keeps track of the layers in your application. To draw all the layers, just ask the layer manager to draw itself.

11.3 Tiled Layers

A tiled layer is a grid of cells. You specify what image goes in each cell, kind of like creating a picture from a set of stamps. The images are *tiles*. To create a TiledLayer, specify how many cells you want and supply the tile images. The tile images are packed together in one image. Figure 11.2, for example, shows a 64×32 image that contains eight 16×16 tiles, numbered for your convenience.

You can arrange the tiles differently if you wish. For example, these tiles could have been created as four rows of two tiles each. Tiles are numbered as you

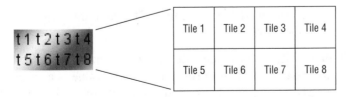

Figure 11.2 A set of tile images

would read English text, from left to right in rows from top to bottom. Tile numbers start at one! They start at one because zero is reserved for an empty tile.

Here is how you could use the example image to create a TiledLayer that is 20 cells wide and 12 cells high:

```
Image tiles = Image.createImage("/tiles.png");
TiledLayer background = new TiledLayer(20, 12, tiles, 16, 16);
```

A freshly created TiledLayer is empty. To assign tiles to cells, call setCell() or fillCells(). For example, to put tile 2 in the cell in the second column and first row, you could do this:

```
background.setCell(1, 0, 2);
```

The row and column numbering for cells is zero-based.

To fill a rectangular region of cells with a tile, use fillCells(). For example, you could fill the bottom row of the TiledLayer like this:

```
background.fillCells(0, 11, 20, 1, 1);
```

This code fills a region starting at column 0, row 11, and extending for 20 cells horizontally and 1 cell vertically. The cells are filled with tile 1.

Here is a series of cell assignments.

```
background.fillCells(0, 0, 20, 1, 1);
background.setCell(1, 0, 2);
background.fillCells(0, 0, 1, 12, 1);
background.fillCells(19, 0, 1, 12, 1);
background.fillCells(0, 11, 20, 1, 1);
background.fillCells(4, 4, 1, 6, 4);
background.fillCells(5, 7, 8, 1, 7);
background.fillCells(16, 4, 2, 2, 5);
```

Figure 11.3 shows what the result would look like if you could see the entire TiledLayer.

Cells that don't have an assigned tile are empty. If you want to make a cell empty, assign the tile value 0 to it.

There is one additional twist. You can animate cells or groups of cells. To do so, pass a tile number to createAnimatedTile(). The return value is a special tile number that you can assign to cells. Those cells will initially look like the tile number you supplied to createAnimatedTile().

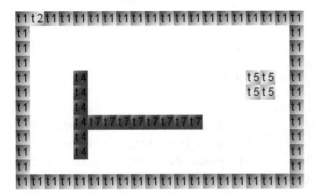

Figure 11.3 The whole TiledLayer

When you want to animate the cells, call setAnimatedTile() with the animated tile number and the new regular tile number you want to assign. All cells that contain the animated tile number will be updated at the same time.

You can draw a TiledLayer using paint(), but it's more likely that a Layer-Manager will take care of drawing all of your layers.

11.4 Sprites

In computer games, a sprite is a small, animated graphic element, like a space-ship or a superhero. Animation is accomplished by showing different *frames* in sequence.

Create a Sprite by supplying an image that contains the sprite frames. Just specify the size of each frame and Sprite will take care of extracting frames from the image. Here is an example that creates a Sprite from an image with 16 × 16 frames:

```
Image frames = Image.createImage("/frames.png");
Sprite s = new Sprite(frames, 16, 16);
```

Frames are numbered starting at 0. (Tiles were numbered starting at 1.)

A Sprite has a *frame sequence*. When you call nextFrame() or prevFrame(), the frame sequence determines which frame is shown next. By default, the frame sequence includes every available frame, in order. You can change the default by passing an integer array containing the new sequence to setFrameSequence().

The following example sets the frame sequence to show frame 4, then frame 1, then frame 0.

```
// Sprite s = ...
int[] sequence = { 4, 1, 0 };
s.setFrameSequence(sequence);
```

To jump to a particular frame, use setFrame(). Note that the method accepts an index, not a frame number, into the current frame sequence. Using the previous frame sequence, the following call would make frame 0 the current frame (because a 0 is at position 2 in the frame sequence):

```
s.setFrame(2);
```

A sprite's position is defined by its upper left corner. It inherits setPosition(), getX(), and getY() from its parent Layer class. The upper right corner is not always a very useful location, however, so Sprite includes the concept of a *reference pixel*. The reference pixel is defined in the sprite's coordinate space. By default, it is 0, 0, which is the upper left corner of the sprite. You can place the sprite in its containing coordinate space by specifying where you want the reference pixel to be. For example, a call to defineReferencePixel(20, 15) specifies the location of the reference pixel in the sprite's coordinate space. Now, a call to setRefPixelPosition(50, 50) places the reference pixel at 50, 50. The actual location of the upper left corner of the sprite would be 30, 35.

The reference pixel gets really useful when you start mirroring and rotating sprites. The Sprite class supports transformation of its frames. The transformations are defined by constants. You already met them in Chapter 9, "Creating Custom Screens":

- TRANS_NONE does nothing.
- TRANS_ROT90, TRANS_ROT180, and TRANS_ROT270 rotate the sprite clockwise by the specified number of degrees.
- TRANS_MIRROR flips the sprite horizontally.
- TRANS_MIRROR_ROT90, TRANS_MIRROR_ROT180, and TRANS_MIRROR_ROT270 flip the sprite and subsequently rotate it.

All you have to do is call setTransform(). The jazzy part is that you can *still* use setRefPixelPosition() to place the reference pixel wherever you want. Sprite correctly handles the transformation of the reference pixel and places the sprite in the right place.

Although you can draw a Sprite directly using paint(), you will probably delegate this responsibility to a LayerManager instead.

11.5 Detecting Collisions

Sprite has three methods for detecting collisions with other sprites, Tiled-Layers, or images.

```
public boolean collidesWith(Sprite s, boolean pixelLevel)
public boolean collidesWith(TiledLayer t, boolean pixelLevel)
public boolean collidesWith(Image, int, int y,
    boolean pixelLevel)
```

Each method returns true if the sprite is colliding with the other object. When pixelLevel is false, collisions are detected by determining if the sprite's collision rectangle intersects with the other object's collision rectangle.

A sprite's collision rectangle is usually the same as the sprite's bounds, but you can set it explicitly with defineCollisionRectangle().

When pixelLevel is true, the pixels in the sprite's current frame are compared with the pixels in the other object. If any two opaque pixels collide, the method returns true. Comparing the pixels is more accurate but slower. If you're having trouble with the speed of your game, see if pixelLevel as false will work for you instead.

11.6 Assembling a Game Scene

To put all your TiledLayers and Sprites together, use a LayerManager. Layer-Manager keeps track of an ordered list of layers. Layers with smaller indices are closer to the user, so the layer at index 0 is on top. You can put a layer at the back of the stack with append(), or you can place a layer at a specific index with insert(). The usual operations are available: you can find the number of layers with getSize(), retrieve a specific layer with getLayerAt(), or remove a layer with remove().

The tricky thing about LayerManager, and the reason this class is useful, is the *view window*. The view window is the portion of the entire scene that the Layer-Manager will draw. You specify the view window in the LayerManager's coordinates with setViewWindow().

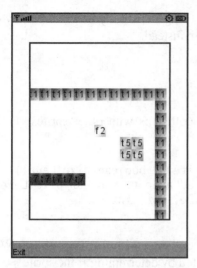

Figure 11.4   It's not Harry Potter, but it's a start.

Draw the scene by calling your LayerManager's paint() method. Pass a Graphics object and the location (in display coordinates) where you want the upper left corner of the view window to appear. The API documentation for LayerManager has a very useful picture that shows the relationship between the view window, contained layers, and drawing on the screen.

11.7   A Blocky Example

To illustrate how TiledLayer, Sprite, and LayerManager work together, the following code is an example called LayersCanvas (see Figure 11.4). It uses rudimentary images for tiles and frames. If you want Harry Potter or Sonic the Hedgehog, you'll have to draw them yourself.

This example has just two layers. A TiledLayer provides the scenery, and an animated Sprite moves around that scenery. The LayerManager, the Tiled-Layer, and the Sprite are created and assembled in the setup() method.

The example responds to key presses by moving the sprite around. However, the sprite always appears in the middle of the screen because the update-GameState() method adjusts the view window of the LayerManager to be centered on the sprite.

updateGameState() also shows how to animate a sprite. Every 10 ticks of the clock, it advances to the next frame.

The paint() method tells the LayerManager to draw its view window. It also draws a blue border around the view window.

In processKeys(), the position of the sprite is updated in response to key presses. However, if the sprite collides with the background TiledLayer, the current move is reversed, which means that movement stops when you reach a wall. Here I've used pixelLevel as false, because my tile and frame images are all rectangles. If you replace them with more interesting images, you might want to set pixelLevel to true.

```java
import java.io.*;
import java.util.*;

import javax.microedition.lcdui.*;
import javax.microedition.lcdui.game.*;

public class LayersCanvas
    extends GameCanvas {
  private Timer mTimer;

  private LayerManager mLayerManager;
  private TiledLayer mBackground;
  private Sprite mSprite;

  private int mViewX, mViewY;

  private int mLMWidth, mLMHeight;

  private int mFrameCounter;

  public LayersCanvas() {
    super(true);

    setup();
  }

  private void setup() {
    int w = getWidth();
    int h = getHeight();

    mLayerManager = new LayerManager();
    mLMWidth = w * 4 / 5;
    mLMHeight = h * 4 / 5;
```

continued

```java
// Create the TiledLayer.
try {
  Image tiles = Image.createImage("/tiles.png");
  TiledLayer background = new TiledLayer(20, 12,
      tiles, 16, 16);
  background.fillCells(0, 0, 20, 1, 1);
  background.setCell(1, 0, 2);
  background.fillCells(0, 0, 1, 12, 1);
  background.fillCells(19, 0, 1, 12, 1);
  background.fillCells(0, 11, 20, 1, 1);
  background.fillCells(4, 4, 1, 6, 4);
  background.fillCells(5, 7, 8, 1, 7);
  background.fillCells(16, 4, 2, 2, 5);
  mBackground = background;
  mLayerManager.append(mBackground);
}
catch (IOException ioe) {
  System.out.println(ioe);
}

// Create the Sprite.
try {
  Image frames = Image.createImage("/frames.png");
  Sprite s = new Sprite(frames, 16, 16);
  s.setPosition(
      (mBackground.getWidth() - 64) / 2,
      (mBackground.getHeight() - 64) / 2);
  mSprite = s;
  mLayerManager.append(mSprite);
}
catch (IOException ioe) {
  System.out.println(ioe);
}
}

public void showNotify() {
  mTimer = new Timer();
  final Graphics g = getGraphics();

  TimerTask task = new TimerTask() {
    public void run() {
      processKeys();
      updateGameState();
      render(g);
      flushGraphics();
    }
  };
  mTimer.schedule(task, 0, 20);
}
```

```
public void hideNotify() {
  if (mTimer != null) {
    mTimer.cancel();
    mTimer = null;
  }
}

private void processKeys() {
  int w = mBackground.getWidth();
  int h = mBackground.getHeight();
  int d = 4;

  int dx = 0, dy = 0;

  int keys = getKeyStates();
  if ((keys & LEFT_PRESSED) != 0) dx = -d;
  if ((keys & RIGHT_PRESSED) != 0) dx = d;
  if ((keys & UP_PRESSED) != 0) dy = -d;
  if ((keys & DOWN_PRESSED) != 0) dy = d;

  mSprite.move(dx, dy);

  if (mSprite.collidesWith(mBackground, false))
    mSprite.move(-dx, -dy);
}

private void updateGameState() {
  mFrameCounter = (mFrameCounter + 1) % 10;
  if (mFrameCounter == 0)
    mSprite.nextFrame();

  mViewX = mSprite.getX() -
      (mLMWidth - mSprite.getWidth()) / 2;
  mViewY = mSprite.getY() -
      (mLMHeight - mSprite.getHeight()) / 2;
  mLayerManager.setViewWindow(mViewX, mViewY,
      mLMWidth, mLMHeight);
}

public void render(Graphics g) {
  int w = getWidth();
  int h = getHeight();

  g.setColor(0xffffff);
  g.fillRect(0, 0, w, h);

  int x = w / 10;
  int y = h / 10;
```

continued

```
        // Draw a frame around the LayerManager.
        g.setColor(0x0000ff);
        g.drawRect(x - 1, y - 1, mLMWidth + 1, mLMHeight + 1);
        g.drawRect(x - 2, y - 2, mLMWidth + 3, mLMHeight + 3);

        // Draw the layers.
        mLayerManager.paint(g, x, y);
    }
}
```

11.8 Summary

MIDP's Game API provides support for 2D games. GameCanvas, an extension of Canvas, can draw to the screen immediately and can query the current state of the keys. A system of layers allows applications to build a game scene from TiledLayers and Sprites. TiledLayers are large scenes built from a palette of tiles, and Sprites are small animated images. Sprites can detect collisions with other Sprites, TiledLayers, or Images. A LayerManager is useful for assembling scenes. Overall, the Game API provides useful tools for novice game developers.

12

Scalable Vector Graphics

YOU can do some jazzy stuff with images using the Game API, but images have some significant shortcomings on small devices:

- Images cannot be resized in MIDP. Your application is likely to run on devices with different screen sizes. While it is possible to construct resizable screens at runtime from a handful of images, it's a little tricky.

- Images cannot be rotated by arbitrary amounts. Although you can mirror images and rotate them in increments of 90 degrees, MIDP does not offer anything fancier. This limitation makes sense, because small devices are not usually equipped with the memory and processing power to perform these types of transformations on images.

- Images are not an efficient representation of some pictures. For some pictures, it makes more sense to describe the picture (a *vector* format) than to describe every pixel in an image (a *raster* format).

- Images do not allow for the easy manipulation of the elements of a picture.

These shortcomings are addressed by JSR 226, the Scalable 2D Vector Graphics API for J2ME. Scalable Vector Graphics (SVG) is a kind of XML for describing pictures. Because it is essentially a programming language, SVG can also describe animations and user interactions. JSR 226 is a standard API for displaying and manipulating SVG documents.

The JSR 226 SVG API applies to a specific subset of SVG called SVG Tiny. SVG and SVG Tiny are both defined by the World Wide Web Consortium. This chapter is not about SVG itself. For more information, consult the specifications:

http://www.w3.org/TR/SVG11/
http://www.w3.org/TR/SVGMobile/

In most cases, a graphic artist will create SVG documents. You probably will not have to know anything about SVG documents except for the IDs of different pieces of the document. Some information about authoring tools is available here:

https://meapplicationdevelopers.dev.java.net/uiLabs/ Tools.html

As of September 2007, 28 devices are shipping with JSR 226. As part of the MSA subset, however, JSR 226 should become much more widely distributed in the near future. A list of JSR 226 devices is here:

http://svg.org/special/226_phones

The SVG API is relatively small. A half dozen classes and interfaces in `javax.microedition.m2g` supply tools for rendering and manipulating SVG documents. The rest of the API, in `org.w3c.dom` and two subpackages, represents the structure of an SVG document.

12.1 The Simplest Way to Show SVG Content

The simplest possible case is that you just want to display an SVG file. Your graphic artist generates the file and all you want to do is stick it on the screen.

In this case, your best friend is `SVGAnimator`. `SVGAnimator` takes care of a lot of details for you and just hands you a `Canvas` that you can put on the device's display.

Before you can create an `SVGAnimator`, you must first load an SVG document with `SVGImage`. `SVGImage` inherits two static creation methods from its parent class, `ScalableImage`.

```
public static ScalableImage createImage(InputStream stream,
    ExternalResourceHandler handler) throws IOException
public static ScalableImage createImage(String url,
    ExternalResourceHandler handler) throws IOException
```

The `ExternalResourceHandler` knows how to retrieve any content that is referenced from within the document. You can supply `null`, in which case the device tries to do something reasonable to locate external resources.

If you plan to use SVG documents that reference external resources that are part of your MIDlet suite JAR file, you must supply an implementation of `External-`

`ResourceHandler` that retrieves the external resources from the JAR file. You have to supply a `requestResource()` method that obtains an `InputStream` for a given URI. The `InputStream` should be passed back to the image's `request-Completed()` method.

If you point one of the `createImage()` methods at an SVG document, the returned object will of course be an `SVGImage`. To load an SVG document from the MIDlet suite JAR file, you could do something like this:

```
String name = "thumbsUp.svg";
InputStream in = getClass().getResourceAsStream(name);
SVGImage svgi = (SVGImage)ScalableImage.createImage(in, null);
```

The image has a *viewport*, which is simply the size in pixels that is used to display the image. In general, you will want to fill the available screen space, but you don't know how much that is until later when you get a `Canvas`.

Once you've got the image, creating an `SVGAnimator` is easy.

```
SVGAnimator svga = SVGAnimator.createAnimator(svgi);
```

To get the `Canvas` that shows the image, call `getTargetComponent()` and cast the result to `Canvas`. The SVG API is designed to be flexible enough to run on Connected, Limited Device Configuration (CLDC) devices as well as on Connected Device Configuration (CDC) devices, so the return type of `getTarget-Component()` is deliberately vague. This means that the SVG API can be used in a variety of GUI environments. In the MIDP world, though, the return value will always be a `Canvas`.

If the SVG document you are displaying contains animation, you can tell the `SVGAnimator` to show it by calling `play()`. The animation runs until you call `pause()` or `stop()`. The example in the next section demonstrates how to correctly handle animations.

Here is a complete example that loads an SVG document and displays it.

```
import java.io.*;

import javax.microedition.lcdui.*;
import javax.microedition.midlet.MIDlet;

import javax.microedition.m2g.*;

public class SimplePlayerMIDlet
    extends MIDlet
    implements CommandListener {
  private Displayable mDisplayable;
```

continued

```java
public void startApp() {
  if (mDisplayable == null) {
    try {
      mDisplayable = showSVGImage("thumbsUp-spin.svg");
    }
    catch (IOException ioe) {
      Form f = new Form("Oops");
      f.append(ioe.toString());
      mDisplayable = f;
    }
    Command exitCommand =
        new Command("Exit", Command.EXIT, 0);
    mDisplayable.addCommand(exitCommand);
    mDisplayable.setCommandListener(this);
  }

  Display.getDisplay(this).setCurrent(mDisplayable);
}

public void pauseApp() {}

public void destroyApp(boolean unconditional) {}

private Canvas showSVGImage(String name)
    throws IOException {
  InputStream in = getClass().getResourceAsStream(name);
  if (in == null)
    throw new IOException("Could not find " + name);
  SVGImage svgi =
      (SVGImage)ScalableImage.createImage(in, null);

  SVGAnimator svga = SVGAnimator.createAnimator(svgi);
  Canvas c = (Canvas)svga.getTargetComponent();
  svgi.setViewportWidth(c.getWidth());
  svgi.setViewportHeight(c.getHeight());

  return c;
}

public void commandAction(Command c, Displayable s) {
  if (c.getCommandType() == Command.EXIT){
    destroyApp(true);
    notifyDestroyed();
  }
}
}
```

Figure 12.1   The `SimplePlayerMIDlet` example

Figure 12.1 shows the result in Sun's emulator. The document is a picture of Duke, the Java platform mascot.

12.2 Working with Animated Documents

The previous MIDlet is fine for showing static content, but part of the fun about SVG is documents that *move*. The `thumbsUp-spin.svg` document from the previous example includes an animation, but `SimplerPlayerMIDlet` just shows a single still frame.

You need to kick off `SVGAnimator` with the `play()` method. That's easy enough, but finding the right place to call `play()` is a challenge. Ideally, you would call `play()` from the `showNotify()` method of the `Canvas`. The problem is that the `Canvas` comes from the `SVGAnimator` and you can't override the `showNotify()` method.

Fortunately, you can supply an `SVGEventListener` to the `SVGAnimator`. This listener receives the usual `Canvas`-like event notifications, such as key events, pointer events, `showNotify()`, and `hideNotify()`.

The next example, `SimpleAnimatorMIDlet`, demonstrates this technique. The `MIDlet` itself is an `SVGEventListener`. When the associated `Canvas` is shown, the animation is played, and when the `Canvas` is hidden, the animation is paused.

Furthermore, SVGAnimatorMIDlet makes the Canvas full-screen and removes the **Exit** command. Instead, hit any key to exit the MIDlet.

```java
import java.io.*;

import javax.microedition.lcdui.*;
import javax.microedition.midlet.MIDlet;

import javax.microedition.m2g.*;

public class SimpleAnimatorMIDlet
    extends MIDlet
    implements SVGEventListener {
  private Displayable mDisplayable;

  private SVGAnimator mSVGAnimator;

  public void startApp() {
    if (mDisplayable == null) {
      try {
        mDisplayable = showSVGImage("thumbsUp-spin.svg");
      }
      catch (IOException ioe) {
        Form f = new Form("Oops");
        f.append(ioe.toString());
        Command exitCommand =
            new Command("Exit", Command.EXIT, 0);
        f.addCommand(exitCommand);
        f.setCommandListener(new CommandListener() {
          public void commandAction(Command c, Displayable s) {
            destroyApp(true);
            notifyDestroyed();
          }
        });
        mDisplayable = f;
      }
    }

    Display.getDisplay(this).setCurrent(mDisplayable);
  }

  public void pauseApp() {}

  public void destroyApp(boolean unconditional) {
    if (mSVGAnimator != null)
      mSVGAnimator.stop();
    mDisplayable = null;
```

```
      mSVGAnimator = null;
  }

  private Canvas showSVGImage(String name)
        throws IOException {
    InputStream in = getClass().getResourceAsStream(name);
    if (in == null)
      throw new IOException("Could not find " + name);
    SVGImage svgi =
        (SVGImage)ScalableImage.createImage(in, null);

    mSVGAnimator = SVGAnimator.createAnimator(svgi);
    Canvas c = (Canvas)mSVGAnimator.getTargetComponent();
    c.setFullScreenMode(true);
    svgi.setViewportWidth(c.getWidth());
    svgi.setViewportHeight(c.getHeight());
    mSVGAnimator.setSVGEventListener(this);

    return c;
  }

  // SVGEventListener methods.

  public void showNotify() {
    if (mSVGAnimator != null)
      mSVGAnimator.play();
  }

  public void hideNotify() {
    if (mSVGAnimator != null)
      mSVGAnimator.pause();
  }

  public void keyPressed(int keyCode) {
    destroyApp(true);
    notifyDestroyed();
  }
  public void keyReleased(int keyCode) {}

  public void pointerPressed(int x, int y) {}
  public void pointerReleased(int x, int y) {}

  public void sizeChanged(int width, int height) {}
}
```

On Sun's emulator, Duke will spin around jauntily (see Figure 12.2). Just hit a key to exit the application.

Figure 12.2 Whoa, Dukey!

12.3 Digging into an SVG Document

SVG documents can be accessed and manipulated using the `org.w3c.dom.svg` package. For the most part, its interfaces extend the standard DOM interfaces in `org.w3c.dom` and `org.w3c.dom.event`.

The fundamental interface for SVG documents is `SVGElement`. It contains methods for getting and setting traits, which means you can make modifications to an SVG document on the fly. `SVGAnimator` is smart enough to detect changes to a document and update the screen.

Once you've loaded an `SVGImage`, call `getDocument()` to retrieve the document. You can then retrieve the top-level element (an instance of `SVGSVGElement`) with `getDocumentElement()`, or search for a specific element with `getElementById()`.

For example, the SVG document in the previous example contains one element that defines the trademark symbol (TM). Here is the beginning of the element definition for the trademark symbol.

```
      .
      .
      .
<g id="tm">
  <path d="M177.773,167.22v7...
  <path d="M186.568,175.173c0...
    .
    .
    .
```

To find the SVGElement for the trademark symbol, all you have to do is this:

```
// SVGImage svgi = ...
Document document = svgi.getDocument();
SVGElement svge =
    (SVGElement)document.getElementById("tm");
```

Once you've got an interesting SVGElement, you can have all sorts of fun. You can retrieve traits as text. This example retrieves the current transformation of the element:

```
String tx = svge.getTrait("transform");
```

You can also retrieve traits into more specific data types. The org.w3c.dom.svg package includes five handy data type classes: SVGMatrix, SVGPath, SVGPoint, SVGRect, and SVGRGBColor. If you wanted to deal with the element's transformation as a matrix rather than a string, you could do this:

```
SVGMatrix txmatrix = svge.getMatrixTrait("transform");
```

SVGElement has a corresponding set of set methods so that you can assign element traits using either strings or the more complex data types.

To rotate the trademark symbol around the point 182, 172, do this:

```
svge.setTrait("transform", "rotate(55, 182, 172)");
```

TMTweakerMIDlet is identical to SimplePlayerMIDlet except for showSVG-Image(), which contains extra code to rotate the trademark symbol:

```
private Canvas showSVGImage(String name)
        throws IOException {
    InputStream in = getClass().getResourceAsStream(name);
    if (in == null)
        throw new IOException("Could not find " + name);
    SVGImage svgi =
        (SVGImage)ScalableImage.createImage(in, null);

    Document document = svgi.getDocument();
    SVGElement svge =
        (SVGElement)document.getElementById("tm");

    svge.setTrait("transform", "rotate(55, 182, 172)");

    SVGAnimator svga = SVGAnimator.createAnimator(svgi);
    Canvas c = (Canvas)svga.getTargetComponent();
```

continued

```
        svgi.setViewportWidth(c.getWidth());
        svgi.setViewportHeight(c.getHeight());

        return c;
    }
```

On Sun's emulator, the result looks like Figure 12.3.

If you plan to modify an SVG document while the SVGAnimator is playing, you should take care to make those modifications in the animator's thread. Use invokeLater() and invokeAndWait() for this purpose. Each method takes a Runnable object whose run() method is called by the animator's thread. invokeLater() returns immediately, while invokeAndWait() will not return until the Runnable has been run.

12.4 Displaying an SVG Document on Your Own Canvas

SVGAnimator creates a Canvas whose sole purpose in life is to display an SVG document. If you'd prefer, you can create your own Canvas and use part of it to display the SVG document.

The magic that makes it possible is ScalableGraphics, which knows how to render an SVGImage on a Graphics object. To get one, call the static factory method createInstance().

```
    ScalableGraphics sg = ScalableGraphics.createInstance();
```

Figure 12.3   TMTweakerMIDlet rotates the trademark symbol.

Inside your `paint()` method, you have to *bind* the `ScalableGraphics` to the `Graphics` you are using.

```
sg.bindTarget(g);
```

Then render as many `SVGImages` as you wish. You have to specify where you want the image. The width and height of the image are determined by its viewport width and height.

```
sg.render(30, 50, svgi);
```

When you're finished, let the `ScalableGraphics` know that it doesn't need the `Graphics` any more.

```
sg.releaseTarget();
```

It's prudent to place `releaseTarget()` inside a `finally` clause. Even if something goes wrong in `render()`, you must release the `ScalableGraphics`.

Here is a canvas that frames an `SVGImage` with a border of blue diamonds (see Figure 12.4).

```
import javax.microedition.lcdui.*;

import javax.microedition.m2g.*;

public class DiamondFrameCanvas extends Canvas {
  private SVGImage mSVGImage;
  private ScalableGraphics mScalableGraphics;

  public DiamondFrameCanvas(SVGImage svgi) {
    mSVGImage = svgi;
    mScalableGraphics = ScalableGraphics.createInstance();

    int w = getWidth();
    int h = getHeight();
    mSVGImage.setViewportWidth(w * 3 / 4);
    mSVGImage.setViewportHeight(h * 3 / 4);
  }

  public void paint(Graphics g) {
    int w = getWidth();
    int h = getHeight();
```

continued

```
        g.setColor(0xffffff);
        g.fillRect(0, 0, w, h);

        g.setColor(0x0000ff);
        int s = 5;
        for (int x = 0; x < w; x += 20) {
          for (int y = 0; y < h; y+= 20) {
            int cx = x + 10;
            int cy = y + 10;
            g.fillTriangle(cx - s, cy, cx, cy - s, cx + s, cy);
            g.fillTriangle(cx - s, cy, cx, cy + s, cx + s, cy);
          }
        }

        g.setColor(0xffffff);
        g.fillRect(w / 8, h / 8, w * 3 / 4, h * 3 / 4);
        g.setColor(0x0000ff);
        g.drawRect(w / 8, h / 8, w * 3 / 4 - 1, h * 3 / 4 - 1);

        mScalableGraphics.bindTarget(g);
        try { mScalableGraphics.render(w / 8, h / 8, mSVGImage); }
        finally { mScalableGraphics.releaseTarget(); }
      }
    }
```

The code having to do with showing an SVG document is minimal, just one line in the constructor and three in paint().

Figure 12.4 It's easy to show SVG documents in your own canvas.

12.5 Creating New SVG Elements

To add new elements to a document, first obtain the document element and the root element as SVGSVGElement.

```
// SVGImage svgi = ...
Document document = svgi.getDocument();
SVGSVGElement svge =
    (SVGSVGElement)document.getDocumentElement();
```

Now you can create an element with the Document's createElementNS() method. Set attributes on the new element with the setTrait() methods.

```
String nsuri = "http://www.w3.org/2000/svg";
SVGElement circle = (SVGElement)
    document.createElementNS(nsuri, "circle");
SVGRGBColor fgColor = svge.createSVGRGBColor(0, 0, 255);
circle.setRGBColorTrait("fill", fgColor);
circle.setFloatTrait("cx", 50);
circle.setFloatTrait("cy", 50);
circle.setFloatTrait("r", 20);
```

To add the newly created element into the document, use appendChild() or insertBefore() on the root element.

```
svge.appendChild(b);
```

Updates to a playing document should be made in the SVG document update thread. SVGAnimator includes invokeAndWait() and invokeLater() methods for this purpose. You have to create a Runnable to do some work, then pass the Runnable to invokeAndWait() or invokeLater() to get the job done in the correct thread.

It is also possible to create an entirely new SVG document. If you want to explore this topic further, take a look at CreateEmptyImageDemo, one of the MIDlets in SVGDemo, an example bundled with the Sun Java Wireless Toolkit.

The following example, BubblesMIDlet, shows how to add new elements to an existing image. It is an adaptation of SimpleAnimatorMIDlet, so it uses a full-screen Canvas. Hit any key to exit the application.

```
import java.io.*;
import java.util.Random;

import javax.microedition.lcdui.*;
import javax.microedition.midlet.MIDlet;
```

continued

```java
import javax.microedition.m2g.*;

import org.w3c.dom.*;
import org.w3c.dom.svg.*;

public class BubblesMIDlet
    extends MIDlet
    implements SVGEventListener {
  private Displayable mDisplayable;

  private SVGAnimator mSVGAnimator;

  public void startApp() {
    if (mDisplayable == null) {
      try {
        mDisplayable = showSVGImage("thumbsUp-spin.svg");
      }
      catch (IOException ioe) {
        Form f = new Form("Oops");
        f.append(ioe.toString());
        Command exitCommand =
            new Command("Exit", Command.EXIT, 0);
        f.addCommand(exitCommand);
        f.setCommandListener(new CommandListener() {
          public void commandAction(Command c, Displayable s) {
            destroyApp(true);
          }                notifyDestroyed();
        });
        mDisplayable = f;
      }
    }

    Display.getDisplay(this).setCurrent(mDisplayable);
  }

  public void pauseApp() {}

  public void destroyApp(boolean unconditional) {
    if (mSVGAnimator != null)
      mSVGAnimator.stop();
    mDisplayable = null;
    mSVGAnimator = null;
  }

  private Canvas showSVGImage(String name)
      throws IOException {
    InputStream in = getClass().getResourceAsStream(name);
    if (in == null)
      throw new IOException("Could not find " + name);
```

```
SVGImage svgi =
    (SVGImage)ScalableImage.createImage(in, null);

mSVGAnimator = SVGAnimator.createAnimator(svgi);
Canvas c = (Canvas)mSVGAnimator.getTargetComponent();
c.setFullScreenMode(true);
int w = c.getWidth();
int h = c.getHeight();
svgi.setViewportWidth(w);
svgi.setViewportHeight(h);
mSVGAnimator.setSVGEventListener(this);

Document document = svgi.getDocument();
SVGSVGElement svge =
    (SVGSVGElement)document.getDocumentElement();

Random random = new Random();
for (int i = 0; i < 20; i++) {
  int cx = Math.abs(random.nextInt()) % w;
  int cy = Math.abs(random.nextInt()) % h;
  int r = Math.abs(random.nextInt()) % 20 + 10;
  SVGElement b = makeBubble(document, svge,
      cx, cy, r);
  svge.appendChild(b);
}

return c;
}

private SVGElement makeBubble(Document document,
    SVGSVGElement svge, int cx, int cy, int r) {
  String nsuri = "http://www.w3.org/2000/svg";
  SVGElement circle = (SVGElement)
      document.createElementNS(nsuri, "circle");
  SVGRGBColor fgColor = svge.createSVGRGBColor(0, 0, 255);
  circle.setRGBColorTrait("fill", fgColor);
  circle.setFloatTrait("cx", cx);
  circle.setFloatTrait("cy", cy);
  circle.setFloatTrait("r", r);
  return circle;
}

// SVGEventListener methods.

public void showNotify() {
  if (mSVGAnimator != null)
    mSVGAnimator.play();
}
```

continued

```
public void hideNotify() {
  if (mSVGAnimator != null)
    mSVGAnimator.pause();
}

public void keyPressed(int keyCode) {
  destroyApp(true);
  notifyDestroyed();
}
public void keyReleased(int keyCode) {}

public void pointerPressed(int x, int y) {}
public void pointerReleased(int x, int y) {}

public void sizeChanged(int width, int height) {}
}
```

When run on Sun's emulator, it looks like Figure 12.5.

12.6 SVG Event Handling

You have already seen how to capture Canvas-related events in your application by using an SVGEventListener. In addition, SVG documents themselves can respond to a few kinds of events. The SVGImage class contains corresponding methods.

- activate() delivers a DOMActivate event to the document.
- dispatchMouseEvent() tells the document that a pointer event has occurred.

Figure 12.5 Adding new elements to an SVG document

- `focusOn()` delivers a `DOMFocusIn` event to the specified `SVGElement`. It also delivers a `DOMFocusOut` event to the element that previously had the focus.

- `incrementTime()` sets the time used for animations.

If you are displaying an SVG document with a playing `SVGAnimator`, `increment-Time()` is automatically called, so a document with animations will play automatically. If you are displaying an SVG document using `ScalableGraphics`, you must call `incrementTime()` yourself to animate the document.

You must call the other event methods yourself if you need the SVG document to respond to them. Because few MIDP devices support pointer events, you might need to provide an alternate method for simulating pointer events. The only type of pointer event you can deliver to `SVGImage` is a click with x and y coordinates, like this:

```
// SVGImage svgi = ...
svgi.dispatchMouseEvent("click", 53, 77);
```

The x and y coordinates are in the viewport coordinate system, which might not be the same as the `Canvas`'s coordinate system.

The next example shows one way to move focus in a document. Hitting keys toggles the focus between the trademark symbol and Duke. The example document, `thumbsUp-enhanced.svg`, defines some behavior that swells up the trademark symbol when it has focus and shrinks it back down when it loses focus.

```
import java.io.*;

import javax.microedition.lcdui.*;
import javax.microedition.midlet.MIDlet;

import javax.microedition.m2g.*;

import org.w3c.dom.*;
import org.w3c.dom.svg.*;

public class SVGEventMIDlet
    extends MIDlet
    implements SVGEventListener {
  private Displayable mDisplayable;

  private SVGAnimator mSVGAnimator;
  private SVGImage mSVGImage;
  private SVGElement mTMElement, mDukeElement;
  private boolean mSwitcher;
```

continued

```
public void startApp() {
  if (mDisplayable == null) {
    try {
      mDisplayable = showSVGImage("thumbsUp-enhanced.svg");
    }
    catch (IOException ioe) {
      Form f = new Form("Oops");
      f.append(ioe.toString());
      Command exitCommand =
          new Command("Exit", Command.EXIT, 0);
      f.addCommand(exitCommand);
      f.setCommandListener(new CommandListener() {
        public void commandAction(Command c, Displayable s) {
          destroyApp(true);
          notifyDestroyed();
        }
      });
      mDisplayable = f;
    }
  }

  Display.getDisplay(this).setCurrent(mDisplayable);
}

public void pauseApp() {}

public void destroyApp(boolean unconditional) {
  if (mSVGAnimator != null)
    mSVGAnimator.stop();
  mDisplayable = null;
  mSVGAnimator = null;
}

private Canvas showSVGImage(String name)
    throws IOException {
  InputStream in = getClass().getResourceAsStream(name);
  if (in == null)
    throw new IOException("Could not find " + name);
  mSVGImage =
      (SVGImage)ScalableImage.createImage(in, null);

  Document document = mSVGImage.getDocument();
  mTMElement =
      (SVGElement)document.getElementById("tm");
  mDukeElement =
      (SVGElement)document.getElementById("body");

  mSVGAnimator = SVGAnimator.createAnimator(mSVGImage);
```

```
    Canvas c = (Canvas)mSVGAnimator.getTargetComponent();
    c.setFullScreenMode(true);
    mSVGImage.setViewportWidth(c.getWidth());
    mSVGImage.setViewportHeight(c.getHeight());
    mSVGAnimator.setSVGEventListener(this);

    return c;
}

// SVGEventListener methods.

public void showNotify() {
    if (mSVGAnimator != null)
        mSVGAnimator.play();
}

public void hideNotify() {
    if (mSVGAnimator != null)
        mSVGAnimator.pause();
}

public void keyPressed(int keyCode) {
    Canvas c = (Canvas)mDisplayable;
    int action = c.getGameAction(keyCode);
    switch (action) {
        case Canvas.UP:
        case Canvas.DOWN:
        case Canvas.LEFT:
        case Canvas.RIGHT:
        case Canvas.FIRE:
            mSwitcher = !mSwitcher;
            if (mSwitcher) mSVGImage.focusOn(mTMElement);
            else mSVGImage.focusOn(mDukeElement);
            break;
        default:
            destroyApp(true);
            notifyDestroyed();
            break;
    }
}
public void keyReleased(int keyCode) {}

public void pointerPressed(int x, int y) {}
public void pointerReleased(int x, int y) {}

public void sizeChanged(int width, int height) {}
}
```

Figure 12.6   Triggering focus events in a document

When you run this example, you'll see the SVG document of Duke as usual. Hit any arrow key, or the select key, to change the focus. As the trademark symbol gains and loses focus, you'll see it grow and shrink. When Duke gains focus, he jumps up, and when he loses focus, he falls back down. In the screen shot, the MIDlet has just called focusOn() for the trademark symbol (see Figure 12.6). Hit any other key to exit.

12.7 Summary

SVG is a way of describing pictures using XML. It is good for small devices because images can be easily scaled and transformed to fit the available space, and the document files can be compact. The JSR 226 SVG API provides classes for displaying and manipulating SVG documents. SVGImage can be used to load an SVG document. SVGAnimator knows how to display and animate an SVGImage. The SVG API also includes a DOM API that you can use to examine and modify SVG documents. In addition, SVGImage includes methods that allow your application to deliver events to an SVG document. For interactive animations that scale easily to different screen sizes, SVG is hard to beat. The JSR 226 SVG API includes everything you need to work with SVG Tiny documents.

13

3D Graphics

JSR 184, the Mobile 3D Graphics (M3G) API, gives MIDlets the ability to show 3D content. It is a scaled-down version of the desktop Java platform 3D API.

The M3G API is a *scene graph* API, which means it knows how to render scenes that are described as a hierarchy of groups and objects. The API includes all the classes and methods you need to create scenes from the ground up.

A much more likely alternative is that a graphic artist will create a 3D scene. Then your job becomes a lot easier because you just have to display the scene. JSR 184 specifies a comprehensive file format. An entire 3D scene, including lights, cameras, and animation, can be designed by an artist and saved in an M3G file.

The M3G API is contained in a single package, `javax.microedition.m3g`.

13.1 Creating M3G Files

The simplest case is that you want to display some 3D content created by your graphic designer. In this case, you don't need to know anything about 3D graphics. This use of the M3G API is *retained mode*.

Your graphic designer can use standard modeling tools like 3ds Max, Lightwave, or Blender. 3ds Max can export to M3G directly, but other packages might need plug-ins or additional tools. Here are some of the available M3G tools:

- Mascot Capsule M3GConverter
  http://www.mascotcapsule.com/toolkit/m3g/en/
- Blender M3G Exporter
  http://www.nelson-games.de/bl2m3g/default.html

- M3GToolkit
  http://www.java4ever.com/index.php?section=j2me&project=
  m3gtoolkit&menu=main&lang=_en
- M3G Exporter for 3ds Max 5.1 and 6.0
  http://www.m3gexporter.com
- Juinness
  http://sourceforge.net/projects/juinness/

13.2   Displaying 3D Content the Easy Way

Use `Loader` to retrieve a 3D scene from a file. The static `load()` method retrieves an array of `Object3D`s from a file. In most cases, the array contains a single element, an instance of `World`.

```
String name = "/swerve.m3g";
Object3D[] objects = Loader.load(name);
World world = (World)objects[0];
```

M3G files can contain animations. You can control the animation by passing a time value to the `animate()` method that `World` inherits from `Object3D`. Usually the time value is specified as milliseconds, but it can be any unit that the graphic designer and developer agree upon. Calling `animate()` updates everything in the scene to be correct for a certain point in time.

```
world.animate(1000);
```

A `Graphics3D` knows how to draw a scene on the display. You can retrieve a `Graphics3D` from its static factory method.

```
Graphics3D g3 = Graphics3D.getInstance();
```

When it comes time to paint your `Canvas`, you must *bind* the `Graphics3D` to the `Graphics` you are using for painting. Then pass the scene to `render()`. When you're done with 3D drawing, unbind the `Graphics3D` by calling `releaseTarget()`.

```
g3.bindTarget(g);
try { g3.render(world); }
finally { g3.releaseTarget(); }
```

If the M3G file you're displaying is created correctly, this is the whole story. You don't have to understand anything about meshes or cameras or lights. All that information is contained in the M3G file.

Here is a MIDlet and Canvas that take advantage of the Game API (Chapter 11) to animate a World. It also demonstrates that you can choose to animate a world to any point in time. After animating forward for 2 seconds, it animates in reverse for 2 seconds. You can adjust the cycle time with the cycle variable in the tick() method of SimpleM3GCanvas.

```java
import java.io.IOException;
import java.util.*;

import javax.microedition.lcdui.*;
import javax.microedition.lcdui.game.*;
import javax.microedition.midlet.*;

import javax.microedition.m3g.*;

public class SimpleM3GPlayer
    extends MIDlet
    implements CommandListener {
  private Displayable mDisplayable;

  public void startApp() {
    if (mDisplayable == null) {
      try {
        String name = "/swerve.m3g";
        Object3D[] objects = Loader.load(name);
        World world = (World)objects[0];
        SimpleM3GCanvas canvas = new SimpleM3GCanvas(world);
        canvas.setFullScreenMode(true);
        mDisplayable = canvas;
      }
      catch(IOException ioe) {
        Form f = new Form("Oops");
        f.append("Copy swerve.m3g from the Sun Java Wireless " +
            "Toolkit's Demo3D example project to the " +
            "kb-ch13/res directory.");
        mDisplayable = f;
      }
      Command exitCommand =
          new Command("Exit", Command.EXIT, 0);
      mDisplayable.addCommand(exitCommand);
      mDisplayable.setCommandListener(this);
    }
    Display.getDisplay(this).setCurrent(mDisplayable);
  }

  public void pauseApp() {
  }
```

continued

```java
        public void destroyApp(boolean unconditional) {
        }

        public void commandAction(Command c, Displayable s) {
            if (c.getCommandType() == Command.EXIT) {
                destroyApp(true);
                notifyDestroyed();
            }
        }
    }

class SimpleM3GCanvas
        extends GameCanvas {
    private World mWorld;
    private Graphics3D mGraphics3D;

    private Timer mTimer;

    private long mBigBang;

    public SimpleM3GCanvas(World world) {
        super(true);
        mWorld = world;
        mGraphics3D = Graphics3D.getInstance();
    }

    public void showNotify() {
        mTimer = new Timer();
        final Graphics g = getGraphics();

        TimerTask task = new TimerTask() {
            public void run() {
                processKeys();
                tick();
                render(g);
                flushGraphics();
            }
        };
        mBigBang = System.currentTimeMillis();
        mTimer.schedule(task, 0, 20);
    }

    public void hideNotify() {
        if (mTimer != null) {
            mTimer.cancel();
            mTimer = null;
        }
    }
```

```
private void processKeys() {
  // Restart for any game action.
  int keyStates = getKeyStates();
  if (keyStates != 0) mBigBang = System.currentTimeMillis();
}

private void tick() {
  // Find elapsed time.
  long now = System.currentTimeMillis();
  int localTime = (int)(now - mBigBang);

  // Adjust time to alternate forward and reverse.
  int cycle = 2000; // 2 s
  localTime = localTime % (cycle * 2);
  if (localTime > cycle) localTime = cycle * 2 - localTime;

  mWorld.animate(localTime);
}

private void render(Graphics g) {
  Graphics3D g3 = mGraphics3D;

  g3.bindTarget(g);
  try { g3.render(mWorld); }
  finally { g3.releaseTarget(); }
}
}
```

Copy the swerve.m3g file from the Demo3D example that comes with the Sun Java Wireless Toolkit. On Sun's emulator, SimpleM3GPlayer looks like Figure 13.1.

Figure 13.1 The SimpleM3GPlayer example

13.3 Doing It the Hard Way

For data visualization or other applications, use the M3G API's *immediate mode* to create 3D objects on the fly.

An entire scene consists of a hierarchy of 3D *nodes*. A node can be an object, a camera, or a light.

Your own objects will be created from instances of Mesh. Ultimately, a Mesh is assembled from many triangles. A Mesh contains information about every vertex (corner) in your object, how those corners are connected to create triangles, and information about the color and light properties of the vertices.

I won't cover all of this material in great detail, because most of it is standard 3D graphics information. However, to get things rolling for you, I'll walk through an example of creating a cube Mesh and provide sample code for the cube and a sphere.

Consider a cube as shown in Figure 13.2.

Starting from the bottom, then, you could define the eight vertices of a cube like this:

```
short[] positions = {
  -1,  1, -1, // A 0
   1,  1, -1, // B 1
   1, -1, -1, // C 2
  -1, -1, -1, // D 3

  -1,  1,  1, // E 4
   1,  1,  1, // F 5
   1, -1,  1, // G 6
  -1, -1,  1, // H 7
};
```

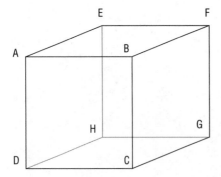

Figure 13.2   The SimpleM3GPlayer example

Each face of the cube is defined by a triangle strip consisting of two triangles. The two triangles are fully defined by four vertices, so each face of the cube is defined by a triangle strip with four vertices.

```
int[] stripLengths = { 4, 4, 4, 4, 4, 4 };
```

Triangle strips are defined by specifying the indices of the corresponding vertices. For example, a single triangle ABD would be defined by the indices 0, 1, and 3. A triangle strip containing ABDC defines two triangles, ABD and DBC. (You might think it would be ABD and BDC, but the odd-numbered triangles in the strip swap the first two vertices.) All six faces of the cube can be defined like this:

```
int[] indices = {
  0, 1, 3, 2, // ABDC
  0, 4, 1, 5, // AEBF
  1, 5, 2, 6, // BFCG
  2, 6, 3, 7, // CGDH
  3, 7, 0, 4, // DHAE
  4, 7, 5, 6  // EHFG
};
```

The ordering is a little tricky because the triangles have to be defined correctly so that the device knows which side of the triangle is the outside.

Finally, you can define a color for each vertex by creating an array that has three bytes of RGB color information per vertex.

```
byte ff = (byte)0xff;
byte df = (byte)0x80;

byte[] colors = {
  ff,  0,  0, // Red
   0, ff,  0, // Green
   0,  0, ff, // Blue
  ff, ff,  0,
  ff,  0, ff,
   0, ff, ff,
  ff, ff, ff, // White
  df, df, df  // Gray
};
```

The vertex positions and vertex colors can be assembled into a VertexBuffer like this:

```
int vc = positions.length / 3;

VertexBuffer vertexBuffer = new VertexBuffer();
```

continued

```
// Assign positions.
VertexArray vaPositions = new VertexArray(vc, 3, 2);
vaPositions.set(0, vc, positions);
vertexBuffer.setPositions(vaPositions, 1.0f, null);

// Assign colors.
VertexArray vaColors = new VertexArray(vc, 3, 1);
vaColors.set(0, vc, colors);
vertexBuffer.setColors(vaColors);
```

The indices into the vertices are likewise assembled in a `TriangleStripArray`, which is a type of `IndexBuffer`:

```
IndexBuffer indexBuffer =
    new TriangleStripArray(indices, stripLengths);
```

With the vertices and indices all nicely packaged, you can now create a `Mesh` to contain everything. An `Appearance` object specifies the light properties of the object. This example uses a default `Appearance`.

```
Appearance appearance = new Appearance();
Mesh mesh = new Mesh(vertexBuffer, indexBuffer, appearance);
```

Once you've got a `Mesh`, it can be added to your `World` just like any other 3D object. Here the mesh is added to a `Group` and then to a `World`:

```
World world= new World();
Group rotateGroup = new Group();
world.addChild(rotateGroup);
rotateGroup.addChild(mesh);
```

The following class, `CubeMeshGenerator`, encapsulates most of this code. Call `generate()` to create a cube. Pass in the length of a side.

```
import javax.microedition.m3g.*;

public class CubeMeshGenerator {
  public static Mesh generate(int s) {
    short[] vertices = createVertices();
    int[] stripLengths = { 4, 4, 4, 4, 4, 4 };
    int[] indices = createIndices(s);
    byte[] colors = createVertexColors();

    VertexBuffer vertexBuffer =
        createVertexBuffer(vertices, colors, s);
```

```
    IndexBuffer indexBuffer =
        new TriangleStripArray(indices, stripLengths);
    Appearance appearance = new Appearance();

    Mesh mesh =
        new Mesh(vertexBuffer, indexBuffer, appearance);
    return mesh;
}

private static short[] createVertices() {
    short[] positions = {
        -1,   1,  -1,  // A 0
         1,   1,  -1,  // B 1
         1,  -1,  -1,  // C 2
        -1,  -1,  -1,  // D 3

        -1,   1,   1,  // E 4
         1,   1,   1,  // F 5
         1,  -1,   1,  // G 6
        -1,  -1,   1,  // H 7
    };
    return positions;
}

// Map vertex indices to triangle strips.
private static int[] createIndices(int n) {
    int[] indices = {
        0, 1, 3, 2, // ABDC
        0, 4, 1, 5, // AEBF
        1, 5, 2, 6, // BFCG
        2, 6, 3, 7, // CGDH
        3, 7, 0, 4, // DHAE
        4, 7, 5, 6  // EHFG
    };
    return indices;
}

private static byte[] createVertexColors() {
    byte ff = (byte)0xff;
    byte df = (byte)0x80;

    byte[] colors = {
        ff,  0,  0, // Red
         0, ff,  0, // Green
         0,  0, ff, // Blue
        ff, ff,  0,
        ff,  0, ff,
         0, ff, ff,
```

continued

```
            ff, ff, ff, // White
            df, df, df  // Gray
        };
        return colors;
    }

    private static VertexBuffer createVertexBuffer(
        short[] positions, byte[] colors, int s) {
        int vc = positions.length / 3;

        VertexBuffer vertexBuffer = new VertexBuffer();

        // Assign positions.
        VertexArray vaPositions = new VertexArray(vc, 3, 2);
        vaPositions.set(0, vc, positions);
        vertexBuffer.setPositions(
            vaPositions, (float)s / 2.0f, null);

        // Assign colors.
        VertexArray vaColors = new VertexArray(vc, 3, 1);
        vaColors.set(0, vc, colors);
        vertexBuffer.setColors(vaColors);

        return vertexBuffer;
    }
}
```

The result is a colorful cube, as in Figure 13.3.

Figure 13.3   The result of CubeMeshGenerator

And here is a MIDlet and Canvas that display the cube and spin it around. They
look very similar to the MIDlet and Canvas you used before to play an M3G file.

```
import java.util.*;

import javax.microedition.lcdui.*;
import javax.microedition.lcdui.game.*;
import javax.microedition.midlet.*;

import javax.microedition.m3g.*;

public class MeshMIDlet
    extends MIDlet
    implements CommandListener {
  private Displayable mDisplayable;

  public void startApp() {
    if (mDisplayable == null) {
      MeshCanvas canvas = new MeshCanvas();
      mDisplayable = canvas;

      Command exitCommand =
          new Command("Exit", Command.EXIT, 0);
      mDisplayable.addCommand(exitCommand);
      mDisplayable.setCommandListener(this);
    }
    Display.getDisplay(this).setCurrent(mDisplayable);
  }

  public void pauseApp() {
  }

  public void destroyApp(boolean unconditional) {
  }

  public void commandAction(Command c, Displayable s) {
    if (c.getCommandType() == Command.EXIT) {
      destroyApp(true);
      notifyDestroyed();
    }
  }
}

class MeshCanvas
    extends GameCanvas {
  private World mWorld;
  private Group mRotateGroup;
  private Graphics3D mGraphics3D;
```

continued

```java
private Timer mTimer;
private float mAngle;

public MeshCanvas() {
  super(true);
  createWorld();
  mGraphics3D = Graphics3D.getInstance();
}

public void showNotify() {
  mTimer = new Timer();
  final Graphics g = getGraphics();

  TimerTask task = new TimerTask() {
    public void run() {
      tick();
      render(g);
      flushGraphics();
    }
  };
  mTimer.schedule(task, 0, 20);
}

public void hideNotify() {
  if (mTimer != null) {
    mTimer.cancel();
    mTimer = null;
  }
}

private void tick() {
  mRotateGroup.setOrientation(mAngle, 1, 1, 1);
  mAngle = (mAngle + 1) % 360;
}

private void render(Graphics g) {
  Graphics3D g3 = mGraphics3D;

  int w = getWidth();
  int h = getHeight();
  int vs = Math.min(w, h) * 9 / 10;
  int vx = (w - vs) / 2;
  int vy = (h - vs) / 2;

  g3.bindTarget(g);
  g3.setViewport(vx, vy, vs, vs);
  g3.render(mWorld);
  g3.releaseTarget();
}
```

```
private void createWorld() {
  mWorld = new World();
  mRotateGroup = new Group();
  mWorld.addChild(mRotateGroup);

  Mesh sphere = SphereMeshGenerator.generate(12, 5);
  sphere.setTranslation(5f, 0, 0);
  Mesh cube = CubeMeshGenerator.generate(5);
  cube.setTranslation(-5f, 0, 0);
  mRotateGroup.addChild(sphere);
  mRotateGroup.addChild(cube);

  Camera camera = new Camera();
  camera.setParallel(20.0f, 1.0f, -200, 200);
  camera.setTranslation(0, 0, 100);
  camera.setOrientation(0, 0, 0, -1);
  mWorld.addChild(camera);
  mWorld.setActiveCamera(camera);
  }
}
```

You should also notice that MeshMIDlet also contains some code to create a sphere using SphereMeshGenerator. I won't reproduce the class here, because it's a lot of trigonometry and index twiddling, but you can find it in the source code download if you want to take a look. For fun, try using peppermintColors instead of rainbowColors in SphereMeshGenerator's createVertexColors() method. Figure 13.4 shows MeshMIDlet in action.

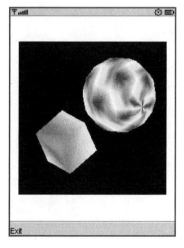

Figure 13.4　A cube and a sphere

13.4 Summary

The M3G API is a scene graph 3D graphics API. A graphic designer can use a 3D authoring package to create a 3D scene in an M3G file. Loading and showing an M3G file (retained mode) is relatively easy. Applications that need to generate 3D scenes at runtime can use immediate mode to create a complete scene.

Sony Ericsson has lots of information on the JSR 184 M3G API here:

http://developer.sonyericsson.com/site/global/techsupport/tipstrickscode/ mobilejava3d/p_mobilejava3d_tips_new.jsp

Section V

Storage and Resources

14

Record Stores

MSA devices provide three ways to work with persistent storage.

- *Record stores* are tiny databases that contain records. The official name for this API is the Record Management System (RMS).

- The FileConnection API provides access to the device's file system.

- The Personal Information Management (PIM) API allows your application to manipulate the device's contact list, calendar, and to-do list.

RMS is part of MIDP. In the old days before MSA, RMS was the only persistent storage available to MIDlets. JSR 75 defines both the FileConnection API and the PIM API. Both MSA and MSA subset devices support the FileConnection and PIM APIs.

In the MSA world, RMS and FileConnection both provide persistent storage for MIDlets. FileConnection has some good things going for it:

- FileConnection is cleaner and simpler than RMS. It's easier to use from the application side, and its behavior is likely to be more consistent across a range of devices.

- FileConnection can provide access to images, sounds, and other files on the device that could be useful for your application.

On the other hand, RMS offers three advantages over FileConnection, and the first one is a biggie.

- Reading and writing files requires appropriate permissions, which means you have to cryptographically sign your application to make sure your users aren't plagued by security prompts. As you read in Chapter 5, signing is expensive in terms of time and money. By contrast, your application can use RMS for free.

- If you want your application to run on plain old MIDP devices rather than on MSA devices, the JSR 75 FileConnection API might not be available. Your only option is RMS.

- If the data you wish to store naturally fits the record model, RMS might be more appropriate than FileConnection for persistent storage.

This chapter is about the RMS API. The next two chapters describe the File-Connection and PIM APIs.

14.1   Itsy Bitsy Teenie Weenie Databases

The RMS API is contained in `javax.microedition.rms` and centers on the `RecordStore` class. A record store is something like a database table and consists of records, which are simply byte arrays.

Record stores belong to MIDlet suites. A MIDlet suite's record stores are not visible to any other MIDlet suites unless they are explicitly shared. In theory, a MIDlet suite's private record stores should not be visible to any other applications on the device, including native applications. If you store particularly sensitive data in a record store, consider obfuscating or encrypting the data before writing it to a record store.

The `RecordStore` class contains a group of static methods that are useful for managing record stores. In addition, `RecordStore` also contains methods for manipulating records inside a record store.

14.2   Working with Record Stores

To open or create a record store, just supply its name to the static `openRecord-Store()` method. A `boolean` argument determines whether the record store will be created if it does not exist. This example opens or creates a record store named cache:

```
RecordStore rs = RecordStore.openRecordStore("cache", true);
```

If something goes wrong, `RecordStoreException` is thrown. Most methods in `RecordStore` can throw this exception.

You can get a list of all the record stores belonging to the current MIDlet suite by calling the static `listRecordStores()`, which returns the names as a string array. This method will not tell you about shared record stores created by other MIDlet suites.

Normally, record stores will be visible only in the MIDlet suite which created them. If you want to create a record store that will be visible to other MIDlet suites, you need to use a fancier version of `openRecordStore()`:

```
String name = "cache";
int authmode = RecordStore.AUTHMODE_ANY;
RecordStore rs = RecordStore.openRecordStore(
    name, true, authmode, true);
```

The last two arguments are only used if the record store does not already exist. Use `AUTHMODE_ANY` to create a record store that will be visible to other MIDlet suites. The other alternative, `AUTHMODE_PRIVATE`, creates a record store that is visible only in the current MIDlet suite. The fourth argument determines whether other MIDlet suites will be able to make changes in the record store. If it is `false`, other MIDlet suites will be able to read information from the record store but cannot make changes. When it is `true`, anyone can make changes.

To open a record store created by another MIDlet suite, you need to know the name of the record store as well as the creating MIDlet suite's vendor and name. The next example opens a record store named `shared-cache`, created by a MIDlet suite `kickbutt-ch14-other` from `Funky Chicken`:

```
RecordStore rs = RecordStore.openRecordStore(
    "shared-cache",
    "Funky Chicken",
    "kickbutt-ch14-other");
```

You can change the sharing and writable aspects of an existing record store with `setMode()`. It accepts a mode (`AUTHMODE_ANY` or `AUTHMODE_PRIVATE`) and a `boolean` that indicates whether other MIDlet suites can make changes to the record store.

To close an open `RecordStore`, call `closeRecordStore()`.

To completely remove a record store, pass its name to the static `deleteRecord-Store()` method. If the record store is open when you are trying to remove it, a `RecordStoreException` is thrown.

Exactly how much space is available for record stores depends a lot on the device. One of the MIDlet suite descriptor values, `MIDlet-Data-Size`, provides a way for your application to request a certain amount of space for record stores. At runtime, you can call `getSizeAvailable()` (not static, oddly enough) to find out how much space remains for the current MIDlet suite's record stores.

If you are using record stores from multiple threads, you might want to find out when a record store is modified. You can do this by supplying an implementation of `RecordStoreListener` to `addRecordStoreListener()`. Consult the API documentation for more information.

14.3 Manipulating Records

A record is an array of bytes. Each record has an identification number (ID), which is unique in the record store.

To add a record, pass a byte array to `addRecord()`. The ID of the new record is returned. To use a portion of the byte array for the record, specify a starting index and a length. The example here uses the entire `recordData` array.

```
// RecordStore rs = ...
// byte[] recordData = ...
int id = rs.addRecord(recordData, 0, recordData.length);
```

You can modify an existing record if you know its ID using `setRecord()`. Likewise, you can pass an ID to `deleteRecord()` to remove the record from the record store.

To retrieve a record, call `getRecord()`. A freshly created byte array that contains the record data will be returned:

```
// RecordStore rs = ...
// int id = ...
byte[] record = rs.getRecord(id);
```

Alternatively, you can retrieve a record into your own byte array. Find out the size of a record by calling `getRecordSize()`. The last argument to `getRecord()` is the starting index in the array where the record data will be placed.

```
// RecordStore rs = ...
// int id = ...
int size = rs.getRecordSize(id);
byte[] record = new byte[size];
rs.getRecord(id, record, 0);
```

14.4 Making Queries

Most record manipulation is done using record IDs, but when your MIDlet first starts, you have no idea what record IDs are contained in a record store.

You can retrieve a list of records in a record store by calling `enumerate-Records()`. To retrieve every record in the record store, do this:

```
// RecordStore rs = ...
RecordEnumeration re = rs.enumerateRecords(null, null, false);
```

The first argument to `enumerateRecords()` is a `RecordFilter` implementation. You can use `RecordFilter` to examine records and return only some subset of them in the `RecordEnumeration`. The second argument is a `RecordComparator`. You can provide an implementation if you want the records in the `Record-Enumeration` to be sorted. Finally, the third argument to `enumerateRecords()` indicates whether the `RecordEnumeration` should be kept current with ongoing changes in the underlying record store. Use `true` for this argument if you expect to be modifying the record store as you're working your way through the `RecordEnumeration`.

Bear in mind that if you expect a record store to be accessed from multiple threads, you should implement your own synchronization to make sure everyone's view of the data remains consistent.

Consult the API documentation for more information about `RecordFilter` and `RecordComparator`.

14.5 Iterating through Records

Once you've got a `RecordEnumeration`, you can use it to retrieve the records themselves as well as their IDs.

Use the `hasNextElement()` and `hasPreviousElement()` methods to see if you're at the beginning or end of the `RecordEnumeration`. When a `Record-Enumeration` is first returned, it is positioned just before the first record.

Call `nextRecord()`, `previousRecord()`, `nextRecordId()`, and `previous-RecordId()` to navigate through the records.

Interestingly, you cannot retrieve both a record and its ID at the same time. Because you can move forward and backward, however, it is possible to retrieve a record and its ID through some trickery.

14.6 A Place to Keep Your Stuff

The following class encapsulates RMS access, providing a clean interface to
store key and value string pairs. It's useful for storing application preferences.

```java
import java.io.*;
import java.util.*;

import javax.microedition.rms.*;

public class Cache {
  private final String mName;
  private Hashtable mMap;

  public Cache(String name) throws RecordStoreException {
    mName = name;
    read();
  }

  // Public methods.

  public void set(String key, String value)
      throws RecordStoreException {
    Object old = mMap.put(key, value);
    if (old == null || !old.equals(value))
      write();
  }

  public void remove(String key) throws RecordStoreException {
    if (mMap.remove(key) != null)
      write();
  }

  public String get(String key) {
    return (String)mMap.get(key);
  }

  // Implementations.

  private void read() throws RecordStoreException {
    RecordStore rs = RecordStore.openRecordStore(mName, true);
    mMap = new Hashtable();
    try {
      RecordEnumeration re =
          rs.enumerateRecords(null, null, false);
      while (re.hasNextElement()) {
        byte[] record = re.nextRecord();
```

```
      parseRecord(record);
    }
  }
  finally { rs.closeRecordStore(); }
}

private void parseRecord(byte[] record) {
  try {
    ByteArrayInputStream raw =
        new ByteArrayInputStream(record);
    DataInputStream in = new DataInputStream(raw);
    String key = in.readUTF();
    String value = in.readUTF();
    mMap.put(key, value);
  }
  catch (IOException ioe) {
    System.out.println("Bad record in " + mName + ".");
  }
}

private void write() throws RecordStoreException {
  // Draconian: delete the old one, write a new one.
  try { RecordStore.deleteRecordStore(mName); }
  catch (RecordStoreNotFoundException rsfe) {} // No problem.

  RecordStore rs = RecordStore.openRecordStore(mName, true);
  try {
    Enumeration keys = mMap.keys();
    while (keys.hasMoreElements()) {
      String key = (String)keys.nextElement();
      String value = (String)mMap.get(key);
      try {
        byte[] record = packRecord(key, value);
        rs.addRecord(record, 0, record.length);
      }
      catch (IOException ioe) {
        System.out.println("Error packing in " + mName + " : " +
          key + " -> " + value);
      }
    }
  }
  finally { rs.closeRecordStore(); }
}

private byte[] packRecord(String key, String value)
    throws IOException {
  ByteArrayOutputStream raw = new ByteArrayOutputStream();
```

continued

```
        DataOutputStream out = new DataOutputStream(raw);
        out.writeUTF(key);
        out.writeUTF(value);
        return raw.toByteArray();
    }
}
```

This class provides a simpleminded implementation that is easy to use from your own application. Each of the public operations (set(), get(), and remove()) is designed to be self-contained, so the record store is never left open. Every set() writes the entire record store on the basis of the contents of an internal Hashtable.

Here is a very simple MIDlet that uses Cache to store a name and a zip code. You can see how easy it is to load the values in startApp():

```
Cache cache = new Cache("cache");
String name = cache.getString("name");
String zip = cache.getString("zip");
```

And it's just as easy to save the values in destroyApp(). Here is the complete MIDlet (see Figure 14.1 on page 204):

```
import javax.microedition.lcdui.*;
import javax.microedition.midlet.*;
import javax.microedition.rms.*;

public class CacheMIDlet
    extends MIDlet
    implements CommandListener {
  private Displayable mDisplayable;

  private TextField mNameField;
  private TextField mZipField;

  public void startApp() {
    if (mDisplayable == null) {
      String name = "";
      String zip = "";

      try {
        Cache cache = new Cache("cache");
        name = cache.get("name");
        zip = cache.get("zip");
      }
```

```
      catch (RecordStoreException rse) {
        System.out.println(rse);
      }

      Form f = new Form("CacheMIDlet");
      mNameField = new TextField("Name:", name,
          512, TextField.ANY);
      f.append(mNameField);
      mZipField = new TextField("Zip:", zip,
          5, TextField.NUMERIC);
      f.append(mZipField);
      mDisplayable = f;

      Command exitCommand =
          new Command("Exit", Command.EXIT, 0);
      mDisplayable.addCommand(exitCommand);
      mDisplayable.setCommandListener(this);
    }
    Display.getDisplay(this).setCurrent(mDisplayable);
  }

  public void pauseApp() {
  }

  public void destroyApp(boolean unconditional) {
    String name = mNameField.getString();
    String zip = mZipField.getString();
    try {
      Cache cache = new Cache("cache");
      cache.set("name", name);
      cache.set("zip", zip);
    }
    catch (RecordStoreException rse) {
      System.out.println(rse);
    }
  }

  public void commandAction(Command c, Displayable s) {
    if (c.getCommandType() == Command.EXIT) {
      destroyApp(true);
      notifyDestroyed();
    }
  }
}
```

Each time you run CacheMIDlet, it loads the last name and zip code values from the record store.

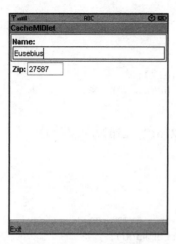

Figure 14.1   The field values are kept in persistent storage.

14.7 Summary

Record stores are MIDP's solution for persistent storage. Record stores belong to MIDlet suites, although they can be explicitly shared with other MIDlet suites. Inside a record store, each record is a byte array. Records can be filtered and sorted when they are retrieved from a record store. The Cache example is a simple persistent map of String key and value pairs.

15

Reading and Writing Files

MIDP devices often have some kind of hierarchical file system. Data lives in files that belong to directories. Directories can contain other directories. File system *roots* contain all the directories.

JSR 75, the PDA Optional Packages, defines a FileConnection API that provides access to a device's file system. It is a mandatory part of MSA and MSA subset.

For the actual work of reading files and writing files, you use the familiar stream classes from java.io. The FileConnection API gives you the streams you need from the device's file system.

Remember, though, that using FileConnection means your application must be signed. If you are sure you need the FileConnection API, make sure your project budget includes the time and money you'll need to make signing happen.

15.1 The Quick Story

Let's say you want to read some data from the file system. First, you have to create a string that represents the filename. FileConnection strings always begin with file://. The rest of the string is an absolute file path.

To create a FileConnection object, you use something called the Generic Connection Framework (GCF). You'll learn all about it in Chapter 18. All you need to know now is that when you pass a file URL to the open() method in javax.microedition.io.Connector, you get back a FileConnection object.

For example, let's say you wanted to read from a file /root1/photos/mango. png. You would do something like this to make the initial connection:

```
String url = "file:///root1/photos/mango.png";
FileConnection fc = (FileConnection)Connector.open(url);
```

The FileConnection object can supply an InputStream for reading or an OutputStream for writing. Here is how you can get an InputStream for reading from the file:

```
InputStream in = fc.openInputStream();
```

Now you can read from in as much as you like. When you're done, close everything up as usual. Use try and finally blocks to make sure the input stream and the FileConnection are closed no matter what happens. In this example, use nested blocks like this:

```
String url = "file:///root1/photos/mango.png";
FileConnection fc = (FileConnection)Connector.open(url);
try {
  InputStream in = fc.openInputStream();
  try {
    // Read from in.
  }
  finally { in.close(); }
}
finally { fc.close(); }
```

15.2 Working with Files and Directories

FileConnection inherits methods from StreamConnection for retrieving streams:

```
public InputStream openInputStream()
    throws IOException
public DataInputStream openDataInputStream()
    throws IOException
public OutputStream openOutputStream()
    throws IOException
public DataOutputStream openDataOutputStream()
    throws IOException
```

The real mojo of FileConnection, however, is its additional methods that pertain directly to files and directories.

You can create files and directories with create() and mkdir() respectively. You must first create a FileConnection with the URL of the file or directory you wish to create. You can check to see if the file or directory already exists by calling `exists()`. Then call `create()` or `mkdir()` as appropriate. Here is a simple method that creates a file and writes some text into it:

```
private void createFile(String url) throws IOException {
  FileConnection fc = (FileConnection)Connector.open(url);
  try {
    if (!fc.exists())
      fc.create();
    OutputStream rawOut = fc.openOutputStream();
    PrintStream out = new PrintStream(rawOut);
    try { out.println("Kick Butt with MSA and MIDP!"); }
    finally { out.close(); }
  }
  finally { fc.close(); }
}
```

You can remove a file or a directory by calling `delete()`. Use `rename()` to assign a new name to a file or directory.

One interesting method is `truncate()`, which chops off the contents of the file after the specified number of bytes.

To find out if a `FileConnection` represents a file or directory, call `isDirectory()`. To list the contents of a directory, use one of the `list()` methods. Each returns an `Enumeration` of strings. Each string in the `Enumeration` represents a file or directory. The directory names have a trailing slash (/).

The size of the files in a directory is computed by `directorySize(false)`. If you call `directorySize(true)` instead, you'll get the size of all files, including those in subdirectories.

You can use an existing directory `FileConnection` to navigate to a contained file or subdirectory. Call `setFileConnection()` with the name of the file or subdirectory, or use `..` for the parent directory.

Files may or may not be readable or writable. Use `canRead()` and `canWrite()` to check, or modify these attributes with `setReadable()` and `setWritable()`.

Some file systems also support the concept of hidden files, which are files that exist but are not normally listed in directory listings. Use `isHidden()` and `setHidden()` to test or modify this attribute.

The size of a file is returned by `fileSize()`. If the file system supports it, you can find out the last time a file was changed with `lastModified()`.

Three additional methods supply information about the file system itself: `total-Size()`, `usedSize()`, and `availableSize()`.

15.3 Somewhere, a Place for Us

MSA guarantees that a MIDlet suite has its own private directory that can be used for storage. As with record stores, this directory should not be visible to other MIDlet suites or applications.

The URL for the directory is given by the system property `fileconn.dir.private`. A human-readable name for this directory is contained in the system property `fileconn.dir.private.name`.

In the Sun Java Wireless Toolkit, use `Run via OTA` to test `FileConnection` MIDlets. When run this way, the emulator will supply a URL for `fileconn.dir.private` where you can store information.

15.4 Finding Pictures, Music, and Other Goodies

MSA defines a handful of system properties that point the way to interesting directories on a device. Each system property, if it is not `null`, contains a URL for a directory. The property names are self-explanatory:

- `fileconn.dir.photos`
- `fileconn.dir.videos`
- `fileconn.dir.graphics`
- `fileconn.dir.tones`
- `fileconn.dir.music`
- `fileconn.dir.recordings`

For example, on the Sun Java Wireless Toolkit emulator, the `fileconn.dir.photos` property contains `file:///root1/photos`, a default location for photograph files. Any of these properties can be `null`, which means the device does not have a default location for the corresponding item.

URLs and pathnames are confusing to most users. If you need to represent one of these locations on the screen, you should use a descriptive name instead. MSA defines a separate set of system properties that contain descriptive names in a language appropriate for the device. Just append `.name` to the system property names above to retrieve the corresponding descriptive name.

For example, on Sun's emulator, the property `fileconn.dir.music.name` is `Music`. On a German MSA device, it might be `Musik`.

15.5 Starting from the Top

Instead of examining "favorite" locations like the ones described previously, you might want to navigate through the file system by starting at the *roots*. Each root is usually a physical device, like a memory card or a hard disk drive.

`FileSystemRegistry` contains a static method, `listRoots()`, which returns an `Enumeration` of strings, one per root. Each string is a full URL that can be passed to `Connector.open()`.

If you want to display the roots to a user, you should use descriptive names instead. The system property `fileconn.dir.roots.names` contains these descriptive names, separated by semicolons. The descriptive names are returned *in the same order* as in the `Enumeration` returned by `FileSystemRegistry.listRoots()`.

File systems can come and go, particularly in devices that have slots for memory cards. To receive notifications, create an implementation of `FileSystemListener` and pass it to `FileSystemRegistry.addFileSystemListener()`. Your listener will be notified when roots arrive and depart via the `rootChanged()` method. Check the API documentation for all the details.

Unless you have a really good reason, you should not expose your users to the complexities of a hierarchical file system. If you can help it, you probably should shield them from the file system roots, even the nice display names. Whenever possible, just store things in the MIDlet suite's private directory and don't bother the user about the details. Applications should *just work*. Users on mobile phones will be even less understanding and patient than users on desktop computers. If your application is the slightest bit difficult or inconvenient, users will discard it and seek out a simpler solution.

15.6 Ask for Permission

Reading and writing local files is, of course, a sensitive operation. If you plan to distribute an application that makes use of the file system, make sure you request one or both of the file-related permissions in the application descriptor:

```
javax.microedition.io.Connector.file.read
javax.microedition.io.Connector.file.write
```

Sign your MIDlet suite so that the user will not be drowned in prompts for access to the file system.

15.7 An Example

The FileExerciserMIDlet shows how to create a directory, create a file, write and read a file, remove a file, and remove a directory. It will give you a start in reading and writing files in your own applications.

```java
import java.io.*;
import java.util.*;

import javax.microedition.io.*;
import javax.microedition.io.file.*;
import javax.microedition.lcdui.*;
import javax.microedition.midlet.*;

public class FileExerciserMIDlet
    extends MIDlet
    implements CommandListener {
  private Displayable mDisplayable;

  public void startApp() {
    if (mDisplayable == null) {
      Form f = new Form("FileExerciserMIDlet");

      try {
        String url = getRoot();
        String durl = url + "kickbutt/";
        String furl = durl + "hello.txt";
        appendln(f, "getRoot() = " + url);
        createDirectory(durl);
        appendln(f, "Created directory.");
        createFile(furl);
        appendln(f, "Created file.");
        String text = readFile(furl);
        appendln(f, "File contents: " + text);
        removeFile(furl);
        appendln(f, "Removed file.");
        removeDirectory(durl);
        appendln(f, "Removed directory.");
      }
      catch (IOException ioe) {
        appendln(f, ioe.toString());
        ioe.printStackTrace();
      }
```

```
      mDisplayable = f;

      Command exitCommand =
          new Command("Exit", Command.EXIT, 0);
      mDisplayable.addCommand(exitCommand);
      mDisplayable.setCommandListener(this);
    }
    Display.getDisplay(this).setCurrent(mDisplayable);
}

public void pauseApp() {
}

public void destroyApp(boolean unconditional) {}

private void appendln(Form f, String s) {
    StringItem si = new StringItem(null, s);
    si.setLayout(Item.LAYOUT_2 | Item.LAYOUT_NEWLINE_AFTER);
    f.append(si);
}

// CommandListener method.

public void commandAction(Command c, Displayable s) {
    if (c.getCommandType() == Command.EXIT) {
      destroyApp(true);
      notifyDestroyed();
    }
}

// Implementation methods.

// Retreieves an appropriate root directory.
private String getRoot() {
    // First try the private directory.
    String url = System.getProperty("fileconn.dir.private");
    // Otherwise get the first root.
    if (url == null) {
      Enumeration e = FileSystemRegistry.listRoots();
      if (e.hasMoreElements()) {
        String root = (String)e.nextElement();
        url = "file:///" + root;
      }
    }
    return url;
}
```

continued

```
private void createDirectory(String url) throws IOException {
  FileConnection fc = (FileConnection)Connector.open(url);
  try {
    if (fc.exists() == false)
      fc.mkdir();
  }
  finally { fc.close(); }
}

private void createFile(String url) throws IOException {
  FileConnection fc = (FileConnection)Connector.open(url);
  try {
    if (!fc.exists())
      fc.create();
    OutputStream rawOut = fc.openOutputStream();
    PrintStream out = new PrintStream(rawOut);
    try { out.println("Kick Butt with MSA and MIDP!"); }
    finally { out.close(); }
  }
  finally { fc.close(); }
}

private String readFile(String url) throws IOException {
  FileConnection fc = (FileConnection)Connector.open(url);
  StringBuffer sb = new StringBuffer();
  try {
    InputStream in = fc.openInputStream();
    try {
      int c;
      while ((c = in.read()) != -1)
        sb.append((char)c);
    }
    finally { in.close(); }
  }
  finally { fc.close(); }
  return sb.toString();
}

private void removeFile(String url) throws IOException {
  FileConnection fc = (FileConnection)Connector.open(url);
  try { fc.delete(); }
  finally { fc.close(); }
}

private void removeDirectory(String url) throws IOException {
  removeFile(url);
}
}
```

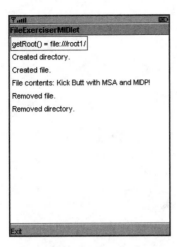

Figure 15.1 Using the private application directory for file storage

You can run this MIDlet directly in the Sun Java Wireless Toolkit emulator, but you'll be inundated with prompts to allow access to the file system. To get around the prompts, register the read and write permissions, sign the MIDlet suite, and use Run via OTA to get the full experience.

You'll also notice that the example uses a different root directory depending on whether you run it directly or use Run via OTA. When run directly, the private directory is not defined, so the application uses the first available root. When using Run via OTA, the private directory is available (see Figure 15.1).

15.8 Summary

The FileConnection API provides your application with the ability to manipulate files and directories. You can read files, write files, create directories, and remove directories. You can examine the file system roots available on a device and receive notifications when roots come and go. MSA provides some system properties that point to commonly used file directories on a device, like directories for pictures, music, or videos. To avoid lots of security prompts, include the file permissions in your application descriptor and cryptographically sign your MIDlet suite.

16

Contacts
and Calendars

MOBILE phones have contact lists (address books) that you can use to keep track of all the people you usually call. Many phones also keep track of calendar appointments (event lists) and to-do lists as well. I would probably miss most of my meetings if my phone didn't beep at me at the right time.

Contact, calendar, and to-do lists are a goldmine of useful information. Suppose you write a jazzy application for text messaging. It won't be much good unless you can allow your users to send messages to people they've already entered in their contact lists.

JSR 75's Personal Information Management (PIM) API provides access to contact lists, calendars, and to-do lists on devices. The API comprises ten dense classes and four exceptions in the `javax.microedition.pim` package.

16.1 Understanding the PIM API

The PIM API has a very general, flexible design. Contacts, calendar appointments, and to-do items are all subclasses of `PIMItem` and work pretty much the same way.

A `PIMItem` is a collection of *fields*, where a field is something with a key and one or more values. Each field has a certain type, such as string, integer, or boolean. The field keys are integers, with constants defined in the subclasses of `PIMItem`.

For example, `Contact` is one of the subclasses of `PIMItem`. Let's say you want to add a nickname to an existing contact. The nickname field is identified by the `NICKNAME` constant in `Contact`. According to the API documentation, the field type for `NICKNAME` is string, which means you'll use the `addString()` method. Finally, you need to specify *attributes* for the value. You could use attributes to distinguish between a work phone number and a home phone number. For a nickname, just use `PIMItem.ATTR_NONE`.

To add a nickname to a contact, then, you would do this:

```
// Contact c = ...
c.addString(Contact.NICKNAME, PIMItem.ATTR_NONE,
    "Handsome Rob");
```

You can change fields as much as you like, but the item won't be stored on the device until you call `commit()`:

```
c.commit();
```

One of the tricky parts to this is that a field can have *more than one* value. You can find out how many values are allowed in a field by asking the list, as you'll see later. In the following example, you could add home, work, and mobile phone numbers by using different attribute values defined in `Contact`:

```
private void addTelephone(Contact c,
    String home, String work, String mobile)
    throws PIMException {
  c.addString(Contact.TEL, Contact.ATTR_HOME, home);
  c.addString(Contact.TEL, Contact.ATTR_WORK, work);
  c.addString(Contact.TEL, Contact.ATTR_MOBILE, mobile);

  c.commit();
}
```

There are corresponding add methods for other field types: `addBoolean()`, `addDate()`, and `addInt()` are a few examples.

To retrieve a value from a `PIMItem`, call one of its `get` methods. You have to specify the field key, and you have to make sure to use the method for the correct type. Finally, you have to supply the *index* of the item you wish to retrieve. Remember, fields can have multiple values. It's not enough to ask a contact for the nickname field. You have to ask for the *first* nickname field, or the *second*, or whichever. Some fields won't even have any values defined.

First, find out how many values exist in a field with `PIMItem`'s `countValues()` method. For example, you could find out if any nickname values are defined on a contact like this:

```
// Contact c = ...
int count = c.countValues(Contact.NICKNAME);
```

If `count` is greater than zero, you can retrieve the very first nickname value like this:

```
String nickname = c.getString(Contact.NICKNAME, 0);
```

Removing values is simply a matter of specifying the field key and index of the value you want to remove. You don't even have to worry about the field type in this case. To remove the first nickname value in a contact, do this:

```
c.removeValue(Contact.NICKNAME, 0);
```

Here is a method that removes all values for a field:

```
private void clearField(PIMItem pimi, int field) {
  while (pimi.countValues(field) > 0)
    pimi.removeValue(field, 0);
}
```

16.2 Working with Lists

The PIM API knows about contact lists, calendars, and to-do lists, but they are all very similar. The parent class for lists is `PIMList`, and it contains most of the methods you'll need for any type of list.

16.2.1 Item Queries

Three `items()` methods provide a way to retrieve items from a list. You could use these to retrieve contacts from the address book, appointments from the calendar, or items from a to-do list. All of the `items()` methods return an `Enumeration`, which you can use to work through the results.

Items are returned as a type that matches the list. For example, calling `items()` on a `ContactList` will give you an `Enumeration` full of `Contacts`. You can retrieve the entire contents of the list by calling `items()` with no arguments.

For simple searching, pass a `String` to `items()`. Items with any string field that contains the search string will be returned. This search is not sensitive to case. For example, if you call `items("roy")` on a contact list, you are likely to get back an item for Roy Rogers as well as an item for Helen, whose address is Troy.

The third variety of `items()` accepts a `PIMItem`. You can set as many fields (of any type) in a `PIMItem` as you wish. When you pass it into `items()`, it will be used to find matching items in the list. This is useful for more specific searches, such as finding someone with a certain last name and zip code.

It's also possible to retrieve items based on category, which is explained soon. Also, calendars (`EventLists`) and to-do lists have their own versions of the `items()` method so that you can retrieve items based on start and end dates.

16.2.2 String Array Fields

String array fields are slightly more complicated. These fields can contain multiple string arrays (arrays of arrays, oh my). One example of a string array field is the `NAME` field in `Contact`. A `NAME` string array can contain a family name, given name, prefix, suffix, and more.

Each string in the array has a specific meaning based on its index. The array indices themselves are represented by constants. So, for example, `Contact` defines `NAME_FAMILY`, `NAME_GIVEN`, `NAME_PREFIX`, and others as indices into the string array field `NAME`.

Feeling dizzy yet? Me too.

Let's suppose you want to add a string array field to an item. How do you know how big to make the string array for the field? To answer this question, you have to ask the list itself. Pass the field key to `PIMList`'s `stringArraySize()` method, and you'll get back the correct size for the string array.

Here's an example that demonstrates how to work with a string array field. This code creates a string array for a contact's name field and adds the field value to the contact.

```
// ContactList cl = ...
// Contact c = ...
int namesize = cl.stringArraySize(Contact.NAME);
String[] names = new String[namesize];

names[Contact.NAME_FAMILY] = "Finch";
names[Contact.NAME_GIVEN] = "Atticus";
```

```
c.addStringArray(Contact.NAME, PIMItem.ATTR_NONE, names);
c.commit();
```

16.2.3 Labels

Field *labels* are human-readable strings that can be shown in your user interface to identify fields to people. Your PIMList can tell you all about them.

Pass a field key constant to getFieldLabel() to get back the matching label. For string array fields, pass the field key and array index to getArrayElementLabel().

You can get a human-readable name for an attribute by passing the attribute key to getAttributeLabel().

16.2.4 Categories

PIMList also knows how to work with *categories*. A category is a way of grouping items. For example, you might have appointments in your calendar that are for work. These could all be assigned to a category "Work." Other appointments might be assigned to "Home," or "Fun," or something else. Similarly, contacts and to-do items can be assigned to categories. Categories make it easy for users to sift through the information in their contact lists, calendars, and to-do lists.

You can get a string array containing all the categories for a list by calling get-Categories(). Modify the list by calling addCategory() or deleteCategory(). Lists have a limit on the number of categories allowed; this limit is returned from maxCategories().

PIMItem has addToCategory() and removeFromCategory() methods so you can manage an item's category or categories.

To retrieve all items for a specific category from a PIMList, pass the category name to itemsByCategory(), which returns an Enumeration of items.

16.2.5 Special Methods for Contact Lists

ContactList includes three methods in addition to the many it inherits from PIMList.

To create a new, empty Contact, call createContact(). The returned contact is not quite real, but you can add fields to it. To save the Contact as part of the ContactList, call commit().

Use removeContact() to immediately remove a Contact from a ContactList.

To copy a Contact into the ContactList, use importContact(). This method is useful if you load Contacts from a file, as described later in this chapter.

16.2.6 Special Methods for Calendars and Appointments

EventList includes methods that are specific to calendars and appointments. Similar to ContactList, EventList includes createEvent(), removeEvent(), and importEvent() methods that work much like their Contact counterparts.

EventList also includes another version of items() that accepts parameters for querying appointments by date. See the API documentation for details.

Also, Events support a RepeatRule, which describes recurring events, like a weekly meeting. RepeatRule itself is moderately complex and supports fields that are similar to PIMItem fields. EventList's getSupportedRepeatRuleFields() can tell you which RepeatRule fields are supported. Use Event's setRepeat() and getRepeat() methods to examine and modify the repeat rule for an appointment. Consult the API documentation for the full details on RepeatRule.

16.2.7 Special Methods for To-Do Lists

ToDoList has methods for managing ToDoItems, just like ContactList and EventList. The methods are createToDo(), removeToDo(), and importToDo().

In addition, ToDoList defines another items() method so that you can retrieve to-do items based on a range of dates.

16.3 Where Do Lists Come From?

All lists come from PIM. Call the static method getInstance() to get your hands on a PIM you can use to retrieve lists.

All you have to do is say what kind of list you want and whether you want to read it, write to it, or both. Use PIM's constants CONTACT_LIST, EVENT_LIST, and TODO_LIST to specify the type, and use READ_ONLY, WRITE_ONLY, and READ_WRITE to describe the type of access.

For example, to open the device's default contact list (address book) for reading and writing, do this:

```
PIM pim = PIM.getInstance();
ContactList cl = (ContactList)
    pim.openPIMList(PIM.CONTACT_LIST, PIM.READ_WRITE);
```

When you're all done with a list, you should explicitly `close()` it to release any open resources.

Some devices might have more than one of any type of list. For example, it's possible that a mobile phone has one contact list stored in internal memory and a different contact list stored on a SIM card.

Multiple lists are identified by name. `PIM` can furnish a string array of list names if you pass the desired list type to `listPIMLists()`. To open a named list, use the alternative form of `openPIMList()` that also accepts a list name.

16.4 Importing and Exporting

The PIM API supports importing and exporting contact information and calendar events using the standard vCard 2.1 and vCalendar 1.0 formats. These formats are defined by the Internet Mail Consortium. More information is here:

> http://www.imc.org/pdi/

The methods you need are in the `PIM` class. Importing an item is the simplest procedure. All you need to do is supply an `InputStream` and the character encoding of the file to the `fromSerialFormat()` method, which returns an array of `PIMItems`.

For example, you could import a calendar appointment like this:

```
// EventList el = ...
InputStream in =
    getClass().getResourceAsStream("/meeting.vcs");
String encoding = "UTF-8";

PIMItem[] items = pim.fromSerialFormat(in, encoding);

for (int i = 0; i < items.length; i++) {
  Event e = (Event)items[i];
  Event addedEvent = el.importEvent(e);
  addedEvent.commit();
}
```

Notice how you have to call two import methods to get items from a file into a list. First you have to call `fromSerialFormat()` to get items that are not part of any list. Then you pass these to the list's import method, which returns corresponding items that belong to the list. Finally, you have to call `commit()` on the new items to make them stick.

The PIM API implementation on a device might support more than the required vCard and vCalendar formats. To find a complete list, pass a list type to PIM's `supportedSerialFormats()` method. A string array of supported formats is returned.

You can export items to files or other destinations. Just supply an item, an `Output-Stream`, a file encoding, and the data format name to PIM's `toSerialFormat()` method.

16.5 What's Supported?

With all the flexibility designed into the PIM API, it can be hard for an application developer to figure out what is supported on a device at runtime. Which lists can you use? What fields are supported? Fortunately, the MSA specification lays down the law in several areas.

First, MSA says that devices must support all three types of lists. It also specifies the fields that must be supported for each type of item.

- Contacts must support ADDR, TEL, EMAIL, URL, NOTE, and PHOTO fields. In addition, contacts must support one or both of NAME and FORMATTED_NAME.
- Events must support START and SUMMARY. The first (default) `EventList` returned by PIM's `listPIMLists()` method must also support END, LOCATION, and ALARM.
- ToDos must support DUE, SUMMARY, PRIORITY, COMPLETED, and COMPLETION_DATE.

These specifications are really useful because they give you a practical minimum set of fields to manipulate with the PIM API.

If you need to find out which other fields are supported, or if you are writing a PIM API application on a non-MSA device, you can find out exactly which fields are supported and which are not. Pass the field key to PIMList's `isSupportedField()` to find out who's naughty and who's nice. A return of `true` indicates that the given field is supported. Likewise, `isSupported-Attribute()` and `isSupportedArrayElement()` provide more detailed information about the PIM API implementation.

16.6 Don't Forget Permissions

Reading and writing the device's contact, calendar, and to-do lists are sensitive operations. You don't want to allow every application off the street access to your personal information.

To give your users some peace from security prompts, you need to cryptographically sign your application and include the appropriate permissions in the MIDlet suite JAR. The permissions applicable to the PIM API are:

```
javax.microedition.pim.ContactList.read
javax.microedition.pim.ContactList.write
javax.microedition.pim.EventList.read
javax.microedition.pim.EventList.write
javax.microedition.pim.ToDoList.read
javax.microedition.pim.ToDoList.write
```

16.7 Example

This chapter's example, `SeraphimMIDlet`, presents a menu of simple PIM API tasks (see Figure 16.1).

Each menu item has a corresponding method in the source code. For example, **Edit nickname** calls a method `editNickname()`. Here is a brief description of each method:

- `showCalendar()` displays every item in the default `EventList`. It shows a `DateField` for the date of each item and the summary text.
- `showContacts()` does a similar thing for the default `ContactList`. It shows the name and nickname for each contact. Getting the contact's name is not as easy as you might think. MSA says that at least one of the

Figure 16.1 Main menu of `SeraphimMIDlet`

FORMATTED_NAME and NAME fields must be supported. However, NAME is a string array field, which makes things more complicated. In this example, the helper function getContactName() retrieves a name either from FORMATTED_NAME or NAME.

- information() displays the PIM API version (from a system property) and the supported import and export formats.

- addContact() creates a new contact and adds it to the contact list. You can verify the addition by showing the contact list.

- editNickname() searches through the default contact list for "Jonathan Knudsen," removes any existing nickname, and changes the nickname to "Buster." The contact list search is performed using one of the alternate forms of items(). You can verify that the nickname is changed by showing the contact list.

- importAppointment() demonstrates how to import an Event from a vCalendar file. In a real application, the vCalendar file would be loaded from a file or a URL, but in this case it is a resource file in the MIDlet suite JAR file. You can verify that the appointment was imported by showing the calendar.

- cleanCalendar() removes every appointment whose summary is "Big New York City Publisher meeting," which is the summary of the appointment that gets imported in the previous method.

- cleanContacts() removes any contact whose name is "Jonathan Knudsen" from the default contact list.

Here is the full listing of SeraphimMIDlet:

```java
import java.io.*;
import java.util.*;

import javax.microedition.lcdui.*;
import javax.microedition.midlet.*;

import javax.microedition.pim.*;

public class SeraphimMIDlet
    extends MIDlet
    implements CommandListener, Runnable {
    private Display mDisplay;
    private List mList;

    private static String kShowCalendar = "Show calendar";
    private static String kShowContacts = "Show contacts";
    private static String kInformation = "Information";
    private static String kAddContact = "Add contact";
```

```java
private static String kEditNickname = "Edit nickname";
private static String kImportAppointment =
    "Import appointment";
private static String kCleanCalendar = "Clean calendar";
private static String kCleanContacts = "Clean contacts";

public void startApp() {
  if (mList == null) {
    mList = new List("SeraphimMIDlet", List.IMPLICIT);
    mList.append(kShowCalendar, null);
    mList.append(kShowContacts, null);
    mList.append(kInformation, null);
    mList.append(kAddContact, null);
    mList.append(kEditNickname, null);
    mList.append(kImportAppointment, null);
    mList.append(kCleanCalendar, null);
    mList.append(kCleanContacts, null);

    Command exitCommand =
        new Command("Exit", Command.EXIT, 0);
    mList.addCommand(exitCommand);
    mList.setCommandListener(this);

    mDisplay = Display.getDisplay(this);
  }
  mDisplay.setCurrent(mList);
}

public void pauseApp() {
}

public void destroyApp(boolean unconditional) {}

public void commandAction(Command c, Displayable s) {
  if (c.getCommandType() == Command.EXIT) {
    destroyApp(true);
    notifyDestroyed();
  }
  else if (c.getCommandType() == Command.BACK) {
    mDisplay.setCurrent(mList);
  }
  else if (c == List.SELECT_COMMAND) {
    Form f = new Form("Working...");
    mDisplay.setCurrent(f);
    Thread t = new Thread(this);
    t.start();
  }
}
```

continued

```
public void run() {
  int index = mList.getSelectedIndex();
  if (index == -1) return;
  String command = mList.getString(index);
  if (command.equals(kShowCalendar)) showCalendar();
  else if (command.equals(kShowContacts)) showContacts();
  else if (command.equals(kInformation)) information();
  else if (command.equals(kAddContact)) addContact();
  else if (command.equals(kEditNickname)) editNickname();
  else if (command.equals(kImportAppointment))
    importAppointment();
  else if (command.equals(kCleanCalendar)) cleanCalendar();
  else if (command.equals(kCleanContacts)) cleanContacts();
}

private void showCalendar() {
  Form f = new Form("Calendar");

  PIM pim = PIM.getInstance();

  try {
    EventList calendar = (EventList)
        pim.openPIMList(PIM.EVENT_LIST, PIM.READ_ONLY);
    Enumeration appointments = calendar.items();
    while (appointments.hasMoreElements()) {
      Event appointment = (Event)appointments.nextElement();
      long start = appointment.getDate(Event.START, 0);
      DateField df =
          new DateField("Start", DateField.DATE_TIME);
      df.setDate(new Date(start));
      String summary =
          appointment.getString(Event.SUMMARY, 0);
      f.append(df);
      appendln(f, "Summary:", summary);
    }
    calendar.close();
  }
  catch (PIMException pime) {
    appendln(f, "PIMException", pime.toString());
  }

  showForm(f);
}

private void showContacts() {
  Form f = new Form("Contacts");

  PIM pim = PIM.getInstance();
```

```
try {
  ContactList contactList = (ContactList)
      pim.openPIMList(PIM.CONTACT_LIST, PIM.READ_ONLY);
  Enumeration contacts = contactList.items();
  while (contacts.hasMoreElements()) {
    Contact contact = (Contact)contacts.nextElement();
    String name = getContactName(contact);
    String nickname = "";
    try {
      nickname = contact.getString(Contact.NICKNAME, 0);
    }
    catch (Throwable t) {}
    appendln(f, "Name:", name);
    appendln(f, "Nickname:", nickname);
  }
  contactList.close();
}
catch (PIMException pime) {
  appendln(f, "PIMException", pime.toString());
}

showForm(f);
}

private void information() {
  Form f = new Form("PIM Information");

  String version =
      System.getProperty("microedition.pim.version");
  appendln(f, "microedition.pim.version:", version);

  int[] types = { PIM.CONTACT_LIST, PIM.EVENT_LIST,
      PIM.TODO_LIST };
  String[] typeNames = { "CONTACT_LIST", "EVENT_LIST",
      "TODO_LIST" };

  PIM pim = PIM.getInstance();

  for (int i = 0; i < types.length; i++) {
    String[] formats = pim.supportedSerialFormats(types[i]);
    StringBuffer formatbuffer = new StringBuffer();
    for (int j = 0; j < formats.length; j++) {
      if (j > 0) formatbuffer.append(':');
      formatbuffer.append(formats[j]);
    }
    String plural = formats.length > 1 ? "s" : "";
    appendln(f, typeNames[i] + " format" + plural + ":",
        formatbuffer.toString());
  }
```

continued

```
      showForm(f);
    }

    private void addContact() {
      Form f = new Form("Add contact");

      String first = "Jonathan";
      String last = "Knudsen";
      String nickname = "Cowboy Flash";
      String url = "http://kickbutt.jonathanknudsen.com/";

      try {
        PIM pim = PIM.getInstance();
        ContactList cl = (ContactList)
            pim.openPIMList(PIM.CONTACT_LIST, PIM.WRITE_ONLY);

        Contact c = cl.createContact();

        int namesize = cl.stringArraySize(Contact.NAME);
        String[] names = new String[namesize];
        names[Contact.NAME_FAMILY] = last;
        names[Contact.NAME_GIVEN] = first;

        int a = PIMItem.ATTR_NONE;
        c.addStringArray(Contact.NAME, a, names);
        c.addString(Contact.NICKNAME, a, nickname);
        c.addString(Contact.URL, a, url);

        c.commit();
        cl.close();

        appendln(f, null, "Created new contact.");
      }
      catch (PIMException pime) {
        appendln(f, "PIMException", pime.toString());
      }

      showForm(f);
    }

    private void editNickname() {
      Form f = new Form("Edit nickname");

      String first = "Jonathan";
      String last = "Knudsen";
      String newNickname = "Buster";
```

```
    try {
      PIM pim = PIM.getInstance();
      ContactList cl = (ContactList)
          pim.openPIMList(PIM.CONTACT_LIST, PIM.READ_WRITE);

      // Look for the first matching contact.
      Contact match = cl.createContact();

      int namesize = cl.stringArraySize(Contact.NAME);
      String[] names = new String[namesize];
      names[Contact.NAME_FAMILY] = last;
      names[Contact.NAME_GIVEN] = first;

      int a = PIMItem.ATTR_NONE;
      match.addStringArray(Contact.NAME, a, names);

      Enumeration e = cl.items(match);
      if (e.hasMoreElements() == false) {
        appendln(f, null, "Could not find contact.");
      }
      else {
        Contact c = (Contact)e.nextElement();
        // Clean the existing nickname.
        int n = c.countValues(Contact.NICKNAME);
        while (n > 0) {
          c.removeValue(Contact.NICKNAME, 0);
          n--;
        }
        // Add the new nickname.
        c.addString(Contact.NICKNAME, a, newNickname);
        appendln(f, "Changed nickname:", newNickname);
        c.commit();
      }
      cl.close();
    }
    catch (PIMException pime) {
      appendln(f, "PIMException", pime.toString());
    }

    showForm(f);
  }

  private void importAppointment() {
    Form f = new Form("Importing");

    PIM pim = PIM.getInstance();
```

continued

```
        InputStream in =
            getClass().getResourceAsStream("/meeting.vcs");
        String encoding = "UTF-8";

        if (in == null) {
          appendln(f, "Missing resource",
              "Couldn't find /meeting.vcs");
        }
        else {
          try {
            PIMItem[] items = pim.fromSerialFormat(in, encoding);

            EventList el = (EventList)
                pim.openPIMList(PIM.EVENT_LIST, PIM.WRITE_ONLY);
            for (int i = 0; i < items.length; i++) {
              Event e = (Event)items[i];
              String summary = e.getString(Event.SUMMARY, 0);
              appendln(f, "Found event:", summary);
              Event addedEvent = el.importEvent(e);
              addedEvent.commit();
              appendln(f, "Added event", null);
            }
          }
          catch (PIMException pime) {
            appendln(f, "PIMException", pime.toString());
          }
          catch (Throwable t) {
            appendln(f, "Throwable", t.toString());
          }
        }

        showForm(f);
      }

      private void cleanCalendar() {
        Form f = new Form("Clean Calendar");

        PIM pim = PIM.getInstance();

        try {
          EventList calendar = (EventList)
              pim.openPIMList(PIM.EVENT_LIST, PIM.READ_WRITE);
          Enumeration appointments = calendar.items();
          while (appointments.hasMoreElements()) {
            Event appointment = (Event)appointments.nextElement();
            String summary =
                appointment.getString(Event.SUMMARY, 0);
```

```
        if (summary.equals(
            "Big New York City Publisher meeting"))
          calendar.removeEvent(appointment);
        appendln(f, "Removed item:", summary);
      }
      calendar.close();
    }
    catch (PIMException pime) {
      appendln(f, "PIMException", pime.toString());
    }

    showForm(f);
  }

  private void cleanContacts() {
    Form f = new Form("Clean Contacts");

    PIM pim = PIM.getInstance();

    try {
      ContactList contactList = (ContactList)
          pim.openPIMList(PIM.CONTACT_LIST, PIM.READ_WRITE);
      Enumeration contacts = contactList.items();
      while (contacts.hasMoreElements()) {
        Contact contact = (Contact)contacts.nextElement();
        String name = getContactName(contact);
        if (name.indexOf("Knudsen") != -1 &&
            name.indexOf("Jonathan") != -1)
          contactList.removeContact(contact);
        appendln(f, "Removed contact:", name);
      }
      contactList.close();
    }
    catch (PIMException pime) {
      appendln(f, "PIMException", pime.toString());
    }

    showForm(f);
  }

  private String getContactName(Contact c) {
    String name = null;

    try { name = c.getString(Contact.FORMATTED_NAME, 0); }
    catch (Throwable t) {}

    if (name != null) return name;
```

continued

```
      try {
        String[] names = c.getStringArray(Contact.NAME, 0);
        String family = names[Contact.NAME_FAMILY];
        String given = names[Contact.NAME_GIVEN];
        name = family + ", " + given;
      }
      catch (Throwable t) {}

      return name;
    }

    private void appendln(Form f, String t, String s) {
      StringItem si = new StringItem(t, s);
      si.setLayout(Item.LAYOUT_2 | Item.LAYOUT_NEWLINE_AFTER);
      f.append(si);
    }

    private void showForm(Form f) {
      Command backCommand = new Command("Back", Command.BACK, 0);
      f.addCommand(backCommand);
      f.setCommandListener(this);
      mDisplay.setCurrent(f);
    }
  }
```

16.8 Summary

The PIM API provides access to a device's phone book (contact list), calendar (event list), and to-do list. These lists are retrieved from a top-level PIM object. Lists contain items that represent contacts, appointments (events), or to-do items. You can retrieve field values by calling the get method of the correct type and specifying a field key. MSA sets some ground rules for which fields are supported in the different types of list items. Appointments and contacts can be imported and exported from standard vCard and vCalendar files.

17

Mobile Internationalization

MOBILE *internationalization* is a fancy phrase that means making your application run in different langauges. *Localization* is the process of creating phrases, images, and other resources for a specific language. *Internationalization* (abbreviated i18n) is what you do to your application so that it can be localized easily.

The Mobile Internationalization API (MIA) is defined by JSR 238, and it includes four elements:

1. A `ResourceManager` provides the plumbing your application needs to retrieve resource strings, images, and other objects.

2. The MIA specification also defines a resource file format that describes how localized resources are stored.

3. `Formatter` knows how to represent numbers, currency, dates, and times in a specific language or region.

4. `StringComparator` understands how to sort strings according to the rules for a particular language.

MIA is relatively compact and resides in the `javax.microedition.global` package.

17.1 About Locales

Resources are based on *locales*, which are combinations of a language and a country or region. A locale, in essence, is a language, but it can be made more specific by adding a country as well. This makes sense because the same language is used differently in different parts of the world. Spanish in Mexico, for example, is different from Spanish in Spain.

Languages are represented using two-letter codes as defined by ISO 639. A list is here:

http://ftp.ics.uci.edu/pub/ietf/http/related/iso639.txt

Countries are represented using two-letter codes defined by ISO 3166. The list of country codes is here:

http://userpage.chemie.fu-berlin.de/diverse/doc/ISO_3166.html

A locale code is simply a language code, a hyphen, and a country code. For example, en-US represents English in the United States of America.

The system property microedition-locale contains the default locale code for a device. It is allowed to be null, in which case you must fall back on appropriate default behavior.

17.2 Using Resources

In the absence of MIA, you might create a simple user interface like this:

```
Form f = new Form("ApplicationName");
f.append("Hello, nurse!");
Command exitCommand = new Command("Exit", Command.EXIT, 0);
f.addCommand(exitCommand);
```

This little code snippet contains three hardcoded strings. Let's assume that "ApplicationName" will be shown regardless of the language of the rest of the user interface. The other two strings should be retrieved from a resource file so that they can easily be localized.

A resource file is represented by ResourceManager. ResourceManager contains strings and byte arrays, each of which has an identification (ID) number. You can retrieve a resource from ResourceManager by passing the ID to get() or getString(). A globalized version of the previous example looks like this:

```
// ResourceManager resources = ...
Form f = new Form("ApplicationName");
String message = resources.getString(1);
f.append(message);
String exit = resources.getString(2);
Command exitCommand = new Command(exit, Command.EXIT, 0);
f.addCommand(exitCommand);
```

It's good practice to use `static final` constants for resource IDs instead of embedding the numbers directly in your code. Here is an even more correct version:

```
// public static final int R_MESSAGE = 1;
// public static final int R_EXIT = 2;
// ResourceManager resources = ...
Form f = new Form("ApplicationName");
String message = resources.getString(R_MESSAGE);
f.append(message);
String exit = resources.getString(R_EXIT);
Command exitCommand = new Command(exit, Command.EXIT, 0);
f.addCommand(exitCommand);
```

17.3 Finding Resources

To load a resource file, pass a *base name* to one of `ResourceManager`'s static `getManager()` factory methods. `ResourceManager` attempts to use the default locale (from the `microedition.locale` system property) if you don't specify a locale. If you do, you can pass either a single locale or an array of locales.

Resource files are stored in a binary format in the MIDlet suite JAR file. They are located under the `global` directory. The location and format of resource files is defined in the JSR 238 specification. You should not have to know the details, because developer tools that support MIA include some kind of resource editor.

In general, resource files have the same base name and are located in directories that are named for locales.

In the Sun Java Wireless Toolkit, navigate to the resource editor (Figure 17.1) by choosing **File > Utilities** from the KToolbar menu, then selecting **i18n Resources Manager** and pressing **Launch**. Select your project from the **Projects** combo box and you are ready to edit resources. See the documentation for more details.

In NetBeans, choose **Tools > Java Platform Manager** from the menu. Select the Sun Java Wireless Toolkit from the list of platforms. Click on the **Tools & Extensions** tab, then press **Open Utilities**. Select **i18n Resources Manager** and press **Launch**.

The example at the end of this chapter shows a resource file with the base name "Babble," which is defined at the top level (right under `global`) and for the en-US and de-DE locales. The contents of the de-DE resource file are shown in the bottom part of the window. You can see the IDs and the corresponding resource. All of them are strings except for 3, which is an image byte array.

Figure 17.1 The Sun Java Wireless Toolkit's resource editor

Typically, your application will attempt to load resources for the device's locale with code like this:

```
String locale = System.getProperty("microedition.locale");
if (locale == null) locale = "";
ResourceManager resources = null;
try {
    resources = ResourceManager.getManager("baseName", locale);
}
catch (ResourceException re) {
    // No resources found at all!
}
```

It is possible that microedition.locale is null. ResourceManager will throw an exception if the requested locale is null, so this example tests for the condition and assigns an empty string if needed. The empty string will at least match the default resource file for the given base name.

17.4 Resource Inheritance

ResourceManager tries hard to honor requests for resources. This commitment to customer service begins at the call to getManager(). ResourceManager attempts to find a resource file that exactly matches the locale you request (or the default locale if you did not specify one).

If an exact match cannot be found, ResourceManager will try to find a resource file that matches just the language part of the locale. If it can't find that, it will see if there is a default resource file, one with no associated locale, located at the root of the global directory.

Supplying a default resource file is therefore a very good idea, because it allows your application to function even when a resource file matching the requested locale does not exist.

Once you have an appropriate ResourceManager, another inheritance scheme takes effect. Let's say, for example, that you've obtained a ResourceManager for en-US and you request string resource 2. If the resource does not exist, ResourceManager will look for it in an en resource file (if it is available) or the default resource file.

To support both British and American English, then, you could create an en resource file that contains most of the phrases and resources for your application. Then you could also create an en-US resource file with all the Americanisms and an en-GB resource file with the specifically British resources.

The example at the end of this chapter demonstrates this technique. The default resource file contains phrases in English. The en-US resource file contains an image of the American flag but does not define any of the phrases. When the application attempts to retrieve the phrases from the en-US ResourceManager, they are returned from the default resource file.

17.5 Formatting Numbers and Dates

A separate class in MIA, Formatter, knows how to format numbers, currency, dates, times, and percentages in different locales.

To get a Formatter, just pass a locale to its constructor. If an appropriate Formatter does not exist, an UnsupportedLocaleException is thrown. You can also use the Formatter constructor with no arguments, which attempts to use microedition.locale. Finally, if you pass null for the locale, you'll get a Formatter that works in a locale-neutral way.

The actual formatting is straightforward. Use the `formatCurrency()` methods for money, the `formatNumber()` methods for numbers, and `formatPercentage()` for percentages.

Note: Using floating-point variables for currency is asking for trouble, but MIA embraces it. A safer approach is to use an `int` or `long` to store pennies (or the equivalent). Consult the following sources for more information.

Representing money

    http://www.javapractices.com/Topic13.cjp

Beware of floating-point numbers

    http://www.javapractices.com/Topic213.cjp

Working with money in Java

    http://www.javaranch.com/newsletter/July2003/ MoneyInJava.html

Currency

    http://mindprod.com/jgloss/currency.html

Floating Point

    http://mindprod.com/jgloss/floatingpoint.html

The `formatDate()` method can create a variety of date and time styles. Pass in a `java.util.Calendar` and one of the style constants from `Formatter`, either `DATE_LONG`, `DATE_SHORT`, `TIME_LONG`, `TIME_SHORT`, `DATETIME_LONG`, or `DATETIME_SHORT`.

The trickiest method in `Formatter` is `formatMessage()`, which is useful for inserting parameters into a fixed message. For example, you might want to localize the message "You now have *n* points." The key is to put the parameters in curly braces. In this example, you could create a string resource like this:

```
You now have {0} points.
```

The parameters should be numbered starting from 0 and counting up. You can use as many as 100 parameters in a message. When you want to show the message, pass the message and a string array of parameters to `Formatter`'s `formatMessage()` method.

It looks something like this:

```
// ResourceManager resources = ...
// Formatter formatter = ...
// int R_POINT_MESSAGE = ...
```

```
// int points = ...
String template = resources.getString(R_POINT_MESSAGE);
String pointsNumber = formatter.formatNumber(points);
String[] parameters = { pointsNumber };
String pointsMessage =
    formatter.formatMessage(template, parameters);
```

17.6 Sorting Strings

Different languages have different alphabets and their own rules about how strings should be sorted (alphabetized). MIA's `StringComparator` encapsulates these rules for a locale.

To use `StringComparator`, pass a locale to its constructor. To compare two strings, pass them to the `compare()` method. The method returns a negative number if the strings are already in ascending alphabetical order, a positive number if they are in descending order, and zero if the two strings are identical.

You can use `StringComparator` to sort a list of strings in a manner that is appropriate for a particular locale.

The Sun Java Wireless Toolkit includes a demonstration of this technique. In the `i18nDemo` project, take a look at the **String Comparator** example. It shows a list of cities. Choose the **Sort - default** command to sort the cities using default rules. Now choose **Sort - slovak** and notice how the sorting changes.

17.7 Take It Out for a Spin

`BabbleMIDlet` includes examples of most of the techniques you've been reading about. It will be useful to you if you are writing an internationalized application. It shows how to retrieve a `ResourceManager`, how to obtain a `Formatter`, and how to use both.

```
import java.util.*;

import javax.microedition.lcdui.*;
import javax.microedition.midlet.MIDlet;

import javax.microedition.global.*;

public class BabbleMIDlet
    extends MIDlet
    implements CommandListener {
```

continued

```
private Form mForm;
private Command mExitCommand;

private static final String RESOURCE_NAME = "Babble";
private ResourceManager mResources;
private Formatter mFormatter;

private static final int R_MESSAGE_LABEL = 1;
private static final int R_MESSAGE = 2;
private static final int R_FLAG = 3;
private static final int R_DATE = 4;
private static final int R_TIME = 5;
private static final int R_MONEY = 6;
private static final int R_EXIT = 7;
private static final int R_POINT_MESSAGE = 8;

public void startApp() {
  if (mForm == null) {
    boolean success = getResources();
    getFormatter();

    if (!success) return;

    buildForm();
  }

  Display.getDisplay(this).setCurrent(mForm);
}

public void pauseApp() {}

public void destroyApp(boolean unconditional) {}

public void commandAction(Command c, Displayable s) {
  if (c.getCommandType() == Command.EXIT) {
    destroyApp(true);
    notifyDestroyed();
  }
}

private boolean getResources() {
  String locale = System.getProperty("microedition.locale");
  if (locale == null) locale = "";
  try {
    mResources =
        ResourceManager.getManager(RESOURCE_NAME, locale);
  }
  catch (ResourceException re) {
```

```java
      Form f = new Form("Exception");
      f.append("Could not find " +
          RESOURCE_NAME + " resources.");
      f.append(re.toString());
      mExitCommand = new Command("Exit", Command.EXIT, 0);
      f.addCommand(mExitCommand);
      f.setCommandListener(this);
      Display.getDisplay(this).setCurrent(f);
      return false;
    }
    return true;
  }

  private void getFormatter() {
    String locale = System.getProperty("microedition.locale");
    try { mFormatter = new Formatter(locale); }
    catch (UnsupportedLocaleException ue) {
      mFormatter = new Formatter(null);
    }
  }

  private void buildForm() {
    StringItem si;
    mForm = new Form("Babble");
    int layout = Item.LAYOUT_2 |
        Item.LAYOUT_NEWLINE_AFTER | Item.LAYOUT_CENTER;

    String messageLabel =
        mResources.getString(R_MESSAGE_LABEL);

    String message = mResources.getString(R_MESSAGE);

    si = new StringItem(messageLabel, message);
    si.setLayout(layout);
    mForm.append(si);

    try {
      byte[] raw = mResources.getData(R_FLAG);
      Image image = Image.createImage(raw, 0, raw.length);
      ImageItem ii = new ImageItem(null, image, layout, "Flag");
      mForm.append(ii);
    }
    catch (ResourceException re) {}

    Calendar now = Calendar.getInstance();

    String dateLabel = mResources.getString(R_DATE);
    String date =
        mFormatter.formatDateTime(now, Formatter.DATE_LONG);
```

continued

```
        si = new StringItem(dateLabel, date);
        si.setLayout(layout);
        mForm.append(si);

        String timeLabel = mResources.getString(R_TIME);
        String time =
            mFormatter.formatDateTime(now, Formatter.TIME_LONG);
        si = new StringItem(timeLabel, time);
        si.setLayout(layout);
        mForm.append(si);

        double moneyAmount = 1234.56;
        String moneyLabel = mResources.getString(R_MONEY);
        String money = mFormatter.formatCurrency(moneyAmount);
        si = new StringItem(moneyLabel, money);
        si.setLayout(layout);
        mForm.append(si);

        int points = 4789;
        String template = mResources.getString(R_POINT_MESSAGE);
        String pointsNumber = mFormatter.formatNumber(points);
        String[] parameters = { pointsNumber };
        String pointsMessage =
            mFormatter.formatMessage(template, parameters);
        si = new StringItem(null, pointsMessage);
        si.setLayout(layout);
        mForm.append(si);

        String exit = mResources.getString(R_EXIT);
        mExitCommand = new Command(exit, Command.EXIT, 0);

        mForm.addCommand(mExitCommand);
        mForm.setCommandListener(this);

        Display.getDisplay(this).setCurrent(mForm);
    }
}
```

Run it with the emulator's locale as en-US, and the result will look like Figure 17.2.

The flag image comes from the en-US resource file, while the text phrases are inherited from the default resource file. The Formatter knows about American dollars and successfully formats the points value by inserting a comma.

To really appreciate the talents of this application, you need to change the default locale (the microedition.locale system property) for the emulator. In the Sun Java Wireless Toolkit, choose **Edit > Preferences...** from the KToolbar menu and click on the **i18n** category.

Figure 17.2 `BabbleMIDlet` in en-US

In NetBeans, choose **Tools > Java Platform Manager** from the menu. Select the Sun Java Wireless Toolkit from the list of platforms. Click on the **Tools & Extensions** tab, then press **Open Preferences**. Click on the **i18n** category.

Fill in de-DE for the locale and run `BabbleMIDlet` again (see Figure 17.3).

As you can see, the text phrases and the flag image come from the de-DE resource file. However, the toolkit's emulator does not include an appropriate formatter.

Figure 17.3 `BabbleMIDlet` in de-DE

Figure 17.4   BabbleMIDlet in cs-CZ

Default behavior, produced from new Formatter(null), occurs instead. The date, time, currency, and number formatting are all plain vanilla, locale-neutral.

For another perspective, try cs-CZ, shown in Figure 17.4.

This time, no appropriate resource file is available, so all the text prompts come from the default resource file, and the image is not defined at all. Notice how the code in buildForm() catches the ResourceException and will not attempt to add the flag image when it is not available.

However, an appropriate Formatter is available on the toolkit's emulator. The date, time, currency, and number formatting are correct for cs-CZ, even though the phrases have all been pulled from the default resource file.

17.8 Summary

The Mobile Internationalization API provides the plumbing you need to make applications that can run smoothly in different languages. It defines a scheme for resource files, represented by ResourceManager, which contain phrases and other data. A resource file belongs to a locale, which is a combination of a language and a country. Resource information can be inherited from less specific resource files, including the default. A separate class, Formatter, can format dates, currency, and numbers for a locale. Finally, StringComparator encapsulates string sorting functionality for a locale.

Section VI

Networking

18

The Generic
Connection Framework

$\mathbf{A}$LL network access in MIDP devices works through the Generic Connection Framework (GCF), a simple API that makes quick work of many types of communication. The fundamental idea of GCF is very simple. Your application supplies a connection string, and GCF hands back the corresponding input and output streams.

The MIDP 2.0 specification says that devices must support HyperText Transfer Protocol (HTTP) and secure HTTP (HTTPS) connections, which means your application has two powerful guarantees for connectivity to the awesome power of the Internet.

This chapter describes the simple premise of GCF and provides details on HTTP and HTTPS networking. It also provides some details on optional connection types. Later chapters cover the details of SMS, MMS, Bluetooth, and other network connections.

18.1 Making Connections

GCF is contained in `javax.microedition.io`. The `Connector` class runs the show, and a hierarchy of `Connection` interfaces represent different connection types.

To use GCF, pass a *connection string* to one of `Connector`'s `open()` methods. It hands you back some `Connection` implementation that you can use to get input and output streams. Connection strings are URLs with a protocol, network address, and optional parameters.

Here is an example that attempts an HTTP connection.

```
String url = "http://kickbutt.jonathanknudsen.com/" +
    "images/castiglione.png";
HttpConnection hc = (HttpConnection)Connector.open(url);
```

The object returned from Connector's open() method is an implementation of Connection. Connection isn't useful by itself, so you must cast the return value to a more specific connection type before you can do anything with it. GCF defines many Connection subinterfaces to support serial ports, sockets, datagrams, HTTP, HTTPS, and even server sockets. Optional APIs add even more connection types. JSR 205 defines MessageConnection to support SMS and MMS, JSR 82 defines L2CAPConnection for Bluetooth, and so forth. GCF is so general that it is also used for purposes that are not, strictly speaking, network connections, like the FileConnection you learned about in Chapter 15.

Figure 18.1 shows a diagram of the path from Connection to HttpConnection and the methods defined along the way. It is not a complete diagram of the Connection family.

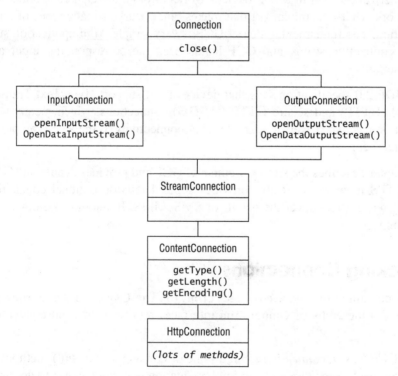

Figure 18.1   Part of Connection's family tree

If you wanted to load the contents of an image file, you could do something like this:

```
String url = "http://kickbutt.jonathanknudsen.com/" +
    "images/castiglione.png";
HttpConnection hc = (HttpConnection)Connector.open(url);
InputStream in = hc.openInputStream();
// in.read() ...
```

In this case, you are using the openInputStream() method that HttpConnection inherits from InputConnection.

Once you've got a stream or two, the rest of your code should be standard java.io programming. GCF, then, provides your application with a way to get streams that connect to interesting things, like Web servers or serial ports or Bluetooth devices.

18.2 Clean Up

Like any other resource, network connections should be closed when you are finished with them. The base Connection interface defines a close() method for this very purpose. It is also a good idea to close any of the Connection's streams independently. Finally, good practice dictates that all this closing take place in a finally block, just to make sure it gets executed. It is a little messy, but it is the safest way to go. Here is a skeleton of a method that reads data from an HTTP network connection and cleans up properly.

```
private void loadBytes(String url) throws IOException {
    HttpConnection hc = (HttpConnection)Connector.open(url);
    try {
        InputStream in = hc.openInputStream();
        try {
            // Read data from in.
        }
        finally { in.close(); }
    }
    finally { hc.close(); }
}
```

The method that calls loadBytes() should catch and handle IOException and SecurityException.

18.3 Use Threads

Network access can take a long time. A typical HTTP connection is subject to the relatively slow speed of today's wireless networks, the whims of the Internet, the speed of the server, the overhead of HTTP connections, and many other factors.

Back in Chapter 4, I told you that you should use a separate thread for any operation that you expect will take a long time. Network access is one of those lengthy operations.

The threading in the examples in this chapter is very simple. Each new network connection is performed in a newly created thread. For more complex applications, a dedicated network thread is more appropriate. You can queue up network requests and let the network thread handle them one at a time. This means you are using only one extra thread and one network connection at a time. This is a good idea on small devices that have limited resources for multiple threads and multiple network connections.

Don't forget about your users, either. They are impatient and needy. They are trying to get something done and network access is slowing them down. Put up a pretty wait screen or an amusing animation. If possible, allow them to keep working while your application hits the network in the background.

18.4 Image Loading via HTTP

Here is an example that loads a small image from a Web server and displays it in a form. The form is created in startApp() with a continuous indefinite gauge, which provides an animation to keep the user enthralled while the image is loading. startApp() also kicks off a thread to do the network access.

The connection is set up in run(), while the actual image data is read using the readAll() method originally presented in Chapter 4.

```
import java.io.*;

import javax.microedition.io.*;
import javax.microedition.lcdui.*;
import javax.microedition.midlet.MIDlet;

public class BaldassareMIDlet
    extends MIDlet
    implements CommandListener, Runnable {
  private String mURL =
    "http://kickbutt.jonathanknudsen.com/" +
    "images/castiglione.png";
```

```java
private Form mForm;
private Command mExitCommand;

public void startApp() {
  if (mForm == null) {
    // Use an application property if it is available.
    String url = getAppProperty("image-url");
    if (url != null && !url.equals("")) mURL = url;
    // Create the main form with a busy indicator gauge.
    mForm = new Form("Baldassare Castiglione");
    Gauge gauge = new Gauge("Loading...", false,
        Gauge.INDEFINITE, Gauge.CONTINUOUS_RUNNING);
    mForm.append(gauge);
    mExitCommand = new Command("Exit", Command.EXIT, 0);
    mForm.addCommand(mExitCommand);
    mForm.setCommandListener(this);
    // Kick off image loading in a separate thread.
    Thread t = new Thread(this);
    t.start();
  }

  Display.getDisplay(this).setCurrent(mForm);
}

public void pauseApp() {}

public void destroyApp(boolean unconditional) {}

public void commandAction(Command c, Displayable s) {
  if (c.getCommandType() == Command.EXIT) {
    destroyApp(true);
    notifyDestroyed();
  }
}

public void run() {
  try {
    byte[] raw = loadBytes(mURL);
    Image image = Image.createImage(raw, 0, raw.length);
    ImageItem ii = new ImageItem(null, image,
        Item.LAYOUT_2 | Item.LAYOUT_CENTER, "Baldy");
    mForm.append(ii);
  }
  catch (IOException ioe) {
    mForm.append(ioe.toString());
  }
  catch (IllegalArgumentException iae) {
    mForm.append("Bad image file.");
```

continued

```
      }
      catch (SecurityException se) {
        mForm.append("Don't have permission.");
      }
      finally { clearGauge(); }
    }

    private byte[] loadBytes(String url) throws IOException {
      HttpConnection hc = (HttpConnection)Connector.open(url);
      try {
        InputStream in = hc.openInputStream();
        try { return readAll(in); }
        finally { in.close(); }
      }
      finally { hc.close(); }
    }

    private void clearGauge() {
      for (int i = 0; i < mForm.size(); i++) {
        Item item = mForm.get(i);
        if (item instanceof Gauge)
          mForm.delete(i--);
      }
    }

    public byte[] readAll(InputStream in) throws IOException {
      ByteArrayOutputStream out = new ByteArrayOutputStream();
      byte[] buffer = new byte[1024];
      for (int n; (n = in.read(buffer)) > 0; )
        out.write(buffer, 0, n);
      return out.toByteArray();
    }
  }
```

The image URL is hardcoded here, but you can override it to try a different image by changing the application property image-url. The hardcoded URL produces the results shown in Figure 18.2.

18.5 Advanced HTTP Techniques

The HttpConnection interface has lots of methods. In theory, you can use these methods to do some fancy stuff:

- You can perform HTTP POSTs from a MIDlet. The default connection type is GET, but a call to setRequestMethod(HttpConnection.POST) makes the change. Unfortunately, you'll have to do your own parameter encoding. Stick with GET if possible.

Figure 18.2 The image has been loaded via HTTP.

- Some Web applications use HTTP cookies for session tracking or other purposes. It's possible to create a cookie-aware MIDlet. You can retrieve cookies sent by the server by calling getHeaderField("Set-cookie") on an HttpConnection. Next time you open an HttpConnection, pass the cookie value by calling setRequestProperty("cookie", value).

- HttpConnection provides access to all of the headers sent in the request and received in the server response. You should be able to perform the same kind of HTTP processing that you would be able to do on any other platform.

Before you get all fired up about this fancy HTTP stuff, though, be aware that HTTP headers might get mangled between your server and your users' devices. Read on for more details.

18.6 Tips for Success

Making HTTP connections consistently across a wide variety of devices is surprisingly difficult for two main reasons:

- Different devices have different implementation behavior and bugs.
- Various gateways lie between your device and the Internet. These gateways sometimes meddle with your requests and responses.

The best way to understand the quirks of particular devices and how to code defensively is to talk with other developers who have already had the pain of discovering the idiosyncrasies of real devices. One enlightening thread on the subject of HTTP connections is here:

http://archives.java.sun.com/cgi-bin/wa?A2=ind0511&L= kvm-interest&P=R2451&I=-3

To protect yourself from meddlesome gateways, don't try to do anything tricky with your HTTP requests and responses. Gateways might modify or remove anything that they don't recognize.

- Don't rely on sending custom headers.
- Don't rely on custom HTTP response messages.
- Don't try to send a response body with anything but 200 OK.
- Don't rely on cookies.

18.7 Using HTTPS

HTTPS is HTTP run on a secure socket connection, typically Transport Layer Security (TLS) or Secure Sockets Layer (SSL). This means that the HTTP requests and responses that pass between the device and the server are encrypted.

HTTPS is powerful and can be complex, but fortunately it's very easy to use in a MIDlet. Most of the time, you can simply use `HttpsConnection` in place of `HttpConnection`, and use the corresponding HTTPS connection string:

```
HttpsConnection hc = (HttpsConnection)
    Connector.open("https://www.nsa.gov/");
```

`HttpsConnection` descends from `HttpConnection`, which means you already know how to use it. If you want more information about the HTTPS connection, `HttpsConnection` defines two additional methods, including one that returns a `SecurityInfo` object.

Here is an example that shows information about an HTTPS connection.

```
import java.io.*;

import javax.microedition.io.*;
import javax.microedition.lcdui.*;
import javax.microedition.midlet.MIDlet;

public class HTTPSInformationMIDlet
    extends MIDlet
    implements CommandListener, Runnable {
```

```
private String mURL = "https://www.cert.org/";
private Form mForm;
private Command mExitCommand;

public void startApp() {
  if (mForm == null) {
    // Use an application property if it is available.
    String url = getAppProperty("https-url");
    if (url != null && !url.equals("")) mURL = url;
    // Create the main form with a busy indicator gauge.
    mForm = new Form("HTTPSInformationMIDlet");
    Gauge gauge = new Gauge("Loading...", false,
        Gauge.INDEFINITE, Gauge.CONTINUOUS_RUNNING);
    mForm.append(gauge);
    mExitCommand = new Command("Exit", Command.EXIT, 0);
    mForm.addCommand(mExitCommand);
    mForm.setCommandListener(this);
    // Kick off image loading in a separate thread.
    Thread t = new Thread(this);
    t.start();
  }

  Display.getDisplay(this).setCurrent(mForm);
}

public void pauseApp() {}

public void destroyApp(boolean unconditional) {}

public void commandAction(Command c, Displayable s) {
  if (c.getCommandType() == Command.EXIT) {
    destroyApp(true);
    notifyDestroyed();
  }
}

public void run() {
  try { getHTTPSInformation(); }
  catch (IOException ioe) {
    appendln("IOException", ioe.toString());
  }
  catch (SecurityException se) {
    appendln("SecurityException", se.toString());
  }
  clearGauge();
}
```

continued

```java
    private void getHTTPSInformation() throws IOException {
      HttpsConnection hc =
          (HttpsConnection)Connector.open(mURL);
      try {
        InputStream in = hc.openInputStream();
        try {
          SecurityInfo secinfo = hc.getSecurityInfo();

          appendln("Port:",
              Integer.toString(hc.getPort()));
          appendln("Cipher suite:",
              secinfo.getCipherSuite());
          appendln("Protocol:",
              secinfo.getProtocolName());
          appendln("Protocol version:",
              secinfo.getProtocolVersion());
          appendln("Server certificate:",
              secinfo.getServerCertificate().toString());
        }
        finally { in.close(); }
      }
      finally { hc.close(); }
    }

    private void clearGauge() {
      for (int i = 0; i < mForm.size(); i++) {
        Item item = mForm.get(i);
        if (item instanceof Gauge)
          mForm.delete(i--);
      }
    }

    private void appendln(String t, String m) {
      StringItem si = new StringItem(t, m);
      si.setLayout(Item.LAYOUT_2 | Item.LAYOUT_NEWLINE_AFTER);
      mForm.append(si);
    }
  }
```

On Sun's emulator, shown in Figure 18.3, you get quite a bit of information.

Most of the time, an HTTPS connection will be sufficient to hide your users' data from prying eyes. If you would like a more detailed story, read this article:

http://developers.sun.com/techtopics/mobility/midp/articles/ security2/

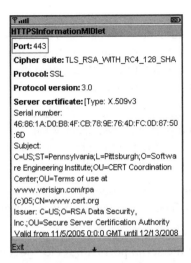

Figure 18.3   Information about an HTTPS connection

18.8 Other Connection Types

MIDP requires support for HTTP and HTTPS connections, but it also defines connection strings and `Connection` subinterfaces for other connection types. The exact format for the connection strings is defined in the API documentation for the corresponding connection interface.

Although socket connections are widely supported, the others are not. None of these connections types are required to be supported, so proceed with caution.

Interface	Example
`SocketConnection`	`socket://kickbutt.jonathanknudsen.com:2048`
`SecureConnection`	`ssl://kickbutt.jonathanknudsen.com:2049`
`DatagramConnection`	`datagram://kickbutt.jonathanknudsen.com:2050`
`CommConnection`	`comm:COM1`

`SocketConnection` is for IP sockets. Just specify a host and port number. `Secure-Connection` works the same way but uses SSL or TLS to make an encrypted connection.

DatagramConnection is a little different. You create the connection by specifying a host and port number, but you don't use streams to write and read data. Instead, use one of the newDatagram() methods in DatagramConnection to create a new Datagram object. Populate the Datagram, then send it out with send(). In a separate thread, you can call receive(), which blocks until a datagram is received.

CommConnection represents a serial port on the device. The serial port could be a physical port or a virtual one like an infrared port. You can specify various connection parameters in the connection string, like data rate, parity, and so forth. Take a look at the CommConnection API documentation for all the details.

You can get a list of all the available serial ports on a device by retrieving the system property microedition.commports. The return value (if it is not null) is a comma-separated list of port names.

The following example shows how to parse the serial port names (see getComm-Ports()) and attempts to open input and output streams on each named port.

```
import java.io.*;
import java.util.Vector;

import javax.microedition.io.*;
import javax.microedition.lcdui.*;
import javax.microedition.midlet.MIDlet;

public class SerialBoxMIDlet
    extends MIDlet
    implements CommandListener {
  private Form mForm;
  private Command mExitCommand;

  public void startApp() {
    if (mForm == null) { buildForm(); }

    Display.getDisplay(this).setCurrent(mForm);
  }

  public void pauseApp() {}

  public void destroyApp(boolean unconditional) {}

  public void commandAction(Command c, Displayable s) {
    if (c.getCommandType() == Command.EXIT) {
      destroyApp(true);
      notifyDestroyed();
    }
  }
```

```
private void buildForm() {
  mForm = new Form("SerialBoxMIDlet");

  String[] commports = getCommPorts();

  for (int i = 0; i < commports.length; i++) {
    String url = "comm:" + commports[i];
    try { openComm(url); }
    catch (IOException ioe) {
      appendln(url, ioe.toString());
    }
    catch (SecurityException se) {
      appendln(url, se.toString());
    }
  }

  mExitCommand = new Command("Exit", Command.EXIT, 0);

  mForm.addCommand(mExitCommand);
  mForm.setCommandListener(this);
}

private void openComm(String url) throws IOException {
  appendln(url, "open");
  CommConnection cc = (CommConnection)
      Connector.open(url);
  try {
    appendln(url, "openInputStream");
    cc.openInputStream();
    appendln(url, "openOutputStream");
    cc.openOutputStream();
  }
  finally { cc.close(); }
}

private String[] getCommPorts() {
  String allports =
      System.getProperty("microedition.commports");
  if (allports == null) return new String[0];
  Vector portsVector = new Vector();
  int index = 0;
  boolean trucking = true;
  while (trucking) {
    // Find the next comma.
    int comma = allports.indexOf(',', index);
    String commport;
```

continued

```
        if (comma != -1) {
          commport = allports.substring(index, comma).trim();
          index = comma + 1;
          if (index >= allports.length()) trucking = false;
        }
        else {
          commport = allports.substring(index).trim();
          trucking = false;
        }
        if (commport.equals("") == false)
          portsVector.addElement(commport);
      }

      String[] portsArray = new String[portsVector.size()];
      for (int i = 0; i < portsVector.size(); i++)
        portsArray[i] = (String)portsVector.elementAt(i);

      return portsArray;
    }

  private void appendln(String t, String m) {
    StringItem si = new StringItem(t, m);
    si.setLayout(Item.LAYOUT_2 | Item.LAYOUT_LEFT |
        Item.LAYOUT_NEWLINE_AFTER);
    mForm.append(si);
  }
}
```

18.9 Incoming Connections

Certain connection strings correspond to incoming connections. You already
caught a glimpse of this in Chapter 6 when you learned about the push registry.

To set up a server socket, for example, use a socket connection string with no
host, like this:

```
socket://:2051
```

Pass this connection string to Connector.open() to receive a ServerSocket-
Connection for port 2051. The acceptAndOpen() waits for an incoming socket
connection and returns it as a StreamConnection. Assuming you have devices
and a wireless network that support socket connections, you could use a Server-
SocketConnection to set up a device-to-device socket connection for a game or
other application. In practice, server sockets are unlikely to be supported.

If you have a device and network that supports it, you can also set up your MIDlet to receive datagram connections. Again, you use a datagram-style connection string but omit the host:

```
datagram://:2052
```

Optional APIs also define connection strings for incoming network connections. For example, the JSR 205 Wireless Messaging API (WMA) 2.0 defines connection strings for applications that wish to receive incoming SMS or MMS messages.

18.10 Connection Permissions

Making network connections is a sensitive operation from a security standpoint. HTTP and HTTPS connections might result in charges to the user, and local connections like Bluetooth or serial port connections can pose security or privacy risks.

Each connection type has a corresponding permission. For example, HTTP connections correspond to the `javax.microedition.io.Connector.http` permission. Don't forget to add the right permissions to your MIDlet suite's descriptor as required permissions or optional permissions.

If you cryptographically sign your application, it is likely to be placed into a security domain where network access is allowed or where the device will ask the user for permission only once at installation time. Leave your application unsigned and your users will probably have to work through a lot of security prompts.

18.11 Summary

The Generic Connection Framework (GCF) allows applications to trade connection strings for input and output streams. Network access should be performed in application threads, and applications should be scrupulous about closing open connections. HTTP and HTTPS must be available, and socket, datagram, serial, and other connection types might also be available via GCF. Server socket and datagram listener connections are also possible. Applications must have appropriate permissions to make network connections.

19

Text and Multimedia
Messaging

T HE Wireless Messaging API (WMA) is a bridge between your MIDlets and the wonderful world of text and multimedia messaging. Most mobile phones are capable of sending and receiving messages. WMA extends this capability to MIDlets.

JSR 120 defines WMA 1.1, which encompasses Short Message Service (SMS), commonly known as *text messaging* or *texting*. JSR 205 defines WMA 2.0, which adds support for Multimedia Messaging Service (MMS).

WMA 2.0 is a superset of WMA 1.1. MSA requires WMA 2.0, but most MIDP devices out in the world today support WMA 1.1 or WMA 1.0. If you are aiming your application at the widest possible audience, stick to the basic SMS functionality provided by WMA 1.1. On the other hand, if you are targeting MSA devices, you can use the full range of MMS supported by WMA 2.0.

Like other network communication, WMA is based on the Generic Connection Framework (GCF) that you read about in Chapter 18. Use `Connector` to get a `MessageConnection`. The `MessageConnection`, in turn, can be used to create, send, and receive messages.

WMA is a compact API that lives in `javax.wireless.messaging`.

19.1 Why Messaging?

WMA is a great solution for some kinds of network communication, although the usual caveats about device testing apply. SMS and MMS travel through a *store-and-forward* network, which means that messages are not lost if the destination is unavailable. For example, if you send a message to your friend when your friend's phone is turned off, the network hangs on to the message until it can be delivered to the phone. One good application for WMA is to transmit turns between players in a slow-moving, turn-based game like chess.

Another advantage to SMS and MMS is that they do not involve a server. You can easily communicate between applications running on different devices with no server-side programming.

Finally, WMA combined with the PIM API is a powerful combination. The PIM API gives your application access to people your user cares about. WMA gives you the ability to send those people messages.

19.2 Sending Messages

It takes longer to explain how to send a message than it takes to write it out in code. Here is the short story:

```
public void sendText(String address, String text)
    throws IOException, InterruptedException {
  String cs = "sms://" + address + ":50000";
  MessageConnection mc = (MessageConnection)
      Connector.open(cs);
  TextMessage tm = (TextMessage)
      mc.newMessage(MessageConnection.TEXT_MESSAGE);
  tm.setPayloadText(text);
  mc.send(tm);
}
```

It's basically four lines, but the casts makes it look bulky. Here are the four steps:

1. Obtain a `MessageConnection` from `Connector`. In the example, `cs` is the connection string, which I'll talk about soon.

2. Get a `Message` from the `MessageConnection` by calling `newMessage()`. In this example, I asked for a text message.

3. Fill up the message. This works differently for different message types. Here I called `setPayloadText()`, a method that is specific to `TextMessage`.

4. Send the message by passing it to the `MessageConnection`'s `send()` method.

The address in the connection string is the telephone number of the device to which you are sending the message. The port number is optional. The example above automatically appends a port number of 50,000.

If you leave off the port number, your message is an ordinary SMS message and will end up in an inbox at the destination. This is nice if you want an actual person to read the message.

If, instead, you are trying to send the message to an application running on the destination device, include a port number. Some port numbers are reserved. They are listed in the WMA specification. Any free port number should work, as long as the sender and recipient agree on that number.

In most cases, the push registry will field an incoming message and launch a MIDlet to respond. Go back to Chapter 6 if you can't remember the push registry. It's possible, but unlikely, that the receiving MIDlet will actually be running and listening for incoming messages. If no running MIDlet is listening for messages on the right port, and if no MIDlet is in the push registry for the right port, the message is likely to disappear entirely.

The people who named SMS were not kidding about the "short" part. Text messages can be, at most, 160 bytes, which allows for 160 characters in a single English message. Different message encodings will decrease the maximum message length. Furthermore, specifying a port number eats up 8 bytes.

Although individual message are small, WMA will actually split apart longer payloads into multiple messages, which will be reassembled at the receiving end. The specification requires implementations to be able to split long payloads into at least three messages. Keep in mind that many users must pay a small fee for each message, so even if it seems like you're sending one payload, your user might have to pay for more than one message.

Check out Table A-1 in the JSR 205 specification for a list of message lengths under different conditions.

19.3 Sending Binary Messages

The payload of an SMS message can carry binary data. You will need a `Binary-Message` instead of a `TextMessage`, but the basic procedure is the same.

```
public void sendBinary(String address, byte[] data)
    throws IOException, InterruptedException {
  String cs = "sms://" + address + ":50001";
  MessageConnection mc = (MessageConnection)
      Connector.open(cs);
  BinaryMessage bm = (BinaryMessage)
      mc.newMessage(MessageConnection.BINARY_MESSAGE);
```

continued

```
        bm.setPayloadData(data);
        mc.send(bm);
    }
```

Remember, you've only got 152 bytes in a message, although longer payloads will be split into multiple messages.

19.4 Sending Multipart Messages

MMS is the next generation of SMS. It enables larger messages, with multiple addresses, a subject, and different parts. In essence, you can use MMS to send one or more files from one device to another. One powerful application for MMS is sending pictures you have just taken with your phone's camera around the world to your friends. Be aware that getting MMS working between different carriers might be a challenge.

The exact size limit on MMS messages depends on the phone and the wireless carrier. Maximum sizes of 100 kB are typical, but some phones and carriers can go as high as 300 kB or 1 MB.

JSR 205, WMA 2.0, adds support for MMS with the MultipartMessage class, a sibling of TextMessage and BinaryMessage. A MultipartMessage keeps track of multiple addresses, a message subject, and some number of MessageParts, which are essentially files with associated content types.

Before you learn about MessagePart, take a look at the basic structure for sending a MultipartMessage.

```
    public void sendMultipart(String address, String subject,
        MessagePart[] parts)
        throws IOException, InterruptedException {
      String cs = "mms://+" + address +
          ":com.jonathanknudsen.Hermes";
      MessageConnection mc = (MessageConnection)
          Connector.open(cs);
      MultipartMessage mm = (MultipartMessage)
          mc.newMessage(MessageConnection.MULTIPART_MESSAGE);
      mm.setSubject(subject);
      for (int i = 0; i < parts.length; i++)
        mm.addMessagePart(parts[i]);
      mc.send(mm);
    }
```

This should look familiar by now: get a MessageConnection, get a message, populate it, and kick it out the door.

The connection string is a little different for multipart messages. It starts with mms instead of sms, for one thing, and it includes an *application identifier*, which is a lot like the port number for SMS messages, but more reliable. In SMS messages, port numbers are used to map to a specific application. For example, if you send a message on port 50,000, you're expecting the receiving application to be listening on port 50,000. There are lots of port numbers from which to choose, but let's face it: sooner or later some kids in a garage are going to write an application that uses the same port number as yours. No central registry exists that ensures port numbers do not overlap between applications.

Instead of port numbers, MMS messages use an application identifier. Messages are sent and received for a specific application identifier. The convention for application identifiers is an inverted domain name plus an application name. In the earlier example, I used com.jonathanknudsen.Hermes to identify my application. The chances of someone else using the same application identifier accidentally are very slim. This is a good system, but note that the application identifier can be a maximum of 32 characters, which is kind of short.

MMS messages are souped-up compared to SMS messages. You can set a message subject, for one thing. Furthermore, you can add more destination addresses. In the earlier example, the message is going to a single address as specified in the connection string. Use addAddress() in MultipartMessage to supply more addresses. You have to specify both an address type and the address itself. The address type is a string, one of to, cc, or bcc, which have the same meanings as for e-mail.

Each file in a multipart message has a *content type*, a *content ID*, an optional *location*, and an optional encoding scheme. The content type is specified as a MIME type, the same type scheme used by Web servers and in e-mail attachments. The content ID should be unique for each part of a multipart message. The location is usually just a filename, and the encoding scheme is useful if you are including encoded text in a part.

Here's a simple case, which encodes a Unicode string using UTF-8 and creates a MessagePart for a text string:

```
private MessagePart makePart(String text, String id)
    throws SizeExceededException,
          UnsupportedEncodingException {
  String encoding = "UTF-8";
  byte[] encoded = text.getBytes(encoding);
  return new MessagePart(encoded, "text/plain", id,
      null, encoding);
}
```

This method creates a `MessagePart` from a byte array. A more common case is to create a `MessagePart` from an `InputStream`. The other parameters in the constructor are the same. Here is a method that creates a `MessagePart` from a resource file in the MIDlet suite:

```
private MessagePart makePart(String filename,
    String type, String id)
    throws IOException, SizeExceededException {
  InputStream in =
      this.getClass().getResourceAsStream(filename);
  return new MessagePart(in, type, id, filename, null);
}
```

19.5 Receiving Messages

To receive messages, create a `MessageConnection` using a messaging connection string without a destination address. For example, to receive SMS messages on port 50,000, use this connection string:

```
sms://:50000
```

To receive MMS messages for the `com.jonathanknudsen.Hermes` application identifier, use this connection string:

```
mms://:com.jonathanknudsen.Hermes
```

Of course, you won't catch most messages with a live `MessageConnection`. Instead, you will put your MIDlet in the push registry, most likely with a static registration in the MIDlet suite descriptor. If this all sounds like gobbledygook, go back to Chapter 6 and read slower.

Picking up incoming messages is a lot like retrieving incoming datagrams or incoming socket connections. There are two ways to do this, both of which involve an additional thread that listens for incoming messages.

The first method is to create a thread that loops on calling `MessageConnection`'s `receive()` method. This works pretty well, except that your thread is blocked at `receive()` until something comes in.

The second method is to use a `MessageListener`. You supply the listener and register it with the `MessageConnection`. Whenever a message arrives, your listener's `notifyIncomingMessage()` is called. Then you go ahead and call `receive()`, knowing full well that there really is a message waiting.

Unfortunately, it's not quite that simple, because you should not call `receive()` from the same system thread that calls `notifyIncomingMessage()`. Remember, when the system invokes one of your callback methods, you should respect its thread and do your own work in your own threads.

It's possible to set up a `MessageListener` in a rational way using `wait()` and `notify()`, but it's not trivial. The example later in this chapter includes such a listener.

`MessageConnection` gives you a `Message` when you call `receive()`, so you might have to do `instanceof` tests and casts if you're not sure what kind of message you are expecting.

19.6   A Simple Messaging Application

`HermesMIDlet` (see Figure 19.1) demonstrates how to send and receive SMS messages. It sends and receives on port 50,000. If you download the example from the book's Web site, the MIDlet suite descriptor has a static push registry entry, but `HermesMIDlet` also attempts to register itself dynamically if the static registration fails for any reason.

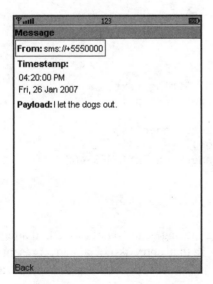

Figure 19.1   Running `HermesMIDlet`

The entire application consists of four classes:

1. HermesMIDlet runs the show. It handles commands and knows how to send messages.

2. HermesMessageReader receives incoming messages in its own thread. It is a MessageListener.

3. HermesForm is the user interface for creating a message.

4. HermesMessageForm is the user interface for displaying an incoming message.

The whole source code is lengthy, so only the interesting parts are here.

Sending a message is straightforward. Two methods in HermesMIDlet get the job done, and that includes the sendText() method you've already seen.

```
public void run() {
  String cs = "sms://" + mHermesForm.getAddress() + ":50000";
  String text = mHermesForm.getMessage();
  try {
    sendText(cs, text);
  }        mDisplay.setCurrent(mHermesForm);
  catch (IOException ioe) {
    showErrorAlert(ioe);
  }
  catch (InterruptedException ie) {
    showErrorAlert(ie);
  }
}

public void sendText(String cs, String text)
    throws IOException, InterruptedException {
  MessageConnection mc =
      (MessageConnection)Connector.open(cs);
  TextMessage tm = (TextMessage)
      mc.newMessage(MessageConnection.TEXT_MESSAGE);
  tm.setPayloadText(text);
  mc.send(tm);
}
```

HermesMessageReader handles incoming messages. Its start() method attempts to place an entry in the PushRegistry if that entry is not already present. In addition, it opens the incoming MessageConnection and registers itself as a listener.

HermesMessageReader maintains two lists, implemented as Vectors. The first is a list of MessageConnections with incoming data. Every time the listener callback method `notifyIncomingMessage()` is called, the connection is added to the list. In addition, the waiting thread in `run()` is awakened.

The second list contains received messages. When the `run()` thread wakes up, it retrieves a message from a waiting `MessageConnection`. The received message is put in the message list. The MIDlet retrieves available messages using the `hasMore()` and `next()` methods.

```java
import java.io.*;
import java.util.*;

import javax.microedition.io.*;

import javax.wireless.messaging.*;

public class HermesMessageReader
    implements MessageListener, Runnable {
  private volatile boolean mTrucking;
  private Vector mConnections;
  private Vector mMessages;
  private HermesMIDlet mMIDlet;

  private MessageConnection mConnection;

  public HermesMessageReader(HermesMIDlet midlet) {
    mConnections = new Vector();
    mMessages = new Vector();
    mMIDlet = midlet;
  }

  public void start() throws IOException {
    mTrucking = true;
    Thread t = new Thread(this);
    t.start();

    // Try push registry registration if static registration
    // did not work.
    String[] registered = PushRegistry.listConnections(false);
    if (registered == null || registered.length == 0) {
      try {
        PushRegistry.registerConnection(
            "sms://:50000", "HermesMIDlet", "*");
      }
      catch (IOException ioe) {
        System.out.println(ioe);
      }
```

continued

```
      catch (ClassNotFoundException cnfe) {
        System.out.println(cnfe);
      }
    }

    // Register as a listener for our connection.
    mConnection =
        (MessageConnection)Connector.open("sms://:50000");
    mConnection.setMessageListener(this);
  }

  public synchronized void stop() {
    mTrucking = false;
    notify();
    try { mConnection.close(); }
    catch (IOException ioe) {
      System.out.println(ioe);
    }
  }

  // MessageListener method.

  public synchronized void notifyIncomingMessage(
      MessageConnection mc) {
    mConnections.addElement(mc);
    notify();
  }

  // Runnable method.

  public synchronized void run() {
    while (mTrucking) {
      try {
        MessageConnection mc = null;
        if (mConnections.size() == 0)
          wait();
        if (mTrucking == false) break;
        mc = (MessageConnection)mConnections.elementAt(0);
        mConnections.removeElementAt(0);
        Message m = mc.receive();
        mMessages.addElement(m);
        mMIDlet.notifyAvailableMessage();
      }
      catch (InterruptedException ie) {
        mTrucking = false;
      }
      catch (IOException ioe) {
        System.out.println("MessageReader.run(): " +
            ioe.toString());
```

```
        }
      }
    }

    // Public API.

    public boolean hasMore() {
      return mMessages.size() > 0;
    }

    public synchronized Message next() {
      Message m = (Message)mMessages.elementAt(0);
      mMessages.removeElementAt(0);
      return m;
    }
  }
```

If you don't have real devices for testing, you can use the Sun Java Wireless Toolkit to simulate a message network. If you launch more than one emulator, you can send messages between emulators. You can also use the WMA Console, available from **File > Utilities**, to send and receive messages.

With my Motorola V3, I was able to send a message to myself, and the message was sent and received by `HermesMIDlet`. However, when I tried to exchange messages between the V3 and my Nokia 6030 (on different wireless networks), the messages were successfully sent but ended up in the recipient's default message box rather than being retrieved by `HermesMIDlet`. The destination port number was lost in transit.

19.7 Summary

WMA gives your application the power to send and receive SMS and MMS messages. Use GCF to obtain a `MessageConnection` that can be used to send and receive messages. SMS messages can include a port number for delivery to a specific application. MMS messages use an application identifier for the same purpose. Use the push registry to invoke specific applications for specific types of incoming messages.

20

Bluetooth and OBEX

BLUETOOTH is short-range wireless technology, good for connecting mobile phones, headsets, keyboards, mice, computers, and other devices together. Many modern mobile phones have Bluetooth hardware, as you have probably noticed by the proliferation of people walking around with those mondo tomorrow Bluetooth headsets tucked in their ears.

JSR 82 defines the Bluetooth API and the OBEX API. The Bluetooth API lives in `javax.bluetooth`, while the OBEX API is in `javax.obex`.

OBEX stands for OBject EXchange. It is a standard for moving data between two endpoints. It is independent of the underlying network transport, so it can run on top of a Bluetooth connection or an infrared data connection.

The Bluetooth and OBEX APIs defined by JSR 82 are entirely independent, but OBEX frequently runs on top of a Bluetooth connection. Nevertheless, there are devices out in the world today that support the JSR 82 Bluetooth API but not the JSR 82 OBEX API. For a list of devices that implement one or both JSR 82 APIs, see here:

```
http://www.javabluetooth.com/jsr82devices.html
```

MSA devices, if they have Bluetooth technology, are required to support both the Bluetooth API and the OBEX API. If the device supports infrared communication or sockets, the OBEX API might be usable over these transports, but it's not required.

Bluetooth is a deep subject all by itself, and the JSR 82 specification does not hide much of its complexity. This chapter teaches you the fundamentals of Bluetooth communication but does not attempt to cover the Bluetooth and OBEX APIs in meticulous detail. For a thorough treatment of JSR 82, consult the specification.

20.1   Control Your Own Bluetoothiness

The device upon which your MIDlet is running is represented by `LocalDevice`. Retrieve an instance like this:

```
LocalDevice bt = LocalDevice.getLocalDevice();
```

Like most methods in the Bluetooth API, this one can throw `BluetoothState-Exception` if something goes wrong. `LocalDevice` has methods for finding the device's name, finding the device's address, determining if the Bluetooth system is turned on, and more.

One useful thing you can do with `LocalDevice` is retrieve a `DiscoveryAgent`, which knows how to find other Bluetooth devices and services.

20.2   Finding Other Bluetooth Devices and Services

Having Bluetooth is great, but it won't do you any good unless you have more than one Bluetooth device.

Discovery is how Bluetooth devices find each other. There are two types of discovery in the Bluetooth API. *Device discovery* lets you find other Bluetooth devices in your immediate vicinity, while *service discovery* is how you find interesting services on specific devices.

Bluetooth devices can control whether or not they are discoverable using `LocalDevice`. If you want other devices to be able to find you, do something like this:

```
LocalDevice bt = LocalDevice.getLocalDevice();
bt.setDiscoverable(DiscoveryAgent.GIAC);
```

There are two kinds of discoverable. `GIAC` means that the device will be discoverable indefinitely, and `LIAC` means the device will be discoverable for some period of time, typically one minute. The exact amount of time is configured outside the scope of the Bluetooth API.

To find other devices, tell the Bluetooth API to start searching and then sit back while the listener object is notified about devices or services.

The listener object is an implementation of DeviceListener. The name is a little misleading, because the listener receives notifications of both device and service discovery.

To kick off device discovery, use the DiscoveryAgent you can get from LocalDevice. Call its startInquiry() method to get the search started.

```
// DiscoveryListener dl = ...
LocalDevice bt = LocalDevice.getLocalDevice();
DiscoveryAgent da = bt.getDiscoveryAgent();
boolean success = da.startInquiry(DiscoveryAgent.GIAC, dl);
```

The DiscoveryListener interface has four methods, two for device discovery and two for service discovery.

Whenever a device is found, the listener's deviceDiscovered() method is called. When the device is done with discovery, inquiryCompleted() is called. Each device found is passed to deviceDiscovered() as a RemoteDevice.

Once you find devices, you can kick off a search for specific services by calling another DiscoveryAgent method, searchServices(). Services are represented by a *universally unique identification number* (UUID). The javax.bluetooth. UUID class encapsulates a UUID. You can create one by specifying a 128-bit hexadecimal number as a string.

```
// DiscoveryListener dl = ...
// RemoteDevice remoteDevice = ...
// UUID uuid = ...
UUID[] uuidSet = { uuid };
LocalDevice bt = LocalDevice.getLocalDevice();
DiscoveryAgent da = bt.getDiscoveryAgent();
da.searchServices(null, uuidSet, remoteDevice, dl);
```

searchServices() looks on the specified device for services that match the supplied list of UUIDs. The first argument to searchServices() is an array of field identifiers if you want to retrieve the values of special fields about the services. In this case, passing null means that just the default field values will be retrieved.

Any matching services are passed to the DiscoveryListener's services-Discovered() method as ServiceRecord objects. When the service search is done, serviceSearchCompleted() is called.

The coolest thing you can do with a `ServiceRecord` is get a connection string that will hook you up with the given service. Call `getConnectionURL()` to retrieve the connection string. You can toss it over to `Connector.open()` to open up a client connection to the service.

In summary, the ultimate result of device and service discovery is `Service-Records`, which provide connection strings for hooking up clients to servers.

20.3 Cheap Shots

Searching for available services is kind of complicated. There are two simplifications of the process that you might consider.

The first is to ask the local device if it remembers talking to any Bluetooth devices in the past. The method to use is `retrieveDevices()` in `Discovery-Agent`. Pass in PREKNOWN or CACHED to retrieve an array of `RemoteDevices`.

The second shortcut is to ask `DiscoveryAgent` to find a service with a given UUID. Call `selectService()` with the UUID, and `DiscoveryAgent` will return a connection string with the very first matching service that it finds. `select-Service()` is a blocking method, which means it won't return until it finds a matching service or gives up. This is different from the behavior of `start-Inquiry()` and `searchServices()`, both of which kick off a search in a different thread and return directly.

20.4 Making a Client Connection

The Bluetooth API supports two types of connections (not counting OBEX, which is covered later). The first type is a packet protocol with the catchy name L2CAP. It is roughly analagous to IP datagrams. A connection string for L2CAP begins with `btl2cap://`, with `bt` standing for Bluetooth.

The second type is RFCOMM, which is a stream-based protocol, roughly analogous to TCP. Connection strings for RFCOMM connections begin with `btspp://`, where `spp` stands for Serial Port Protocol, another name for RFCOMM.

Most of the time, though, you won't create your own connection strings. Instead, you will retrieve a connection string from the `ServiceRecord` of whatever service it is to which you want to connect. Once you've gotten the connection string from `ServiceRecord`'s `getConnectionURL()` method, it's mostly straightforward GCF programming from there.

In the `btspp` case, in particular, everything is gravy once you've got the connection string. You call `Connector.open()`, as usual, and get back a `Stream-Connection`. From there you can get input and output streams and read and write as much as you like. The `BlueChew` example, later in this chapter, shows how to set up `btspp` connections and send and receive data.

The case for `btl2cap` is a little more complicated. `Connector.open()` returns an `L2CAPConnection`, and you use its `send()` and `receive()` methods to send and receive packets of data. You have to make sure you observe the limits on the size of incoming and outgoing packets returned from `getTransmitMTU()` and `getReceiveMTU()`.

20.5 Setting Up a Server

Running a Bluetooth service is accomplished through the GCF. Pass an appropriate connection string to `Connector.open()`. You'll get back an object that can be used to field incoming connections.

For `btl2cap` connections, use a connection string like this (split into two lines for readability):

```
btl2cap://localhost:3B9FA89520078C303355AAA694238F08
                    ;name=L2CAPEx
```

The UUID of the service is a lot like a port number, a very long port number. The `name` parameter is optional.

`Connector.open()` will return an `L2CAPConnectionNotifier`. You can catch incoming connections by calling its `acceptAndOpen()` method, which blocks until a client connects. Then it returns an `L2CAPConnection` that can be used to exchange data with the client.

`btspp` server connections are, again, easier. Here is an example `btspp` server connection:

```
btspp://localhost:3B9FA89520078C303355AAA694238F08
                    ;name=BlueChew
```

For this type of connection string, `Connector.open()` returns a `StreamConnection-Notifier`. Its `acceptAndOpen()` method blocks until a client connects, then returns a `StreamConnection` that can be used to communicate with the client.

In either case (`btl2cap` or `btspp`), the service cannot be discovered by clients until the server is waiting on the `acceptAndOpen()` method.

20.6 Authorization and Encryption

Bluetooth supports several security mechanisms:

- A device can verify the identity of another device, a process called *authentication*.
- Two devices can *encrypt* data that passes between them.
- A device can ask the user for *authorization* to perform an action.

These mechanisms are outside the scope of the Bluetooth API, but you can request one or more of these options for connections. In general, you do so by adding options to the connection string. For example, to create a server that wants encrypted connections, you could use this connection string:

```
btspp://localhost:3B9FA89520078C303355AAA694238F08
               ;name=BlueChew;encrypted=true
```

On the client side, you could create a connection string from a `ServiceRecord` and request authentication and encryption like this:

```
// ServiceRecord sr = ...
String cs = sr.getConnectionURL(
    ServiceRecord.AUTHENTICATE_ENCRYPT, false);
```

20.7 What about OBEX?

OBEX can be layered on Bluetooth, sockets, or an infrared connection. It is a client/server protocol for moving files between devices.

The client side of an OBEX conversation is represented by `ClientSession`. The exact form of the connection string depends on the transport under OBEX. For OBEX over infrared, do something like this:

```
String cs = "irdaobex://discover";
```

You can add *hint bits*, which are described in specifications listed in the References section of the JSR 82 specification. For an example of the use of hint bits, consult the Sun Java Wireless Toolkit's `ObexDemo` application, in the `ObexImage-Sender` class.

For OBEX over sockets, just specify the server address and port number. If you leave off the port number, the default is 650.

```
String cs = "tcpobex://kickbutt.jonathanknudsen.com";
```

Finally, OBEX can run over a Bluetooth RFCOMM connection. In this case, things work as usual: clients discover available services and use the connection strings from the service records to make a connection. The connection string starts with `btgoep`, which stands for Bluetooth Generic Object Exchange Protocol.

Regardless of the underlying transport and connection string, an OBEX connection is represented by a `ClientSession`:

```
ClientSession session = (ClientSession)Connector.open(cs);
```

Clients connect to servers and send a sequence of commands. `ClientSession` has methods that correspond to the available OBEX commands: `connect()`, `put()`, `get()`, `setPath()`, `delete()`, and `disconnect()`.

A client command is answered with a server response. In this respect, OBEX resembles HTTP. Command requests and server responses are composed of headers, represented in the OBEX API as `HeaderSet`.

Most methods in `ClientSession` take a `HeaderSet` argument representing the command and return a `HeaderSet` representing the server response. However, `get()` and `put()` are slightly more complicated. Each returns an `Operation` that can be used to work with streams for sending and receiving data. `Operation` is a subinterface of `ContentConnection`, which means you can retrieve input and output streams from it.

On the server side, connection strings also depend on the underlying transport. For infrared, do something like this:

```
String cs = "irdaobex://localhost";
```

Again, hint bits can be used. See `ObexDemo`'s `ObexImageReceiver` class for an example.

For OBEX over sockets, just leave off the address. Add a port if you don't want the default of 650.

```
String cs = "tcpobex://":
```

For OBEX over Bluetooth RFCOMM, use `localhost` and the UUID of the service you are providing, just as you would do with a regular RFCOMM server.

```
String cs = "btgoep://localhost:
                12AF51A9030C4B2937407F8C9ECB238A";
```

Whichever connection string you use, `Connector.open()` will return a `Session-Notifier`.

```
SessionNotifier session =
    (SessionNotifier)Connector.open(cs);
```

Now you sit in a loop and call `acceptAndOpen()`, which blocks until a client makes a connection. However, the `acceptAndOpen()` method in the OBEX API takes a `ServerRequestHandler` argument that does all the work. In fact, even though `acceptAndOpen()` returns a `Connection`, you won't do anything with it.

The methods in the `ServerRequestHandler` get called whenever the client tries to send a command. For example, `ServerRequestHandler`'s `onConnect()` method is called when a client calls `connect()` on its `ClientSession`.

Except for `onGet()` and `onPut()`, the other on- methods in `ServerRequest-Handler` take two `HeaderSet` arguments, one for the client request and one for the server response. Those of you who have done any server-side programming will immediately recognize the parallel to servlets.

`onGet()` and `onPut()` are a little different. Each receives an `Operation` argument that can be used to directly manipulate the streams between client and server.

20.8   Don't Forget the Push Registry

To make your applications useful even when they are not running, put an entry in the push registry. This works just as you'd expect. You map the server connection string to your MIDlet class name in the push registry. The device takes care of making sure that the corresponding Bluetooth service is discoverable. When clients attempt to connect, your MIDlet is launched to handle the connection.

20.9   Permissions for Bluetooth and OBEX

Incoming and outgoing network connections are sensitive operations with regard to security. The following permissions apply to Bluetooth and OBEX connections:

```
javax.microedition.io.Connector.bluetooth.client
javax.microedition.io.Connector.bluetooth.server

javax.microedition.io.Connector.obex.client
javax.microedition.io.Connector.obex.client.tcp
javax.microedition.io.Connector.obex.server
javax.microedition.io.Connector.obex.server.tcp
```

20.10 The BlueChew Application

The BlueChew application demonstrates how to make devices communicate over Bluetooth. It includes a server, a discovery object, and a client. Devices running BlueChew can find and send short text messages to other devices running BlueChew. The whole application is too long to show here, but you can get the full source code from the book's Web site:

> http://kickbutt.jonathanknudsen.com/download.html

To use BlueChew, run the emulator more than once. Each instance of the emulator will find the other emulators and show them in the list of destinations, as shown in Figure 20.1.

Here, two other running emulators were found. They are listed by their friendly name (which is Wireless Toolkit in both cases) and their Bluetooth addresses. Normally, you probably shouldn't show Bluetooth addresses to a user, but I included them because the friendly names of all the emulator instances are the same.

You can check off all the devices to which you want to send a message. Edit the message itself and choose **Send**. BlueChew uses the connection strings of the corresponding ServiceRecords to make client connections and send the message.

Figure 20.1   Other devices found via Bluetooth discovery

Figure 20.2   A message is received.

On the receiving end, BlueChew accepts incoming connections, reads the message, and shows it on the screen, as in Figure 20.2.

The application is divided into three main classes.

BlueChewMIDlet provides a user interface and coordinates the other objects. It also handles (in the run() method) sending the message to any checked destinations.

```
import java.io.*;
import java.util.*;

import javax.microedition.io.*;
import javax.microedition.lcdui.*;
import javax.microedition.midlet.MIDlet;

import javax.bluetooth.*;

public class BlueChewMIDlet
    extends MIDlet
    implements CommandListener, Runnable {
  private BlueChewServer mBlueChewServer;
  private BlueChewFinder mBlueChewFinder;

  private Form mSendForm;
  private TextField mMessageField;
```

```
private ChoiceGroup mDestinations;
private Command mSendCommand, mBackCommand, mExitCommand;

public void startApp() {
  createUI();
  setupConnections();
  Display.getDisplay(this).setCurrent(mSendForm);
}

private void createUI() {
  if (mSendForm != null) return;

  mSendCommand = new Command("Send", Command.SCREEN, 0);
  mBackCommand = new Command("Back", Command.BACK, 0);
  mExitCommand = new Command("Exit", Command.EXIT, 0);

  mSendForm = new Form("BlueChewMIDlet");
  mMessageField = new TextField("Message:", "Hello, nurse!",
      512, TextField.ANY);
  mDestinations = new ChoiceGroup("Destinations",
      ChoiceGroup.MULTIPLE);
  mSendForm.append(mMessageField);
  mSendForm.append(mDestinations);
  mSendForm.addCommand(mSendCommand);
  mSendForm.addCommand(mExitCommand);
  mSendForm.setCommandListener(this);
}

private void setupConnections() {
  mBlueChewServer = new BlueChewServer(this);
  mBlueChewServer.start();

  mBlueChewFinder = new BlueChewFinder(this);
  mBlueChewFinder.start();
}

public void pauseApp() {}

public void destroyApp(boolean unconditional) {
  mBlueChewServer.stop();
  mBlueChewFinder.stop();
}

public void commandAction(Command c, Displayable s) {
  if (c.getCommandType() == Command.EXIT) {
    destroyApp(true);
    notifyDestroyed();
  }
```

continued

```
      else if (c == mSendCommand) {
        Form waitForm = new Form("Sending...");
        Display.getDisplay(this).setCurrent(waitForm);
        Thread t = new Thread(this);
        t.start();
      }
      else if (c == mBackCommand) {
        Display.getDisplay(this).setCurrent(mSendForm);
      }
  }

  // Runnable method

  public void run() {
    Vector urls = new Vector();

    // Synchronize so reconcile() won't run
    // at the same time.
    synchronized(mBlueChewFinder) {
      int n = mDestinations.size();
      boolean[] flags = new boolean[n];
      mDestinations.getSelectedFlags(flags);
      for (int i = 0; i < n; i++) {
        if (flags[i] == true) {
          String url = mBlueChewFinder.getURL(i);
          urls.addElement(url);
        }
      }
    }

    for (int i = 0; i < urls.size(); i++) {
      String url = (String)urls.elementAt(i);
      try { runURL(url); }
      catch (IOException ioe) {
        Log.log("BlueChewMIDlet.run(): " + ioe);
      }
    }
    Display.getDisplay(this).setCurrent(mSendForm);
  }

  private void runURL(String url) throws IOException {
    StreamConnection sc = null;
    DataOutputStream dataOut = null;

    try {
      sc = (StreamConnection)
          Connector.open(url);
      dataOut = new DataOutputStream(
          sc.openOutputStream());
```

```
        LocalDevice bt = LocalDevice.getLocalDevice();
        String from = bt.getFriendlyName() + ":" +
            bt.getBluetoothAddress();
        dataOut.writeUTF(from);
        dataOut.writeUTF(mMessageField.getString());
      }
      finally {
        try { if (dataOut != null) dataOut.close(); }
        catch (IOException ioe) {}
        try { if (sc != null) sc.close(); }
        catch (IOException ioe) {}
      }
    }

    // BlueChewServer callback

    public void messageReceived(String from, String message) {
      int layout = Item.LAYOUT_NEWLINE_AFTER;
      StringItem si;
      Form messageForm = new Form("Message");
      si = new StringItem("From:", from);
      si.setLayout(layout);
      messageForm.append(si);
      si = new StringItem("Message:", message);
      si.setLayout(layout);
      messageForm.append(si);
      messageForm.addCommand(mBackCommand);
      messageForm.setCommandListener(this);
      Display.getDisplay(this).setCurrent(messageForm);
    }

    // BlueChewFinder callbacks

    public void serviceAdded(BlueChewService bcs) {
      String s = bcs.getName() + ":" + bcs.getAddress();
      mDestinations.append(s, null);
    }

    public void serviceRemoved(BlueChewService bcs, int i) {
      mDestinations.delete(i);
    }
  }
```

BlueChewFinder encapsulates discovery. It implements the DiscoveryListener interfaces. The device discovery is kicked off in start(). For each device found, service discovery is initiated. BlueChewFinder keeps two Vector lists of service records. Each time a device and service discovery cycle completes, the reconcile() method updates the main list on the basis of the latest findings.

During this process, `reconcile()` calls methods in `BlueChewMIDlet` to notify it to add or remove items from the list of destinations.

```java
import java.io.IOException;
import java.util.Vector;

import javax.bluetooth.*;

public class BlueChewFinder implements DiscoveryListener {
  private BlueChewMIDlet mBlueChewMIDlet;

  private Vector mNewServices;
  private Vector mServices;

  private boolean mSearching;
  private int mPendingServiceSearches;

  private boolean mTrucking;

  public BlueChewFinder(BlueChewMIDlet midlet) {
    mBlueChewMIDlet = midlet;
    mNewServices = new Vector();
    mServices = new Vector();
    mSearching = false;
    mPendingServiceSearches = 0;
    mTrucking = true;
  }

  public void start() {
    // Start looking for other devices.
    try {
      LocalDevice bt = LocalDevice.getLocalDevice();
      DiscoveryAgent da = bt.getDiscoveryAgent();
      boolean success = da.startInquiry(DiscoveryAgent.GIAC,
          this);
      mSearching = true;
    }
    catch (BluetoothStateException bse) {
      Log.log("start() threw " + bse);
    }
  }

  public void stop() {
    // Shut down any running inquiries.
    try {
      mTrucking = false;
      LocalDevice bt = LocalDevice.getLocalDevice();
```

```
        DiscoveryAgent da = bt.getDiscoveryAgent();
        da.cancelInquiry(this);
      }
      catch (BluetoothStateException bse) {
        Log.log("stop() threw " + bse);
      }
    }

    public String getURL(int i) {
      BlueChewService bcs = (BlueChewService)
          mServices.elementAt(i);
      String url = bcs.getURL();
      return url;
    }

    // DiscoveryListener methods

    public void deviceDiscovered(RemoteDevice remoteDevice,
        DeviceClass cod) {
      try {
        // Kick off a service search for that device.
        LocalDevice bt = LocalDevice.getLocalDevice();
        DiscoveryAgent da = bt.getDiscoveryAgent();

        UUID[] uuidSet = { BlueChewService.BLUECHEW_UUID };

        mPendingServiceSearches++;
        da.searchServices(
            null,
            uuidSet,
            remoteDevice,
            this);
      }
      catch (IOException ioe) {
        Log.log("deviceDiscovered(): " + ioe);
      }
      catch (Throwable t) {
        Log.log("deviceDiscovered(): " + t);
      }
    }

    public void inquiryCompleted(int discType) {
      mSearching = false;
    }

    public void servicesDiscovered(int transID,
        ServiceRecord[] servRecord) {
```

continued

```java
    for (int i = 0; i < servRecord.length; i++) {
      try {
        RemoteDevice bt = servRecord[i].getHostDevice();
        String name = bt.getFriendlyName(false);
        String address = bt.getBluetoothAddress();
        String url = servRecord[i].getConnectionURL(
            ServiceRecord.NOAUTHENTICATE_NOENCRYPT, false);
        BlueChewService bcs = new BlueChewService(
            name, address, url);
        mNewServices.addElement(bcs);
      }
      catch (BluetoothStateException bse) {
        Log.log("servicesDiscovered(): " + bse);
      }
      catch (IOException ioe) {
        Log.log("servicesDiscovered(): " + ioe);
      }
    }
  }

  public void serviceSearchCompleted(int transID,
      int respCode) {
    mPendingServiceSearches--;

    if (mSearching == false && mPendingServiceSearches == 0) {
      reconcile();

      try { Thread.sleep(1000); }
      catch (InterruptedException ie) {}

      if (mTrucking == true)
        start();
    }
  }

  // BlueChewFinder methods

  public synchronized void reconcile() {
    // Remove items from mServices that are not in mNewServices.
    for (int i = 0; i < mServices.size(); i++) {
      BlueChewService bcs =
          (BlueChewService)mServices.elementAt(i);
      if (contains(mNewServices, bcs) == false) {
        mServices.removeElement(bcs);
        mBlueChewMIDlet.serviceRemoved(bcs, i);
      }
    }
```

```
    // Add items from mNewServices to mServices.
    for (int i = 0; i < mNewServices.size(); i++) {
      BlueChewService bcs =
          (BlueChewService)mNewServices.elementAt(i);
      if (contains(mServices, bcs) == false) {
        mServices.addElement(bcs);
        mBlueChewMIDlet.serviceAdded(bcs);
      }
    }

    mNewServices.removeAllElements();
  }

  // Compares for equality, not the same actual object.
  private boolean contains(Vector v, Object o) {
    boolean contained = false;

    for (int i = 0; i < v.size(); i++) {
      Object oc = v.elementAt(i);
      if (oc.equals(o))
        contained = true;
    }
    return contained;
  }
}
```

BlueChewServer is the service itself. Its run() method obtains the Stream-
ConnectionNotifier and loops around on acceptAndOpen(). Client connections are handled immediately.

```
import java.io.*;

import javax.microedition.io.*;

import javax.bluetooth.*;

public class BlueChewServer implements Runnable {
  private BlueChewMIDlet mBlueChewMIDlet;

  private boolean mTrucking;
  private StreamConnectionNotifier mNotifier;

  public BlueChewServer(BlueChewMIDlet midlet) {
    mBlueChewMIDlet = midlet;
  }
```

continued

```java
public void start() {
  mTrucking = true;
  Thread t = new Thread(this);
  t.start();
}

public void stop() {
  mTrucking = false;
  try { if (mNotifier != null) mNotifier.close(); }
  catch (IOException ioe) {}
}

public void run() {
  // Make sure we're discoverable.
  try {
    LocalDevice bt = LocalDevice.getLocalDevice();
    bt.setDiscoverable(DiscoveryAgent.GIAC);
  }
  catch (BluetoothStateException bse) {
    Log.log("BlueChewServer.run(): " + bse);
  }

  // Start up the server.
  try {
    UUID uuid = BlueChewService.BLUECHEW_UUID;

    String cs = "btspp://localhost:" + uuid.toString()
        + ";name=BlueChew";

    mNotifier =
        (StreamConnectionNotifier)Connector.open(cs);

    while (mTrucking) {
      // Get the next incoming connection.
      StreamConnection sc = mNotifier.acceptAndOpen();

      // Service inline. We could spawn off a thread for
      // each but it seems unnecessary for this type of
      // application.
      DataInputStream dataIn = new DataInputStream(
          sc.openInputStream());
      String from = dataIn.readUTF();
      String message = dataIn.readUTF();
      mBlueChewMIDlet.messageReceived(from, message);
      dataIn.close();
      sc.close();
    }
  }
```

```
      catch (BluetoothStateException bse) {
        Log.log("BlueChewServer.run(): " + bse);
      }
      catch (IOException ioe) {
        if (mTrucking == true)
          Log.log("BlueChewServer.run(): " + ioe);
      }
    }
  }
}
```

Two small utility classes round out BlueChew. Neither is presented here, but you can download and examine the source code if you wish. First, BlueChewService is a compact representation of a ServiceRecord. It holds a name, an address, and a connection string.

The last class, Log, keeps track of a list of messages. It is useful for debugging. It includes a method that returns a Form with all the messages. The Form is good for showing debugging messages on a real device, where there is no console to examine.

If you want to explore further, there are plenty of possible improvements you could make to this application. Here are a few.

- BlueChewFinder keeps a list of devices that are *currently* discoverable. Most devices are discoverable only for a short period of time but are still available for communication even when they are no longer discoverable. A more realistic implementation would keep previously discovered service records in the list and continue to display them in BlueChewMIDlet. If BlueChewMIDlet attempted a connection and was unsuccessful, the service record could be removed from the list on the assumption that the corresponding device is no longer available.

- BlueChewFinder could also use cached and preknown devices in its discovery search. See retrieveDevices() in DiscoveryAgent for details.

- Incoming messages are shown immediately. If a new message arrives while the user is still reading a previous message, the new message is shown and the previous message is lost forever. A more graceful way to handle this would be to keep a list of incoming messages and show them one by one, with each one dismissed by an explicit action from the user.

20.11 Summary

Bluetooth is wireless communication technology for short distances. The Bluetooth API allows your application to discover other Bluetooth devices and communicate with them. Methods in `DiscoveryAgent` start searches for devices and searches for services on specific devices. You supply a `DiscoveryListener` that is notified when devices and services are found. A `ServiceRecord` represents a service and can supply a connection string for hooking up a client and server. Standard GCF and stream programming are used for `btspp` connections. Servers are identified by a UUID, which is part of the server and client connection strings.

The OBEX API provides access to the OBEX protocol, which can run on top of Bluetooth, infrared, or socket connections. OBEX uses a client/server model that is similar to HTTP servlets. It is useful for exchanging files between devices.

21

XML and
Web Services

ONCE upon a time, not so long ago, *Web services* were going to be the next big thing. Web services referred to specific methods of making Web server functionality available to other applications, and everyone fully expected an interoperable nirvana of communicating systems. The air was pungent with the smell of unwieldy acronyms like WS-I, XML-RPC, WSDL, and UDDI, and everyone had to make sure that their products and technologies were going to work with the coming wave of Web services. Collectively, this approach is known as WS-*, and it is more about a distributed computing scheme (think CORBA or DCOM) than anything specific to the World Wide Web.

Web services did turn out to be one of the next big things. As usual, things didn't turn out quite how everyone planned. While the cool kids like Google and Flickr are exposing their functionality to developers, and Web 2.0 seems well underway, the emphasis has faded from WS-*. A different, lighter approach called Representational State Transfer (REST) is a popular way to make Web services available to client applications.

The Extensible Markup Language (XML) is here to stay, regardless of the fate of its various Web services' cousins.

Java ME got caught up in the WS-* hype, and the result was JSR 172, which defines an XML parsing (JAXP) API and a JAX-RPC API for consuming WS-* services. The XML parsing API will probably be useful well into the future, but the JAX-RPC API will most likely appeal only to developers who must connect a MIDlet to some existing SOAP service. Developers of entirely new systems should strongly consider a RESTful approach.

This chapter describes how to use the XML parsing API, how to call WS-* Web services using the JAX-RPC API, and how to work with RESTful Web services. Examples will show how to parse a Rich Site Summary (RSS) feed, how to invoke a WS-* Web service, and how to write a RESTful client for the Flickr photo-sharing service.

21.1 Parsing XML

Regardless of the future of Web services, XML is an important part of the computing world. JSR 172's JAXP API is useful in a wide variety of applications.

Several different flavors of XML parsers are available in the desktop world. The JAXP API conforms to the Simple API for XML (SAX) standard, defined here:

> http://www.saxproject.org/

The SAX parts of the API live in `org.xml.sax`, while the rest of the JAXP API is in `javax.xml.parsers`.

A SAX parser is a *push* parser, which means it runs through an entire document, spitting out events as it goes. In your application, you supply a *handler* (a listener) that gets notified whenever the parser finds something in the document.

The parser itself is `jaxp.xml.parsers.SAXParser`. You can get one from a SAX-ParserFactory, like this:

```
SAXParserFactory spf = SAXParserFactory.newInstance();
SAXParser parser = spf.newSAXParser();
```

You can use methods in `SAXParserFactory` to change the options on the parser returned by `newSAXParser()`. For example, you can specify whether or not you want a validating parser.

21.2 Creating a Handler

Once you've got a parser, you need to supply a handler and give it a document. Your handler should be a subclass of `DefaultHandler` (in `org.xml.sax. helpers`), and the document to be parsed is represented by an `InputStream` or an `InputSource`.

```
// InputStream in = ...
// DefaultHandler dh = ...
parser.parse(in, dh);
```

Your DefaultHandler subclass is where most of the action happens. Default-Handler has empty methods that get called by the parser. To do something interesting, override some or all of these methods in your handler subclass.

Here is a class, CheapHandler, which overrides three of DefaultHandler's methods. It uses the startElement() and endElement() methods to keep track of the current element hierarchy. In addition, it overrides characters() to find out when character data is parsed.

```java
import java.util.Hashtable;

import org.xml.sax.*;
import org.xml.sax.helpers.DefaultHandler;

/**
 * CheapHandler keeps the current hierarchy of tags
 * in a variable, mTree, with nested tags separated
 * by pipe characters. To use this class, create a
 * subclass and override the processCharacters() or
 * processStart() methods.
 */
public abstract class CheapHandler
    extends DefaultHandler {
  // Override these methods in child classes.
  public void processCharacters(String tree, String s) {}
  public void processStart(String tree, Hashtable a) {}

  // Implementation

  private String mTree;

  public void characters(char[] ch, int start, int length) {
    if (length <= 0) return;
    if (mTree == null ||
        mTree.length() == 0)
      return;

    String s = new String(ch, start, length);
    processCharacters(mTree, s);
  }
```

continued

```
    public void startElement(String uri, String localName,
        String qName, Attributes attributes) {
      if (mTree == null) mTree = "";
      if (mTree.length() > 0) mTree += "|";
      mTree += qName;
      Hashtable a = new Hashtable();
      for (int i = 0; i < attributes.getLength(); i++) {
        String qname = attributes.getQName(i);
        String value = attributes.getValue(i);
        a.put(qname, value);
      }

      processStart(mTree, a);
    }

    public void endElement(String uri, String localName,
        String qName) {
      if (mTree == null) return;
      if (mTree.length() == 0) return;

      int pipe = mTree.lastIndexOf('|');
      if (pipe == -1) {
        mTree = "";
        return;
      }

      mTree = mTree.substring(0, pipe);
    }
  }
```

CheapHandler is a simplified handler for XML parsing. I use it in the rest of the examples in this chapter. You can create a simple subclass of CheapHandler and override the processCharacters() method or processStart() method. Each method is passed a tree argument, which represents the parser's current position in the document hierarchy. Nested tags are separated by a pipe character.

21.3 Parsing RSS

RSS is a simple XML format used for summaries of blogs, news Web sites, and other content. RSS files are placed in known locations at a Web site and updated to reflect updates to the main content of the Web site. RSS files are often called *feeds*.

This section presents a MIDlet that retrieves an RSS feed that contains the top ten songs sold in the iTunes music store. You could easily modify this MIDlet to retrieve other types of RSS feeds.

```java
import java.io.*;

import javax.microedition.io.*;
import javax.microedition.lcdui.*;
import javax.microedition.midlet.MIDlet;

import javax.xml.parsers.*;
import org.xml.sax.*;
import org.xml.sax.helpers.*;

public class TopTenMIDlet
    extends MIDlet
    implements CommandListener, Runnable {
  private String mURL =
      "http://ax.phobos.apple.com.edgesuite.net/WebObjects/" +
      "MZStore.woa/wpa/MRSS/topsongs/limit=10/rss.xml";
  private Form mForm;
  private Command mExitCommand;

  public void startApp() {
    if (mForm == null) {
      // Use an application property if it is available.
      String url = getAppProperty("topten-url");
      if (url != null && !url.equals("")) mURL = url;
      // Create the main form with a busy indicator gauge.
      mForm = new Form("iTunes Top Ten Songs");
      Gauge gauge = new Gauge("Loading...", false,
          Gauge.INDEFINITE, Gauge.CONTINUOUS_RUNNING);
      mForm.append(gauge);
      mExitCommand = new Command("Exit", Command.EXIT, 0);
      mForm.addCommand(mExitCommand);
      mForm.setCommandListener(this);
      // Kick off image loading in a separate thread.
      Thread t = new Thread(this);
      t.start();
    }

    Display.getDisplay(this).setCurrent(mForm);
  }

  public void pauseApp() {}
```

continued

```
    public void destroyApp(boolean unconditional) {}

    public void commandAction(Command c, Displayable s) {
      if (c.getCommandType() == Command.EXIT) {
        destroyApp(true);
        notifyDestroyed();
      }
    }

    public void run() {
      try {
        runImpl(mURL);
      }
      catch (IOException ioe) {
        mForm.append(ioe.toString());
      }
      catch (ParserConfigurationException pce) {
        mForm.append(pce.toString());
      }
      catch (SAXException se) {
        mForm.append(se.toString());
      }

      // Remove the gauge.
      for (int i = 0; i < mForm.size(); i++) {
        Item item = mForm.get(i);
        if (item instanceof Gauge)
          mForm.delete(i--);
      }
    }

    // Make the connection, get an InputStream.

    private void runImpl(String url)
        throws IOException,
            ParserConfigurationException, SAXException {
      HttpConnection hc =
          (HttpConnection)Connector.open(mURL);
      try {
        InputStream in = hc.openInputStream();
        try {
          parse(in);
        }
        finally { in.close(); }
      }
      finally { hc.close(); }
    }
```

```
        private void parse(InputStream in)
            throws IOException,
                ParserConfigurationException, SAXException {
          TopTenHandler tth = new TopTenHandler(mForm);
          SAXParserFactory spf = SAXParserFactory.newInstance();
          SAXParser parser = spf.newSAXParser();
          parser.parse(in, tth);
        }
      }

      class TopTenHandler extends CheapHandler {
        private Form mForm;

        public TopTenHandler(Form f) { mForm = f; }

        public void processCharacters(String tree, String s) {
          if (tree.equals("rss|channel|item|title")) {
            StringItem si = new StringItem(null, s);
            si.setLayout(Item.LAYOUT_2 | Item.LAYOUT_NEWLINE_AFTER);
            mForm.append(si);
          }
        }
      }
```

You can see the network connection and XML parsing happens in `run()`, performed in a separate thread.

The SAX handler is `TopTenHandler`, a simple subclass of `CheapHandler`. Whenever characters are encountered that are part of a `title` element, they are appended to the main form.

One of the nice features of `TopTenMIDlet` is that information is placed on the screen as soon as it is parsed (see Figure 21.1). This capability is especially important on wireless devices that are likely to have relatively slow network connections.

21.4 Parsing XML without JSR 172

Not many current devices have support for either of the JSR 172 APIs. However, if you just want to parse XML in a MIDlet, you can embed a small parser in your application. kXML 2 is an excellent choice:

http://kxml.sourceforge.net/

For a dated look at the world of XML parsers in Java ME, try this article:

http://developers.sun.com/techtopics/mobility/midp/articles/ parsingxml/

Figure 21.1   Information is displayed as it is parsed

The size of the XML parser adds directly to your MIDlet suite JAR file size, but if that's not a problem, you can fairly easily incorporate XML parsing in your application without requiring JSR 172 support on your target devices.

The kXML 2 JAR file is only 43 KB, and if you use an obfuscator, the impact on your MIDlet suite JAR can be much smaller.

The example code for this chapter includes a rewritten `TopTenMIDlet` that uses kXML. You can run this version of the application on any MIDP 2.0 device without worrying about JSR 172 support. Look in the `kb-ch21-kxml` project for the rewritten `TopTenMIDlet` and a rewritten `CheapHandler` helper class. The obfuscated JAR file size for this project, including another MIDlet from later in this chapter, is just 16 KB!

Using the kXML parser, `org.kxml2.io.KXmlParser`, is fabulously easy. Create one and point it at a `Reader` using the `setInput()` method:

```
// InputStream in = ...
Reader reader = new InputStreamReader(in);
KXmlParser parser = new KXmlParser();
parser.setInput(reader);
```

Then sit in a loop and call the parser's `next()` method, which parses the next thing in the document. Call methods on the parser to find out what was just read. Here is an example that parses through the document until it reaches the end:

```
boolean trucking = true;
while (trucking) {
  parser.next();
  // Process the read data.
  if (parser.getEventType() == KXmlParser.END_DOCUMENT)
    trucking = false;
}
```

For example, if the event type is KXmlParser.START_TAG, you can find out the name of the tag with getName(). If the event type is KXmlParser.TEXT, you can retrieve the text with getText().

21.5 Using WS-* Web Services

WS-* Web services are a kind of distributed computing. To use a WS-* Web service, you have to generate stub classes (during development) that represent the Web service. At runtime, you call methods on the stub class to invoke methods on the Web service. In the Java platform, this is very similar to Remote Method Invocation (RMI).

WS-* Web services are described by a Web Service Description Language (WSDL) file. To use a Web service in your application, you first must generate stub classes based on the WSDL description. Your development tool should be able to do this for you. In the Sun Java Wireless Toolkit, choose **File > Utilities...**, then launch the **Stub Generator** utility.

In NetBeans Mobility Pack, right-click on your project and choose **Properties**. Select **Platform** in the left pane, then click on **Manage Emulators...** on the right side. Click on the **Tools & Extensions** tab, then click **Open Utilities**. Finally, launch the **Stub Generator**.

You have to specify the location of the WSDL file, the destination for the generated stub classes, and to which package you would like the stubs to belong.

Once you have stubs, using them is pretty easy. Suppose you want to use a Web service that returns speeches from Shakespeare's plays:

http://www.xmlme.com/WSShakespeare.asmx

First, generate the service stubs. Here is how to invoke the service:

```
String fragment = "slings and arrows";
ShakespeareSoap service = new ShakespeareSoap_Stub();
try {
```

continued

```
        String speech = service.getSpeech(fragment);
    }
    catch (RemoteException re) {
      // Handle the exception
    }
```

First, create a `ShakespeareSoap` object that represents the Web service. Then you can call methods, like `getSpeech()`. Methods called on remote objects can throw `RemoteException` if something goes wrong with the network communication.

Following is the complete MIDlet example, `BillMIDlet`. It assumes that the Shakespeare Web service stubs are generated in the `bill` package. The code example downloads for this chapter include the stub package and classes.

The Shakespeare Web service returns results as very simple XML documents, so `BillMIDlet` uses the JAXP API to parse the results and present them on the screen. `BillHandler` is a simple `CheapHandler` subclass that takes care of the details. (See Figure 21.2 on page 307.)

```
import java.io.*;

import javax.microedition.io.*;
import javax.microedition.lcdui.*;
import javax.microedition.midlet.MIDlet;

import java.rmi.*;
import javax.xml.parsers.*;
import org.xml.sax.*;
import org.xml.sax.helpers.*;

import bill.*;

public class BillMIDlet
    extends MIDlet
    implements CommandListener, Runnable {
  private Form mForm;
  private TextField mQuoteField;
  private Command mGoCommand, mExitCommand;

  public void startApp() {
    if (mForm == null) {
      // Create the main form with a busy indicator gauge.
      mForm = new Form("Shakespeare's Speeches");
      mQuoteField = new TextField("Speech fragment",
          "slings and arrows", 512, TextField.ANY);
      mGoCommand = new Command("Go", Command.SCREEN, 0);
      mExitCommand = new Command("Exit", Command.EXIT, 0);
```

```
      mForm.append(mQuoteField);
      mForm.addCommand(mGoCommand);
      mForm.addCommand(mExitCommand);
      mForm.setCommandListener(this);
  }

  Display.getDisplay(this).setCurrent(mForm);
}

public void pauseApp() {}

public void destroyApp(boolean unconditional) {}

public void commandAction(Command c, Displayable s) {
  if (c.getCommandType() == Command.EXIT) {
    destroyApp(true);
    notifyDestroyed();
  }
  else if (c == mGoCommand) {
    Gauge gauge = new Gauge("Loading...", false,
        Gauge.INDEFINITE, Gauge.CONTINUOUS_RUNNING);
    mForm.append(gauge);

    // Remove previous results.
    for (int i = 0; i < mForm.size(); i++) {
      Item item = mForm.get(i);
      if (item instanceof StringItem)
        mForm.delete(i--);
    }

    Thread t = new Thread(this);
    t.start();
  }
}

public void run() {
  ShakespeareSoap service = new ShakespeareSoap_Stub();
  try {
    String fragment = mQuoteField.getString();
    String speech = service.getSpeech(fragment);
    parse(speech);
  }
  catch (RemoteException re) {
    mForm.append(re.toString());
  }
  catch (IOException ioe) {
    mForm.append(ioe.toString());
  }
```

continued

```
        catch (ParserConfigurationException pce) {
          mForm.append(pce.toString());
        }
        catch (SAXException se) {
          mForm.append(se.toString());
        }

        // Remove the gauge.
        for (int i = 0; i < mForm.size(); i++) {
          Item item = mForm.get(i);
          if (item instanceof Gauge)
            mForm.delete(i--);
        }
      }

    private void parse(String speech) throws IOException,
        ParserConfigurationException, SAXException {
      byte[] raw = speech.getBytes("UTF-8");
      ByteArrayInputStream in = new ByteArrayInputStream(raw);

      BillHandler wh = new BillHandler(mForm);
      SAXParserFactory spf = SAXParserFactory.newInstance();
      SAXParser parser = spf.newSAXParser();
      parser.parse(in, wh);
    }
  }

  class BillHandler extends CheapHandler {
    private Form mForm;

    public BillHandler(Form f) { mForm = f; }

    public void processCharacters(String tree, String s) {
      String title = null;

      if (tree.equals("MESSAGE")) title = "Message:";
      else if (tree.equals("SPEECH")) title = null;
      else if (tree.equals("SPEECH|SPEAKER")) title = "Speaker:";
      else if (tree.equals("SPEECH|PLAY")) title = "Play:";

      StringItem si = new StringItem(title, s);
      si.setLayout(Item.LAYOUT_NEWLINE_AFTER);
      mForm.append(si);
    }
  }
```

To run BillMIDlet, enter a few words from a speech and choose the **Go** command.

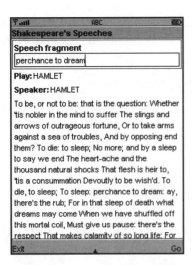

Figure 21.2   Web services and William Shakespeare

21.6 Harness the World

The Web services programming model that is spanking traditional WS-* Web services is Representational State Transfer, or REST. REST is an awful name, and it's hard to understand exactly what it means. Like the Pirate Code, it is more of a set of guidelines than a specification or definition.

The main principles of REST are as follows:

- **Simple URLs.** Clients can retrieve information and make things happen by constructing URLs. This means that it's easy to make things happen, and it's also easy to change the implementation on the server side if the need arises.

- **XML responses.** Information passes from the server to the client as XML, which means it's well-structured and reliable to read. Responses usually include whatever information the client needs to retrieve more information or perform actions on the server side.

- **Good documentation.** A key feature of a RESTful Web service is clear, definitive documentation. This is useful for clients, because it tells them exactly how to use the Web service. It is also useful for the Web service implementers, because it tells them exactly how the Web service must appear to the rest of the world.

In general, REST Web services are lighter and more flexible than WS-* Web services. For an allegorical look at the Web services debate, try Elliotte Harold's essay here:

http://cafe.elharo.com/web/rest-vs-soap-a-parable/

The Java platform community seems to be catching up with the REST philosophy, as evidenced by the recent appearance of JSR 311:

http://jcp.org/en/jsr/detail?id=311

21.7 A Mobile Client for Flickr

The Flickr photo sharing service is a great example of a RESTful Web service. The API for Flickr is documented here:

http://www.flickr.com/services/api/

To use this API, and to run this example, you need to get a *developer key* from Flickr. For experimentation, it is easy and free, but if you're going to create commercial applications, you must follow a more rigorous application process. Consult Flickr's Web site for complete details.

FlickrMIDlet loads the developer key from an application property. To successfully run this example, you must place your developer key in the flickr-apikey application property.

FlickrMIDlet makes three calls into the Flickr API.

1. flickr.people.findByUsername returns an identification number (NSID) that corresponds to a Flickr user name. An example URL for this method is here, split across multiple lines for readability:

```
http://api.flickr.com/services/rest/?
    method=flickr.people.findByUsername&
    username=Tiger+Empress&
    api_key=4c14eb5d14d429069d6e116a9c64d29d
```

This method returns a very brief XML document that associates the user name to an NSID. Here is an example response:

```
<?xml version="1.0" encoding="utf-8" ?>
<rsp stat="ok">
  <user id="27605340@N00" nsid="27605340@N00">
    <username>Tiger Empress</username>
  </user>
</rsp>
```

2. `flickr.people.getPublicPhotos` returns a list of information about the public photos for a given NSID. Here is an example request URL:

```
http://api.flickr.com/services/rest/?
        method=flickr.people.getPublicPhotos&
        user_id=27605340@N00&
        api_key=4c14eb5d14d429069d6e116a9c64d29d
```

The response, again, is a simple XML document, something like this:

```
<?xml version="1.0" encoding="utf-8" ?>
<rsp stat="ok">
  <photos page="1" pages="1" perpage="100" total="10">
                <photo id="390271118" owner="27605340@N00"
        secret="7676416608" server="154" farm="1"
        title="DSCF3704.JPG"
        ispublic="1" isfriend="0" isfamily="0" />
                <photo id="325610335" owner="27605340@N00"
        secret="1aaa6c19ce" server="135" farm="1"
        title="DSCF3697.JPG"
        ispublic="1" isfriend="0" isfamily="0" />
                <photo id="325610284" owner="27605340@N00"
        secret="b97073425d" server="135" farm="1"
        title="DSCF3695.JPG"
        ispublic="1" isfriend="0" isfamily="0" />
    ...
  </photos>
</rsp>
```

3. The photos themselves are retrieved by creating URLs based on the information returned from `flickr.people.getPublicPhotos`. In particular, the `id`, `secret`, `server`, and `farm` attributes are used. The URL scheme is described in the Flickr API documentation. `FlickrMIDlet` uses a special designation to retrieve thumbnail photos, which are at most 100 pixels on a side, great for little mobile screens. Here is the image URL corresponding to the first item in the list above.

http://farm1.static.flickr.com/154/390271118_7676416608_t.jpg

In `FlickrMIDlet`, two handler classes (`FlickrUserHandler` and `FlickrPhoto-ListHandler`) extract the important parts of each XML reply.

The photos themselves are returned as a byte stream of JPEG image data. Many MIDP implementations can decode JPEG data, and MSA requires this capability.

Here is the source code for FlickrMIDlet, which runs the whole show. The network connections are implemented in lookupUser(), lookupPictures(), and lookupPicture(), all of which are called from run(), which lives in a separate application thread. The MIDlet keeps track of the current user name so that it doesn't perform any unnecessary network work.

```java
import java.io.*;
import java.util.Vector;

import javax.microedition.io.*;
import javax.microedition.lcdui.*;
import javax.microedition.midlet.MIDlet;

import javax.xml.parsers.*;
import org.xml.sax.*;
import org.xml.sax.helpers.*;

public class FlickrMIDlet
    extends MIDlet
    implements CommandListener, Runnable {
  private String kURL =
      "http://api.flickr.com/services/rest/?";

  private Form mForm;
  private TextField mUserField;
  private Gauge mWaitGauge;
  private Command mNextCommand, mExitCommand;

  private String mUser;
  private String mNSID;
  private Vector mPhotoURLs;
  private int mPhotoIndex;

  private String mAPIKey;

  public void startApp() {
    if (mForm == null) {
      mForm = new Form("FlickrMIDlet");

      mAPIKey = getAppProperty("flickr-apikey");
      boolean keyavailable = true;
      if (mAPIKey == null || mAPIKey.length() == 0) {
        keyavailable = false;
        mForm.append("FlickrMIDlet cannot run without " +
            "an API key. The flickr-apikey application " +
            "property must contain the API key. To get " +
            "an API key, see " +
            "http://www.flickr.com/services/api/");
      }
```

```
    String user = getAppProperty("flickr-user");
    if (user == null || user.length() == 0)
      user = "cormack13";
    mUserField = new TextField("User name:", user,
        512, TextField.ANY);
    mWaitGauge = new Gauge("Loading...", false,
        Gauge.INDEFINITE, Gauge.CONTINUOUS_RUNNING);

    if (keyavailable) mForm.append(mUserField);
    mNextCommand = new Command("Next", Command.SCREEN, 0);
    mExitCommand = new Command("Exit", Command.EXIT, 0);
    if (keyavailable) mForm.addCommand(mNextCommand);
    mForm.addCommand(mExitCommand);
    mForm.setCommandListener(this);
  }

  Display.getDisplay(this).setCurrent(mForm);
}

public void pauseApp() {}

public void destroyApp(boolean unconditional) {}

public void commandAction(Command c, Displayable s) {
  if (c.getCommandType() == Command.EXIT) {
    destroyApp(true);
    notifyDestroyed();
  }
  else if (c == mNextCommand) {
    mForm.append(mWaitGauge);
    Thread t = new Thread(this);
    t.start();
  }
}

public void run() {
  try {
    runImpl();
  }
  catch (IOException ioe) {
    mForm.append(ioe.toString());
  }
  catch (ParserConfigurationException pce) {
    mForm.append(pce.toString());
  }
  catch (SAXException se) {
    mForm.append(se.toString());
  }
  finally { clearGauge(); }
}
```

continued

```
private void runImpl() throws IOException,
    ParserConfigurationException, SAXException {
  String user = mUserField.getString();
  if (mUser == null || mUser.equals(user) == false) {
    mWaitGauge.setLabel("Looking up " + user + "...");
    String nsid = lookupUser(user);
    if (nsid != null) {
      mUser = user;
      mNSID = nsid;
      mPhotoURLs = null;
    }
    else {
      mUserField.setString(mUser);
      clearGauge();
      return;
    }
  }
  else {
    mPhotoIndex++;
    if (mPhotoIndex >= mPhotoURLs.size())
      mPhotoIndex = 0;
  }

  if (mNSID == null) return;

  if (mPhotoURLs == null) {
    mWaitGauge.setLabel("Getting photo list...");
    mPhotoURLs = lookupPictures(mNSID);
    mPhotoIndex = 0;
  }

  if (mPhotoURLs == null || mPhotoURLs.size() == 0)
    return;

  mWaitGauge.setLabel("Getting photo...");
  String url = (String)mPhotoURLs.elementAt(mPhotoIndex);
  byte[] raw = lookupPicture(url);
  clearImage();
  Image image = Image.createImage(raw, 0, raw.length);
  mForm.append(image);
}

private void clearGauge() {
  for (int i = 0; i < mForm.size(); i++) {
    Item item = mForm.get(i);
    if (item instanceof Gauge)
      mForm.delete(i--);
  }
}
```

```java
private void clearImage() {
  for (int i = 0; i < mForm.size(); i++) {
    Item item = mForm.get(i);
    if (item instanceof ImageItem)
      mForm.delete(i--);
  }
}

private String lookupUser(String username)
    throws IOException,
        ParserConfigurationException, SAXException {
  String nsid = null;
  // Lame attempt at URL encoding.
  username = username.replace(' ', '+');
  String cs = kURL +
      "method=flickr.people.findByUsername&" +
      "username=" + username + "&" +
      "api_key=" + mAPIKey;
  HttpConnection hc = (HttpConnection)Connector.open(cs);
  try {
    InputStream in = hc.openInputStream();

    try {
      FlickrUserHandler fuh = new FlickrUserHandler();
      parseToHandler(in, fuh);
      nsid = fuh.getNSID();
    }
    finally { in.close(); }
  }
  finally { hc.close(); }
  return nsid;
}

private Vector lookupPictures(String nsid)
    throws IOException,
        ParserConfigurationException, SAXException {
  Vector urls = null;
  String cs = kURL +
      "method=flickr.people.getPublicPhotos&" +
      "user_id=" + nsid + "&" +
      "api_key=" + mAPIKey;
  HttpConnection hc = (HttpConnection)Connector.open(cs);
  try {
    InputStream in = hc.openInputStream();

    try {
      FlickrPhotoListHandler fplh =
          new FlickrPhotoListHandler();
```

continued

```
        parseToHandler(in, fplh);
        urls = fplh.getPhotoURLs();
      }
      finally { in.close(); }
    }
    finally { hc.close(); }
    return urls;
  }

  // Helper method for running a parser.

  private void parseToHandler(InputStream in,
      CheapHandler handler) throws IOException,
        ParserConfigurationException, SAXException {
    SAXParserFactory spf = SAXParserFactory.newInstance();
    SAXParser parser = spf.newSAXParser();
    parser.parse(in, handler);
  }

  // Load a single image.

  private byte[] lookupPicture(String cs) throws IOException {
    byte[] raw = null;
    HttpConnection hc = (HttpConnection)Connector.open(cs);
    try {
      InputStream in = hc.openInputStream();
      try { raw = readAll(in); }
      finally { in.close(); }
    }
    finally { hc.close(); }
    return raw;
  }

  public byte[] readAll(InputStream in) throws IOException {
    ByteArrayOutputStream out = new ByteArrayOutputStream();
    byte[] buffer = new byte[1024];
    for (int n; (n = in.read(buffer)) > 0; )
      out.write(buffer, 0, n);
    return out.toByteArray();
  }
}
```

Both parser handler classes inherit from CheapHandler, which you've already seen. Here is the handler that extracts an NSID from a user name query response.

```
import java.util.*;

public class FlickrUserHandler
    extends CheapHandler {
```

```
      private String mNSID;

      public String getNSID() { return mNSID; }

      public void processStart(String tree, Hashtable a) {
        if (tree.equals("rsp|user")) {
          Enumeration keys = a.keys();
          while (keys.hasMoreElements()) {
            String name = (String)keys.nextElement();
            String value = (String)a.get(name);
            if (name.equals("nsid"))
              mNSID = value;
          }
        }
      }
    }
```

The handler for a user's public photo list is a little more complicated. As it reads the document, it creates an URL for retrieving each photo.

```
    import java.util.*;

    public class FlickrPhotoListHandler
        extends CheapHandler {
      private Vector mPhotoURLs;

      public FlickrPhotoListHandler() {
        mPhotoURLs = new Vector();
      }

      public Vector getPhotoURLs() { return mPhotoURLs; }

      public void processStart(String tree, Hashtable a) {
        if (tree.equals("rsp|photos|photo")) {
          String id = getAttribute(a, "id");
          String secret = getAttribute(a, "secret");
          String server = getAttribute(a, "server");
          String farm = getAttribute(a, "farm");

          if (mPhotoURLs == null)
            mPhotoURLs = new Vector();

          String url = "http://farm" + farm +
              ".static.flickr.com/" +
              server + "/" + id + "_" + secret + "_t.jpg";
          mPhotoURLs.addElement(url);
        }
      }
```

continued

```
    private String getAttribute(Hashtable a, String key) {
      return (String)a.get(key);
    }
  }
```

To run `FlickrMIDlet`, just enter a Flickr user name and select the **Next** command. `FlickrMIDlet` retrieves the user's NSID, photo list, and the first photo in the list (see Figure 21.3).

Keep choosing **Next** to see the rest of the photos in the user's list.

In the source code download, the `kb-ch21-kxml` project contains a rewritten version of `FlickrMIDlet` that uses the kXML 2 parser instead of the JSR 172 API. You can run this version of `FlickrMIDlet` on any MIDP 2.0 device.

`FlickrMIDlet` is a nice toy and a great example of infusing a MIDlet with the massive power of the Internet. If you'd like to explore this example further, here are some ideas for improvements:

- Error handling could be better. For example, if you enter a user name that does not exist, `FlickrMIDlet` quietly reverts to the previous user name without telling you why. What about valid user names that have no public photos?

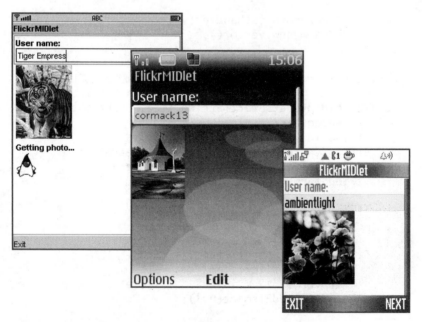

Figure 21.3   Flickr pictures on your phone!

- It would be wise for `FlickrMIDlet` to keep a cache of the current user's images. Network access is expensive in terms of time (and sometimes money), so caching loaded images would enable repeated viewing of a single user's images.

- `FlickrMIDlet` would benefit from a custom `Canvas` user interface for easier browsing and a prettier look.

- It would be nice to save the current user name in a record store so it pops up automatically next time you start `FlickrMIDlet`. A fancier approach would be to keep a list of favorite user names for quick browsing.

21.8 Summary

XML is a great format for structured data. The JSR 172 JAXP API provides basic tools for parsing XML documents. Most of the work is in a `Default-Handler` subclass, which gets notified about interesting events as the parser works through a document. XML is used as the basis for Web services, whether they are the heavy WS-* Web services or lighter RESTful Web services. The JSR 172 JAX-RPC API provides stub-based access to WS-* Web services. RESTful Web services can be invoked with specially constructed URLs, while XML results can be parsed using JAXP.

22

Session
Initiation Protocol

SESSION Initiation Protocol (SIP) is a standard way to set up a call, videoconference, or other session between two network endpoints. Conceptually, SIP interactions resemble call setup in a traditional telephone network: dialing numbers, ringing, busy signals, and hanging up. However, SIP is entirely independent of the type of session that will be set up. In the traditional telephone analogy, SIP has nothing to do with the actual voice conversation.

In today's world of relatively slow wireless data networks, SIP is slightly ahead of its time, as it is good for setting up futuristic communications such as full-motion videoconferencing and CD-quality streaming audio. However, SIP can be used to set up *any* type of communication, including applications like text chat that are feasible on slower networks.

One of the reasons SIP is a good fit for mobile applications is that it recognizes that people don't use the same device all day. SIP clients can query a network of SIP servers to find a network address for a SIP user name. As a user moves from device to device during the day (from a desktop computer to a mobile phone, for example), the device can register the user's current network address with the SIP network.

While SIP setup takes place using a network of SIP servers, the actual communication is more likely to be peer to peer. That is, two endpoints might find each other using SIP, but their actual call or videoconference could be conducted with direct network connections between the endpoints.

SIP and its close relatives are defined by Internet standard RFCs. Core SIP functionality is described in RFC 3261:

http://tools.ietf.org/html/rfc3261

For general information on SIP, try the Wikipedia entry:

http://en.wikipedia.org/wiki/Session_Initiation_Protocol

JSR 180, the SIP API for J2ME, is an optional API that enables your applications to send and receive SIP requests and responses.

22.1 Understanding SIP

SIP is a text-based protocol with similarities to HTTP and SMTP. Like HTTP, it is based around requests and responses. Like HTTP, it uses human-readable headers in both requests and responses. Many of the response codes used in SIP are similar to those in HTTP.

RFC 3261 defines six types of methods, although other standards have added more.

- REGISTER is used to associate a network address with a SIP user name.
- INVITE sends the details of a desired session to the intended recipient. The session details are described any way you want. In many cases, Session Description Protocol (SDP) is used.
- ACK is used to acknowledge a message.
- BYE ends a session.
- CANCEL stops a pending operation.
- OPTIONS queries the SIP capabilities of another device.

The JSR 180 SIP API consists of eight interfaces and four classes, all of which live in javax.microedition.sip. Like other networking APIs, the SIP API has its roots in the Generic Connection Framework.

A secure version of SIP is known as SIPS.

The following permissions are related to the SIP API:

```
javax.microedition.io.Connector.sip
javax.microedition.io.Connector.sips
```

Finally, as with other networking APIs, the push registry can be used to respond to incoming connections.

22.2 Development Tools

SIP is forward-looking technology, which means it's hard to find devices that implement JSR 180. So far, Nokia seems to be most invested in SIP:

http://j2mepolish.org/devices/devices-sip.html
http://forum.nokia.com/main/resources/technologies/sip.html

The JSR 180 SIP API is required by MSA, so devices and applications that use the SIP API will be coming soon.

In the meantime, the Sun Java Wireless Toolkit and NetBeans Mobility offer tools for developing mobile SIP applications.

The toolkit includes an example SIP proxy and registrar server that are extremely useful when you are developing and testing an application on the emulator. To run the SIP server, choose **File > Utilities...** from the KToolbar menu. Select **Start SIP Server** and press **Launch**. The SIP Server will pop up in its own window. It includes a log area that displays received messages.

You can also use the toolkit's network monitor to examine SIP traffic sent and received by the emulator.

In NetBeans Mobility, right-click on your project and choose **Properties**. Select **Platform** in the left pane, then click **Manage Emulators...** in the right pane. Select the **Tools & Extensions** tab, then click **Open Utilities**. Select **Start SIP Server** and press **Launch**.

22.3 Setting Up a Notifier

The first step in a SIP API application is to create a `SipConnectionNotifier` that will be used to handle responses and incoming requests. You can specify a listening port or use the default 5060.

```
SipConnectionNotifier scn = (SipConnectionNotifier)
    Connector.open("sip:");
```

This notifier is used by other parts of the SIP API. Without it, for example, you would not be able to receive a response from a request.

22.4 Sending Requests

To send a SIP request, obtain a `SipClientConnection`, set it up, and call its `send()` method.

The first step in many applications is to register in order to associate a network address with a SIP name. Here is a method that creates a REGISTER request and sends it off. The registrar argument is an IP name or address.

```
// SipConnectionNotifier scn = ...
// SipClientConnectionListener sccl = ...
public void register(String registrar)
    throws SipException, IOException {
  SipClientConnection scc = (SipClientConnection)
      Connector.open("sip:" + registrar);
  scc.setListener(sccl);

  scc.initRequest("REGISTER", scn);
  String address = "Pinky <sip:pinky@acmelab.com>";
  scc.setHeader("To", address);
  scc.setHeader("From", address);
  scc.setHeader("Content-Length", "0");
  scc.setHeader("Max-Forwards", "6");
  scc.send();
}
```

Notice how the SipConnectionNotifier is passed in to initRequest(). It is used to receive a response. When the response arrives, the SipClientConnection-Listener is notified via its notifyResponse() method.

22.5 Receiving SIP Requests and Sending Responses

SIPConnectionNotifier also receives incoming SIP requests. Call its blocking acceptAndOpen() method to retrieve a SIPServerConnection. You can also register a SipServerConnectionListener that is notified when requests arrive.

The SIP API contains a confusing asymmetry with regard to listeners:

- SipClientConnection has an associated SipClientConnectionListener.
- SipConnectionNotifier (not SipServerConnection) has an associated SipServerConnectionListener.

You can find out the request method with getMethod() in SipServerConnec-tion. Other methods can be used to retrieve the value of headers or to examine the payload, if there is one.

To send a response, call initResponse() and pass in the status code you wish to use.

22.6 GoSIP and SIPDemo

The Sun Java Wireless Toolkit and NetBeans Mobility Pack include two example SIP applications, both of which demonstrate different aspects of the SIP API.

- SIPDemo is the simpler of the two examples. It sends SIP messages directly
  between running emulators.
- GoSIP is a more realistic example (see Figure 22.1). You need two instances
  of the emulator and the example SIP Server. You can register as one of two
  users (sippy.a or sippy.b) with the example SIP Server. Then you can
  send an INVITE from one emulator to the other. This exchange results in
  a direct, peer-to-peer socket connection between the two emulators. They
  can then exchange text messages. A SIP BYE message terminates the
  conversation.

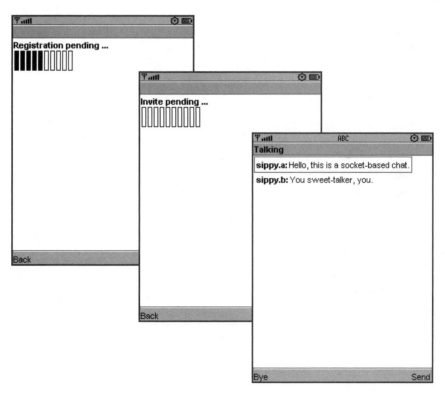

Figure 22.1   Various stages of the GoSIP example

22.7 Summary

SIP is a protocol for setting up communication sessions. It includes the same basic stages as a plain old telephone call: an invitation, ringing, talking, and hanging up. In addition, it includes a way for users to register with a SIP network, which makes it possible to locate users regardless of their current device. The JSR 180 SIP API allows MIDlets to take advantage of SIP functionality.

`SipConnectionNotifier` handles incoming SIP data. Use `SipClientConnection` to send out requests. To respond to incoming requests, get `SipServerConnections` from `SipConnectionNotifier`.

The Sun Java Wireless Toolkit and NetBeans Mobility include an example SIP proxy and registrar server that are useful for testing. The `GoSIP` example shows how to set up a socket-based chat session using SIP.

Section VII

Multimedia

23

Playing and Recording
Sound and Video

$\mathbf{Y}$OU know your phone can make noise. It has a ringer, and you can hear voices
from it. How can your applications make noise with your phone? The answer is
the Mobile Media API (MMAPI).

You can do a lot more with MMAPI than just make noise. MMAPI has a very flexible design that makes it suitable for a wide variety of content, such as images, audio,
and video. The Advanced Multimedia Supplements (AMMS) extend MMAPI's
capabilities with additional camera support, 3D audio, and more.

23.1 Boring Background Information

MSA's multimedia APIs are composed of parts that are related in subtle ways. If
you know that your applications are aimed at MSA devices, then skip this section and read the rest of the chapter, where you learn how to *do* stuff. If you want
the whole story, drink some strong coffee and read this section.

The core of MSA's multimedia capabilities is the MMAPI, defined by JSR 135.
The basic idea is pretty simple. Ask for a `Player` for a certain type of content,
and the API returns an object that knows how to render that content. If the device
can't handle the content, it throws an exception.

If APIs were tools, then MMAPI would be a shiny platinum ratcheted electric
screwdriver that comes without any bits. You can't do anything useful with MMAPI

unless the implementation on the device supports useful content. It's possible, though tragic, that a device could be able to play MP3 files from native applications, such as the Web browser, but not support playing MP3 files via MMAPI. In theory, it's also possible that a device could have MMAPI without being actually able to play anything at all.

The MMAPI specification does not require *any* content types, although most devices that implement MMAPI will take advantage of any available supported content types. The conundrum of supported content is covered in a later section.

MIDP 2.1 includes a subset of MMAPI for playing tones and sampled audio. It is a strict subset of MMAPI, so any audio-related code in MIDlets should also work on an MMAPI device.

MIDP requires that devices can play tones, which at least means you can make some kind of noise. MIDP also requires support for one type of sampled audio, but only halfheartedly. The specification states that if the device can play sampled audio, then MMAPI must support 8-bit, 8KHz, monophonic linear PCM WAV. This is roughly equivalent in sound quality to telephones from a century ago.

The MSA specification is a little more concrete, but not much. It requires MMAPI, and it requires support for the following content types:

- 8kHz, 8-bit linear PCM audio in WAV. This is the same requirement as in MIDP, but this time it *has* to be done.
- AMR-NB. Adaptive Multirate Narrowband (AMR-NB) is a sampled audio format suitable for voice.
- MIDI and SP-MIDI. MIDI is a venerable standard for representing music as a series of tones and durations. SP-MIDI is a variant suitable for small devices. It allows composers to specify portions that can be eliminated on devices that cannot play as many notes simultaneously.

All that is confusing enough, but now another character has come on stage, JSR 234 AMMS. AMMS is not those pills the bulky guy at the gym is offering. It's an API that extends the capabilities of MMAPI. MSA requires AMMS, which means the API is present but its capabilities are mostly dependent on the underlying hardware. Here are a few examples, but not a complete list, of AMMS capabilities:

- If the device has a camera, then the AMMS camera APIs must be supported.
- If the device has a radio, then it must be available through AMMS.
- If the device has 3D audio capabilities, they must be available through AMMS.

In summary, MSA's multimedia APIs come from JSR 135 MMAPI and JSR 234 AMMS. Tones, sampled WAV audio, AMR-NB, and MIDI content must all be supported.

MMAPI lives in `javax.microedition.media` and its child packages. The center of MMAPI is `javax.microedition.media.Manager`.

23.2 Tones

Playing a single tone is pretty easy, but you don't get much control over how it sounds. Use the static `playTone()` method in `Manager`.

You need to specify a note number, which corresponds to a key on a piano. Middle C on a piano is note number 60. This is the same numbering scheme used in the Musical Instrument Digital Interface (MIDI) standard. You also need to say how long the note will be, in milliseconds, and how loud it should be, from 0, silent, to 100, loudest.

This example plays middle C for one second at half volume:

```
try {
  Manager.playTone(60, 1000, 50);
}
catch (MediaException me) {
  // Handle exception.
}
```

If the tone cannot be played, `MediaException` is thrown. This could happen if the device is busy playing some other sound. My Motorola RAZR is a milquetoast in this regard and can't handle quickly repeated calls to `playTone()` without throwing a `MediaException`.

You can also play a *tone sequence*. This technique is described later in the chapter.

23.3 Using Players

The story of MMAPI is very simple for simple tasks. First, ask `Manager` for a `Player` for some content. `Manager` either returns an appropriate `Player` for the content type or throws `MediaException`. Then start the `Player`.

Here is how it works for a MIDI content file:

```
InputStream in = this.getClass().
    getResourceAsStream("/newsong3-anvil.mid");
Player p = Manager.createPlayer(in, "audio/midi");
p.start();
```

A Player has a distinct life cycle, represented by constants in the Player class:

- An UNREALIZED Player has just been created.
- REALIZED means the Player has located all the resources it needs. For example, a Player that is going to render some audio content from a Web server will initiate the communication with the server to become REALIZED.
- A Player gets ready to render content by acquiring device resources or filling buffers. After this work is done, the Player is PREFETCHED.
- When the Player is actually rendering content, it is STARTED. After the Player finishes rendering, it returns to the PREFETCHED state.
- Shut down a Player by calling close(), which releases resources and changes the state to CLOSED.

You can read more about Player's life cycle in the API documentation. In the earlier example, calling start() rocketed the Player through the intermediate states of REALIZED and PREFETCHED to STARTED. To perform these steps explicitly, use the realize() and prefetch() methods. Note that these methods block until the requested state is reached, so you shouldn't call them in an event callback thread.

You can prefetch() a Player to ensure that it can respond quickly when your application is ready to make a noise.

Manager has three createPlayer() methods. The one used in the previous example accepts an InputStream and a content type. You can also just specify a URL, in which case MMAPI will attempt to determine the content type itself and return an appropriate Player. The third createPlayer() method involves a DataSource, which is a lower-level object that you will probably never use. For more information, consult the API documentation.

Creating a Player from a URL is really simple:

```
Player p = Manager.createPlayer(
        "http://kickbutt.jonathanknudsen.com/audio/opti.mid");
```

Of course, you need appropriate permission to make network connections. For efficient use of network content, you want a streaming protocol like Real-Time Streaming Protocol (RTSP). Unfortunately, the MIDP specification, the MMAPI specification, and the MSA specification are all silent on this subject, so support varies from device to device.

You can also use a `file:` URL to load content from a local file using the JSR 75 FileConnection API. The MSA specification defines three system properties that point to likely content locations:

- The `fileconn.dir.tones` property contains the location of ring tones and related audio.
- The `fileconn.dir.music` property points to a directory containing music content such as MP3 or AAC files.
- The `fileconn.dir.recordings` property contains the location of voice recordings.

23.4 Supported Content Types

You know that an MSA device can render WAV, AMR-NB, and MIDI content, but what else is available? At runtime, `Manager` can tell you all the content types and protocols it supports. Use the static `getSupportedContentTypes()` and `getSupportedProtocols()` to find out the device's capabilities.

WAV files are bulky but could be appropriate for short sounds. AMR-NB files have poor sound quality but can be adequate for some applications, particularly podcasts or other voice recordings. AMR-NB is more portable than WAV because it has fewer encoding options. MIDI files are good as a compact representation of songs but are not appropriate for short sound effects.

For music clips, consider using Advanced Audio Coding (AAC) or AAC+, although neither is part of the MSA specification. AAC has been supported on many higher end handsets for a couple years. AAC is CD quality. AAC+ is even more compact but not yet as widely supported as AAC.

In video formats, `.3gp` is the most portable for Global System for Mobile Communications (GSM), and `.3g2` is the most portable for Code Division Multiple Access (CDMA) networks. See Wikipedia for more information:

http://en.wikipedia.org/wiki/3GP

23.5　Threading and Listening

Media rendering usually happens in a separate thread. When you call `start()` on a `Player`, the content starts playing and control returns to your application. However, playing content usually is a heavy load for a small device, so don't expect to do lots of other work at the same time.

A `Player` can notify your application of important events in its life. Just register a `PlayerListener` with the `addPlayerListener()` method. `PlayerListener` has a single callback method, `playerUpdate()`, which gets called when the `Player` reaches the end of its content, when it's stopped, when the volume is changed, and more. Again, it depends on the implementation as to exactly which events trigger a call to `playerUpdate()`.

Generally in your application, you can register a listener, then listen for a specific event and react to it appropriately. For example, you might wait for an END_OF_MEDIA event and then `close()` the corresponding `Player` to free system resources.

23.6　Taking Control

How do you pump up the volume? How can you change the rate of playback? How can you rewind, pause, and restart? The answer is *controls*, another useful abstraction in MMAPI.

You can get a control from a `Player` by passing its class name to `getControl()`. The `javax.microedition.media.control` package contains a toolbox of control types. The `Player` must be REALIZED to supply controls. If the `Player` cannot supply a control of the requested type, it returns `null`.

For example, to adjust the volume for MIDI content, you would do something like this:

```
InputStream in =
    this.getClass().getResourceAsStream("/town.mid");
Player p = Manager.createPlayer(in, "audio/midi");

p.realize();
VolumeControl vc = (VolumeControl)
    p.getControl("VolumeControl");
vc.setLevel(65);

p.start();
```

This example sets the playback volume to 65% of the maximum.

You can retrieve all of a `Player`'s `Control`s by calling `getControls()`, which returns an array of `Control`s. Then you can test each one using `instanceof` to see if it's the type of control you need.

MSA does require any audio player to include a `VolumeControl`, but you cannot rely on the presence of any other type of control.

To make a MIDI file play back faster or slower, use a `RateControl`. The default rate is 100,000, so the following code would make MIDI content play at 120% of its usual rate:

```
RateControl rc = (RateControl)
    p.getControl("RateControl");
if (rc != null)
  rc.setRate(120000);
```

My Motorola V3 returns `null` when I ask for a `RateControl`. Testing for the `null` return value prevents my application from utterly failing with an **Application Error** message. I can't play my MIDI file at a 120% rate, but the application runs without barfing.

23.7 Playing Sampled Audio Content

Now that you understand the basics of `Player`s and `Control`s, playing sampled audio is easy. In fact, the code is nearly identical in many cases.

Just like before, supply a path to the content and kick off the `Player`:

```
InputStream in =
    this.getClass().getResourceAsStream("/quickie-2.wav");
Player p = Manager.createPlayer(in, "audio/wav");
p.start();
```

The same rules apply here. You can ask for `Control`s to change how the audio is rendered. On MSA devices, you know at least a `VolumeControl` is available.

23.8 Playing Video Content

Video content is handled much the same way, except you have to do some magic to make it show up on the screen.

First, create a `Player` as usual, pointing it to some video content.

```
InputStream in =
    this.getClass().getResourceAsStream("/phantom-wee.mpg");
Player p = Manager.createPlayer(in, "video/mpeg");
```

To show the video on the screen, you need a `VideoControl`. You can only get it if the `Player` is REALIZED.

```
p.realize();
VideoControl vc = (VideoControl)p.getControl("VideoControl");
```

Now you have two choices. You can show the video on a `Canvas`, or you can show it as an `Item` in a `Form`. This is one way to show it on a `Canvas`:

```
Canvas c = new Canvas() {
    public void paint(Graphics g) {}
};

vc.initDisplayMode(VideoControl.USE_DIRECT_VIDEO, c);
vc.setVisible(true);

Display.getDisplay(this).setCurrent(c);

p.start();
```

MSA mandates that `VideoControl`'s methods for setting the size and location of the video must be supported, and furthermore, that `setDisplayFullScreen()` must be supported. Figure 23.1 shows it on a canvas in the Sun Java Wireless Toolkit:

To show video on a `Form` instead, use this kind of code:

```
Form f = new Form("Enjoy your video!");
Item vi = (Item)
    vc.initDisplayMode(VideoControl.USE_GUI_PRIMITIVE, null);
vc.setVisible(true);
f.append(vi);
Display.getDisplay(this).setCurrent(f);
```

The video `Item` behaves like any other item. As usual, you are free to add other kinds of items and commands to the `Form`.

Figure 23.1   Video in a Canvas

23.9 The Tone Sequence Player

Two special players, a tone sequence player and an interactive MIDI player, provide useful functionality.

The tone sequence player must be supported. It serves as a base level of audio functionality that must be present on all device. To use the tone sequence player, call Manager's `createPlayer()` method with a special string, `Manager.TONE_DEVICE_LOCATOR`. Then retrieve a `ToneControl` to work with the `Player`.

Tone sequences have a file format, which is described in the API documentation for `ToneControl`. You can either point `Manager` at a file (MIME type is `audio/x-tone-seq`) or define the tone sequence directly in your code.

The core of the tone sequence is a series of note number and duration pairs, although you can do some other stuff, such as define blocks, change volume, and set a tempo.

Here is an example that defines a simple tone sequence in the source code, then plays it:

```
byte[] sequence = {
    ToneControl.VERSION, 1,
    67, 32, // I'm
```

continued

```
    67, 28, // just
    67,  4, // a
    64, 16, // fell -
    67, 16, // a,
    ToneControl.SILENCE, 16,
    67, 16, // a
    65, 16, // fell -
    65, 16, // a
    65, 12, // with
    67,  4, // an
    65, 16, // um -
    62, 16, // brell -
    65, 16, // a
    ToneControl.SILENCE, 16
};

Player p = Manager.createPlayer(Manager.TONE_DEVICE_LOCATOR);
p.realize();
ToneControl tc = (ToneControl)p.getControl("ToneControl");
tc.setSequence(sequence);
p.start();
```

23.10 The Interactive MIDI Player

The *interactive* MIDI player is not the same as the MIDI content player. MSA requires that devices be able to play MIDI content. The interactive MIDI player is more like the tone sequence player. If it's available, you can play notes and send other MIDI events dynamically using MIDIControl.

Obtain the interactive MIDI player by calling Manager.createPlayer() with the special locator value MIDI_DEVICE_LOCATOR. If the interactive MIDI player is not supported on the device, you'll get a MediaException.

Once you've got the interactive MIDI player, prefetch() it and get a MIDI-Control. You can get information about the MIDI device's sounds and sound banks, and you can send short and long messages directly to the device.

Here's an example that plays a cymbal crash for one second.

```
Player p = Manager.createPlayer(Manager.MIDI_DEVICE_LOCATOR);
p.prefetch();
MIDIControl mc = (MIDIControl)p.getControl("MIDIControl");
mc.shortMidiEvent(MIDIControl.NOTE_ON | 9, 57, 127);
try { Thread.sleep(1000); }
catch (InterruptedException ie) {}
mc.shortMidiEvent(MIDIControl.NOTE_ON | 9, 57, 0);
```

23.11 Recording Audio

If a device supports recording audio, the `supports.audio.capture` system property will have the value `true`. In this case, you can find out the content types that are supported for recording by examining the system property `audio.encodings`.

To record audio, use a special locator `capture://audio` to create a `Player`. Then use `RecordControl` to control the recording. Here is an example that records for two seconds into a byte array, then plays the recording back:

```
Player p = Manager.createPlayer("capture://audio");
mPlayer = p;
p.realize();

// Record into a byte array.
RecordControl rc = (RecordControl)
    p.getControl("RecordControl");
ByteArrayOutputStream bout = new ByteArrayOutputStream();
rc.setRecordStream(bout);
rc.startRecord();
p.start();
Thread.sleep(2000);
p.stop();
rc.stopRecord();
rc.commit();
p.close();

// Now play it back.
String type = rc.getContentType();
ByteArrayInputStream bin =
    new ByteArrayInputStream(bout.toByteArray());
p = Manager.createPlayer(bin, type);
mPlayer = p;
p.start();
```

A more accurate implementation would register a listener and wait until the player was started (`RECORD_STARTED`) before kicking off the two-second timer. This example keeps things simpler by starting the timer right after the call to `start()`.

Recording audio is a security-sensitive operation. You don't want any old downloaded application recording your voice or the sounds around you. The device should ask for permission before recording. To avoid security prompts, you need to cryptographically sign your MIDlet suite and get the `javax.microedition.media.control.RecordControl` permission.

23.12 Capturing Video

If your device has a camera, the MSA specification requires that it be available via MMAPI. *Capture* means your application can show the camera's output on the screen. In addition, you can record video (like a camcorder) or take snapshots of the video (like a camera).

If the system property `supports.video.capture` is `true`, then your device has a camera and you are in business.

For recording video, the `video.encodings` property contains a list of supported content types for captured video.

For taking snapshots, the `video.snapshot.encodings` property lists the image encodings that are supported.

Recording video is very similar to recording audio. You need to get a `Record-Control`, tell it where to store the video content, and start it and stop it.

Taking snapshots is even simpler. Use the `getSnapshot()` method in `Video-Control`. You have to supply an encoding, and you get back an array of bytes. It's up to you what to do next. You could use one of the `Image.createImage()` methods, or you could write the byte array to a file or send it out to the network.

Using the camera is security-sensitive, just like recording audio, so you need one or both of the following permissions:

```
javax.microedition.media.control.RecordControl
javax.microedition.media.control.VideoControl.getSnapshot
```

23.13 You Can't Make Everyone Happy

If you want to create an application that makes noise, what kind of content should you package with your application? Your answer will be the result of some tough balancing between application size, performance, and compatibility:

1. Package one of the MSA-mandated formats, either MIDI, WAV, or AMR- NB.

2. Package several different kinds of resources with the application and select appropriate resources at runtime on the basis of the device's capabilities. This technique is likely to result in a large MIDlet suite JAR file.

3. On the basis of the device's capabilities, download appropriate resources from the network. This option is attractive because you can keep the MIDlet suite JAR file small by packaging no content or some mostly compatible content. On the other hand, accessing the network is usually slow, and the

first experience your users will have with your application is waiting for content to download from the network, hardly an auspicious beginning.

4. Create customized MIDlet suite JAR files for different devices, or at least different groups of devices. This is a headache, but if it's handled properly, it is a manageable problem.

The ideal solution is that you expect your target devices will all implement MSA and you can package MIDI, WAV, or AMR content with your application. A more realistic scenario is that you aim your application at both MSA and pre-MSA devices and follow one of the other strategies described above.

23.14 About MMMIDlet

The example application for this chapter, `MMMIDlet`, is an extended version of the snippets of sample code sprinkled throughout this chapter (see Figure 23.2). It presents a menu of options that roughly correspond to the sections in this chapter.

Two projects are included for this chapter. `kb-ch23` contains the full spectrum of examples from this chapter. By contrast, `kb-ch23-midp` contains a pared-down `MMMIDlet` that will run on MIDP 2.0 devices without MMAPI.

`MMMIDlet` keeps the current `Player` as a member variable, `mPlayer`. If a new item is selected before the last one is finished, the current `Player` is stopped before the new one is created.

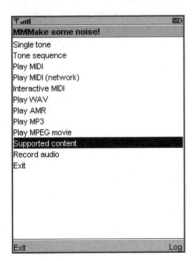

Figure 23.2 The main menu of `MMMIDlet`

To aid in debugging, MMMIDlet also includes a log screen where information and messages about exceptions are printed.

The **Play WAV** item is implemented a little differently from the others. MMMIDlet attempts to play a WAV file using three different content types, just in case your device recognizes one and not another.

Choose **Supported content** from the menu to list all the content types your device can render. This is the output of Manager.getSupportedContentTypes(null) and is shown on MMMIDlet's log screen.

23.15 Summary

The Mobile Media API (MMAPI) is the key to playing and recording sound and video content in MIDP applications. To play a sound or a video, ask Manager for an appropriate Player. You can identify the content with a URL or supply an InputStream and a MIME type. Players have a distinct life cycle, which is partly under your control. To begin playing content, call start(). Register a PlayerListener so you can be sure to call Player methods when the Player is in a known state.

A Player can have controls associated with it that are useful for manipulating the playback. One common control is VolumeControl. Playing video works much the same as playing audio, but you use a VideoControl to display the video on a Canvas or Form. MMAPI also enables recording audio and video and taking snapshots from a device's camera. Although MMAPI is flexible and powerful, content capabilities can vary widely among devices. MSA requires support for MIDI, WAV, and AMR-NB.

24

Advanced Multimedia

THE JSR 234 Advanced Multimedia Supplements (AMMS) specification defines standard extensions to MMAPI. Most of the API is composed of additional `Controls`, but some additional infrastructure is also provided. The AMMS specification defines six *capabilities* that serve as groups of functionality.

- `imagepostprocessing` supplies a structure for applying image effects like blurring, sharpening, or posterization.
- `imageencoding` allows applications to encode images using standard file formats.
- `music` provides volume and equalization controls for audio playback.
- `audio3d` enables your applications to place sound sources in a virtual 3D space surrounding the listener.
- `camera` provides access to camera features like flash and exposure control.
- `tuner` allows applications to control a device's FM or AM radio.

A device that *supports* a capability provides some minimum functionality, which is described in the specification. At runtime, you can find out which capabilities are supported by retrieving the system property `supports.mediacapabilities`. It contains a list of capability names separated by spaces.

The MSA specification requires devices to support `imagepostprocessing` and `imageencoding`. If the device has a camera, the `camera` capability must also be supported. If the device has a radio tuner, the `tuner` capability must also be supported.

24.1 Image Processing

If your platform supports it, applications can use AMMS to perform common image operations like blurring, sharpening, posterizing, resizing, and rotating. Image processing is performed by a MediaProcessor, which knows how to manipulate a certain type of input. You can get a MediaProcessor from GlobalManager by specifying the input type. Both MediaProcessor and GlobalManager are in javax.microedition.amms.

For example, to process JPEG images, you would do this:

```
MediaProcessor mp =
    GlobalManager.createMediaProcessor("image/jpeg");
```

You can find out what input formats are supported by calling GlobalManager's static getSupportedMediaProcessorInputTypes() method. The Sun Java Wireless Toolkit returns image/png, image/jpeg, and image/raw, although only image/jpeg and image/raw are required. *Raw* means that the MediaProcessor will manipulate Image objects rather than manipulating byte streams.

Tell the MediaProcessor about your input (source) image with setInput(). One form of the method accepts an InputStream and a byte length, which can be MediaProcess.UNKNOWN. For example, you can use a JPEG image as input like this:

```
InputStream in = getClass().getResourceAsStream("/orca.jpg");
mp.setInput(in, MediaProcessor.UNKNOWN);
```

The MediaProcessor writes the processed image to an output stream. Use setOutput() to tell MediaProcessor where your output should go.

```
ByteArrayOutputStream bout = new ByteArrayOutputStream();
mp.setOutput(bout);
```

The next step is picking the transformations you want to apply to the image. These are accessible as Controls on the MediaProcessor. You can get useful controls from MediaProcessor by specifying their class names, just like you can with Players. Common photographic effects are encapsulated by ImageEffect-Control, which includes useful *presets*. Choose a preset by passing its name to setPreset(). monochrome and negative must be supported, but other possibilities include emboss, sepia, solarize, and redeyereduction. Call getPreset-Names() for a list of available presets. Take a look at the API documentation for ImageEffectControl for a description of each preset.

In this example, the `emboss` preset is used. Note that you must enable the control for it to affect the output image.

```
String p = "javax.microedition.amms.control.";

ImageEffectControl iec = (ImageEffectControl)
    mp.getControl(p + "imageeffect.ImageEffectControl");
iec.setPreset("emboss");
iec.setEnabled(true);
```

Other controls might be available. The following example shows how to scale an image to 80% of its original size using an `ImageTransformControl`:

```
ImageTransformControl itc = (ImageTransformControl)
    mp.getControl(p + "imageeffect.ImageTransformControl");
int ow = itc.getSourceWidth();
int oh = itc.getSourceHeight();
int w = ow * 80 / 100;
int h = oh * 80 / 100;
itc.setTargetSize(w, h, 0);
itc.setEnabled(true);
```

Useful controls for image processing live in the `javax.microedition.amms.control.imageeffect` package.

You can control the output of the `MediaProcessor` with an `ImageFormatControl`.

When you are finished working with the `Controls` of the `MediaProcessor`, the `start()` method kicks off the processing. If you've registered a `MediaProcessorListener`, you'll be notified when the processing is finished. If you'd prefer to wait instead, you can call `complete()`.

```
mp.complete();
```

If you prefer, you can use a `MediaProcessor` that works with `Image` objects directly instead of a `MediaProcessor` that works on byte streams. In this case, use an `image/raw` `MediaProcessor`. The other form of `setInput()` accepts an `Image` object directly:

```
MediaProcessor mp =
    GlobalManager.createMediaProcessor("image/raw");
InputStream in = getClass().getResourceAsStream("/orca.jpg");
Image i = Image.createImage(in);
mp.setInput(i);
```

In the example code for this chapter, `HanzUndFranzMIDlet` contains two methods that illustrate aspects of image processing:

```
runImagePostProcessingJPEG()
runImagePostProcessingRaw()
```

The first uses a JPEG file as `InputStream` input. The other shows how to pass an `Image` directly to an `image/raw` `MediaProcessor`. In both cases, the source image is shrunk and embossed. The source and processed images are both displayed. See Figure 24.1.

24.2 Controlling Image Format

Unless you say otherwise, `MediaProcessor` spits out the same format you feed it. For example, if you create an `image/png` `MediaProcessor`, the output will be a PNG image.

You can control the output format with an `ImageFormatControl`. Here is an example that sets the output format to PNG:

```
ImageFormatControl ifc = (ImageFormatControl)
    mp.getControl(p + "ImageFormatControl");
ifc.setFormat("image/png");
```

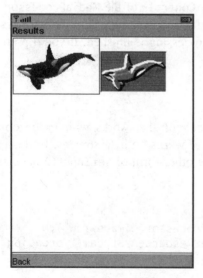

Figure 24.1 Processed fish

This capability can be used without any processing to encode images in any available formats. The available formats are returned by ImageFormatControl's method getSupportedFormats().

24.3 Music

The music capability of AMMS is simple. All it means is that a VolumeControl and an EqualizerControl must be available from GlobalManager. These controls affect all Players.

24.4 3D Audio

The AMMS audio3d capability allows applications to make sounds seem as though they are coming from different locations. A 3D sound engine processes sounds to make the listener perceive that they are in a particular location. The sound is physically delivered using stereo headphones. A sound that emanates from only the left side of the headphones is perceived to be located on the listener's left side. More sophisticated frequency and temporal processing can make a sound appear to be in front, behind, over, or under the listener.

For an excellent introduction to the fascinating topics of sound and audio perception, read the Interactive Audio Special Interest Group (IASIG) guidelines for 3D audio rendering:

> http://www.iasig.org/pubs/3dl1v1.pdf
> http://www.iasig.org/pubs/3dl2v1a.pdf

Many 3D APIs follow the IASIG specifications. Developers who are familiar with such APIs will find the AMMS 3D Audio API easy to understand.

If a device has hardware or software support for 3D audio, the MSA specification requires support for the AMMS 3D Audio API.

The simplest way to use the 3D Audio API is to create a Player, then add it to a SoundSource3D. You can use controls on the SoundSource3D to affect the perceived position of the sound.

For example, you could create a Player as usual, like this:

```
String file = "/newsong3-anvil.mid";
InputStream in = getClass().getResourceAsStream(file);
String type = "audio/midi";
Player p = Manager.createPlayer(in, type);
```

Get a SoundSource3D from GlobalManager and add the Player to it:

```
SoundSource3D ss3d = GlobalManager.createSoundSource3D();
ss3d.addPlayer(p);
```

SoundSource3D can have a variety of Controls. LocationControl must be available, and other control types might also be available. The 3D audio controls all live in javax.microedition.amms.control.audio3d.

Modifying the perceived position of the audio is as simple as obtaining a LocationControl and calling one of its methods:

```
LocationControl lc = (LocationControl)ss3d.getControl(
    "javax.microedition.amms.control.audio3d.LocationControl");
lc.setCartesian(10, 10, -20);
```

Then you can start the Player as usual:

```
p.start();
```

One obvious use of the 3D Audio API is to provides sounds for 3D graphics objects that are shown using the Mobile 3D Graphics API (JSR 184). Just move 3D objects and their corresponding audio sources simultaneously. Remember, mobile devices have slower processors and less memory than desktop computers, so you might need to trade quality for speed in order to produce an application that won't overwhelm a small device.

Together3DCanvas, included in the example code for this chapter, animates a rotating musical tetrahedron (see Figure 24.2).

As with most MIDP applications, device testing is crucial to success. You should run your application on a representative sampling of target devices to observe how it performs and then adjust accordingly.

Recognizing the exact or even approximate location of the sound is very subjective and depends on the listener. Each listener's ears and frequency response are different, and it is impossible for any 3D audio implementation to work perfectly for all listeners. Distinguishing between left, right, front, and back for an audio source is usually possible. It's quite difficult to distinguish between above and below. Providing visual clues to the sound's location greatly increases the chance of convincing the listener of the location of the sound.

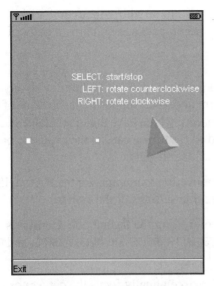

Figure 24.2   A musical tetrahedron

24.5 Audio Special Effects

Special effects like reverberation, chorus, and equalization might be available through AMMS, although they are not explicitly grouped as a capability. These types of audio effects are often available from the same audio engine that handles 3D effects.

The `audio3d` capability requires that a `ReverbControl` be available from `GlobalManager`, but other types of audio effects might or might not be available. As usual, you must be careful when you attempt to use these controls.

The audio effect controls, unsurprisingly, are in the `javax.microedition.amms.controls.audioeffect` package.

24.6 More Camera Control

AMMS does not change the basic technique for using a camera, but it allows your applications to control the camera in much more detail.

You'll still get a Player representing the camera with capture://video. The javax.microedition.amms.control.camera package contains a bevy of useful controls.

- CameraControl provides general methods that will be familiar to anyone with a digital camera. You can learn about the supported resolutions of the camera and supported *exposure modes*, which have understandable names like auto, sunset, portrait, and so forth. You can set the exposure mode and examine the camera's current rotation state.

- ExposureControl allows your application to manipulate the F-Stop, ISO, exposure time, and other photographic settings of the camera.

- FlashControl has methods for controlling the flash mode. Constants represent different modes: AUTO, AUTO_WITH_REDEYEREDUCE, FORCE, and OFF are a few of the possibilities.

- FocusControl enables applications to manually focus the camera or request automatic focus.

- SnapshotControl supports *burst shooting* by which the camera takes pictures as fast as it can and saves them automatically as files.

- Finally, ZoomControl provides methods for querying and setting both the optical and digital zooms of the camera.

Remember that these controls are not necessarily available on all devices. Code defensively, testing the results of getControl() for null and only exposing features to your users that are actually available on the device.

24.7 Plain Old Radio

Mobile phones always have a radio in them, the one that communicates with the cell tower that connects the phone to the rest of the network. Some phones also feature an old-fashioned FM or AM receiver.

You can access a radio tuner as a Player by requesting capture://radio. Once you've got the Player, TunerControl and RDSControl give you methods for using the radio. Both control types live in javax.microedition.amms.control.tuner.

TunerControl allows you to select the radio band and find a specific station, while RDSControl is useful for receiving information about stations and songs.

The system property `tuner.modulations` contains a list of supported radio types, separated by whitespace. The Sun Java Wireless Toolkit emulator returns the following:

```
fm am
```

The emulator doesn't have a real radio, of course, but it simulates one with a few different stations.

This code sets up the radio and seeks an FM station, starting at 99.9 MHz and moving downward:

```
Player p = Manager.createPlayer("capture://radio");

p.start();

TunerControl tc = (TunerControl)p.getControl(
    "javax.microedition.amms.control.tuner.TunerControl");
tc.seek(999000, TunerControl.MODULATION_FM, false);
```

Using `RDSControl` is a little more complicated. First register a `PlayerListener`. When an event comes to the listener that is `RDSControl.RDS_NEW_DATA`, you can use the `RDSControl` to examine the incoming information.

For a comprehensive example, consult `TunerDemo` in `AdvancedMultimedia-Supplements`, part of the Sun Java Wireless Toolkit demonstrations.

24.8 Summary

AMMS expands on the promise of MMAPI with all sorts of goodies. 3D audio, image processing and encoding, camera and radio control are a few of the highlights. MSA requires support for the image encoding and image processing capabilities of AMMS. In addition, if the device has 3D audio infrastructure, a camera, or a radio tuner, MSA requires support for the corresponding AMMS APIs.

Section VIII

Security and Transactions

25

Smart Cards and Cryptography

T HE Security and Trust Services APIs (SATSA) are defined by JSR 177. SATSA actually contains four separate APIs. Two of these are for communicating with smart cards, while the other two relate to cryptography.

- SATSA-APDU is an API for communicating with a smart card using basic data packets called Application Protocol Data Units (APDUs).
- SATSA-JCRMI is also about smart card communication but is based on Java Card Remote Method Invocation, a distributed computing protocol based on Java SE's Remote Method Invocation (RMI).
- SATSA-PKI provides methods for using a smart card to generate digital signatures and manage certificates.
- SATSA-CRYPTO is a compact API for general-purpose cryptography, including message digests, digital signatures, and ciphers.

This chapter provides a brief introduction to SATSA. For more depth, read the *SATSA Developer's Guide*, available here:

http://java.sun.com/j2me/docs/satsa-dg/index.html

Some of the discussion about tools is out of date, but the basic concepts and descriptions are valid.

The MSA specification requires SATSA-CRYPTO. Furthermore, if the device has a smart card or a similar component, then SATSA-APDU and SATSA-PKI are also required.

25.1 Smart Cards? Really?

A smart card is a tiny computer. Many smart cards look just like credit cards with some extra electrical contacts.

A boiled-down view of a smart card is that it is a physical manifestation of a private cryptographic key. One of the big problems of Public Key Infrastructure (PKI) is key management. A smart card is a compact place to store a private key that can be kept physically secure by placing it in a purse or wallet, just like a regular credit card. The smart card, however, can do wonderful things such as digitally sign information *on the card*, which makes it appropriate for all sorts of transactions involving money and important information. A full discussion of PKI is beyond the scope of this book. If you need some background, try the *SATSA Developer's Guide* (mentioned earlier) or this article:

> http://developers.sun.com/techtopics/mobility/midp/articles/ security1/

How do smart cards relate to MIDP devices? All Global System for Mobile Communication (GSM) devices already have a special kind of smart card inside them called a subscriber identity module (SIM) card. Beyond this, some phones may have one or more slots where smart cards could be inserted.

On devices that support SATSA, the `microedition.smartcardslots` system property contains a list of all available slots. The slot is identified by a number followed by a letter that indicates whether cards can be inserted and removed while the device is powered on. This is called *hot swappable*, indicated by H. Slot numbers are separated by commas. The Sun Java Wireless Toolkit returns this list for `microedition.smartcardslots`:

    0H,1H

This list indicates two hot-swappable slots numbered 0 and 1.

25.2 Testing SATSA Applications with the Emulator

The Sun Java Wireless Toolkit supports SATSA, but testing applications that interact with a smart card is a little more complicated than just running the emulator. The key is another program that simulates a running smart card, `cref`.

`cref` is really part of the Java Card Development Kit, which is a set of tools for creating smart card applications. At this writing, the current version is 2.2.2. If you want to explore smart card application development, download the kit here:

http://java.sun.com/products/javacard/dev_kit.html

As a convenience, however, the Sun Java Wireless Toolkit now includes `cref` in its `bin` directory. To test SATSA applications in the toolkit's emulator, use one running instance of `cref` to represent each connected smart card.

The toolkit includes an example application, `SATSADemos`, that has working versions of the concepts outlined in this chapter. Consult the Sun Java Wireless Toolkit *User's Guide*, Appendix A, for instructions on running `SATSADemos`.

25.3 Basic Smart Card Communication

The SATSA-APDU API provides basic communication to smart card applications. It consists of a single interface, `javax.microedition.apdu.APDUConnection`, which is an extension of the Generic Connection Framework (GCF).

To communicate with a smart card application, you need to know its identifier, a magic number expressed as a series of hexadecimal numbers. Then open a connection to the smart card application like this:

```
String url = "apdu:0;target=a0.00.00.00.62.03.01.0c.02.01";
APDUConnection ac = (APDUConnection)Connector.open(url);
```

The connection URL includes the slot number, 0, and the application identifier. Once the connection is established, you can send and receive data using `APDUConnection`'s `exchangeAPDU()` method.

When you're finished talking to the smart card, close the connection. Use a `finally` block to ensure the connection is shut down.

25.4 Smart Card Communication with Java Card RMI

Using SATSA-JCRMI is similar to using SATSA-APDU, but you use a *remote object* to do work on the smart card, which follows RMI's distributed object model. Your application needs a local stub class that contains the same methods exposed by the smart card application.

The SATSA-JCRMI API consists mainly of `javax.microedition.jcrmi.JavaCardRMIConnection` but also includes some RMI-related classes.

Making the connection is similar to using SATSA-APDU. You need to specify the card slot and application identifier:

```
String url = "jcrmi:0;AID=a0.0.0.0.62.3.1.c.8.1";
JavaCardRMIConnection jcrmic =
    (JavaCardRMIConnection)Connector.open(url);
```

Next, get a reference to the remote object (a stub, really) by calling `getInitial-Reference()` on the `JavaCardRMIConnection`. You must cast the returned `Object` to the appropriate stub type. Here is an example:

```
WineAccount ica = (WineAccount)jcrmic.getInitialReference();
```

Now you can call methods on the stub, which invokes methods on the remote object on the smart card. When you're finished working, remember to close the connection.

25.5 Generating Signatures

SATSA-PKI gives your application the ability to sign data using a smart card or to manage certificates. SATSA-PKI has two main classes:

```
javax.microedition.securityservice.CMSMessageSignatureService
javax.microedition.pki.UserCredentialManager
```

CMS refers to the Cryptographic Message Syntax defined by RFC 2630 and RFC 2634.

http://www.ietf.org/rfc/rfc2630.txt
http://www.ietf.org/rfc/rfc2634.txt

Your application uses `CMSMessageSignatureService` by calling its static methods `sign()` or `authenticate()`. The implementation will locate an appropriate key and use a smart card or other appropriate mechanism to sign some data.

The only real difference between `sign()` and `authenticate()` is the type of key that the implementation will find. Bear in mind that the implementation is likely to display one or more prompts to the user, to verify the use of a key, ask for a PIN, and so on.

You can limit the key search by supplying a list of allowed issuing Certificate Authorities (CAs). You can also use options to affect the exact format of the generated signature.

A typical use would be for a client application to sign a small message and send it to a server. The server can verify the signature on the data to be sure the message has not come from an imposter.

25.6 Managing Certificates

The other part of SATSA-PKI is `UserCredentialManager`, which allows applications to manage the keys that are available to `CMSMessageSignatureService`.

Use `UserCredentialManager`'s `addCredential()` method to add a key, represented by a certificate path, to the certificate store. The specification is deliberately vague about the location of the certificate store; it might be on the device, or it might be in a smart card. The certificate path is a byte array, which is normally a CA's response to a Certificate Signing Request (CSR). You have to supply a human-readable name for the key.

The `generateCSR()` method creates a request to a CA for a signed certificate. Most of the time, an attached smart card is used to generate a new key pair, which is then wrapped up in a CSR. Your application can submit the CSR to a CA server for signing. The response can then be passed to `addCredential()` to add it to the certificate store.

Finally, use `removeCredential()` to remove a certificate from the certificate store.

25.7 Cryptography

SATSA-CRYPTO provides three cryptographic tools in an API that resembles Java SE.

25.7.1 Using Message Digests

A *message digest* can be used to generate a "fingerprint" for a set of data. In SATSA-CRYPTO, `java.security.MessageDigest` is the corresponding class.

Get a `MessageDigest` instance by passing an algorithm name to the static `getInstance()` factory method:

```
MessageDigest md = MessageDigest.getInstance("SHA-1");
```

Next, feed the `MessageDigest` data with the `update()` method.

```
// byte[] data = ...
md.update(data, 0, data.length);
```

Generate the digest value by passing an appropriate byte array to `digest()`.

```
byte[] digest = new byte[20];
md.digest(digest, 0, 20);
```

25.7.2 Using Signatures

A signature is a lot like a signed message digest. It acts as a fingerprint of data, but it is generated using a private key and can only be verified using the matching public key.

Back in the world of SATSA-PKI, `CMSMessageSignatureService` is capable of generating signatures. In SATSA-CRYPTO, `java.security.Signature` can verify signatures.

You'll need the correct public key to verify a signature. Loading and manipulating keys is outside the scope of this chapter, but you can find information on this topic in the *SATSA Developer's Guide*.

Obtain a `Signature` object using the `getInstance()` factory method. The following example requests a `Signature` that uses SHA-1 to generate a message digest, then encrypts or decrypts the digest value using an RSA cipher.

```
// PublicKey publicKey = ...
Signature signature = Signature.getInstance("SHA1withRSA");
```

Now initialize the `Signature` for verification with the public key.

```
signature.initVerify(publicKey);
```

Just as you did with `MessageDigest`, pass the data whose signature will be verified using `update()`:

```
// byte[] data = ...
signature.update(data, 0, data.length);
```

Now pass the expected signature value to `verify()`. If everything checks out, this method returns `true`.

```
// byte[] expected = ...
boolean verified = signature.verify(expected);
```

25.7.3 Using Ciphers

The `javax.crypto.Cipher` class allows for general-purpose encryption and decryption using symmetric or asymmetric ciphers.

The basic steps for using `Cipher` are as follows:

1. Create a `Cipher` by passing an algorithm to the factory method `get-Instance()`. Along with the algorithm name, you can also specify a mode and a padding scheme. For example, `AES/CBC/PKCS5Padding` means to use the AES cipher in the CBC mode with PKCS #5 padding.

2. Initialize the `Cipher` with a key and a flag that indicates whether you want to encrypt or decrypt data.

3. Feed the `Cipher` data with the `update()` method.

4. Send the last data to the `Cipher` with `doFinal()`.

Both `update()` and `doFinal()` perform encryption or decryption directly, taking input data and placing output data in arrays you supply.

25.8 Summary

SATSA defines four APIs for smart card communication and cryptographic functionality. SATSA-APDU provides basic smart card communication, while SATSA-JCRMI is a smart card communication API based on remote objects. Both SATSA-APDU and SATSA-JCRMI are extensions of the Generic Connection Framework.

SATSA-PKI allows applications to request digital signatures from a smart card or other security device. In addition, it provides methods for applications to add or remove keys and their associated certificates.

SATSA-CRYPTO provides message digests, digital signature verification, and general-purpose ciphers for applications with sophisticated cryptographic requirements.

26

Mobile Payments

$\mathbf{M}$OBILE applications get really interesting when money changes hands. The initial sale of your application is one way to make money, but applications that allow their users to buy things open up many more possibilities. Here are a few:

- You could sell a game with two or three levels and allow users to buy more levels. You could even distribute the game application for free to get people hooked and then make money by selling levels or other upgrades.

- An online store client could enable its users to order items and pay for them.

- A client that connects to a pay service could allow users to pay for additional service directly.

The JSR 229 Payment API is a flexible API that enables applications to make payments on behalf of their users. Although MSA requires the presence of this API, it makes no demands about available payment mechanisms. Therefore, while your application can use the Payment API, the exact details of payments will depend on the device and its wireless carrier.

JSR 229 defines a compact API located in `javax.microedition.payment`, based around one main class and two interfaces:

- `TransactionModule` provides the main services: processing payments and retrieving payment history.

- Your application must register a `TransactionListener` to receive notifications about payments.

- A `TransactionRecord` represents a single payment.

26.1 Show Me the Money!

Making a payment is straightforward. First, obtain an appropriate `Transaction-Module`. Pass your application's MIDlet class to the constructor.

```
TransactionModule tm = new TransactionModule(this);
```

Next, register a `TransactionListener`. You have to register a `Transaction-Listener` so you will find out whether the payment succeeds or fails.

```
tm.setListener(this);
```

Now submit a payment with one of the `process()` methods. The things that users can buy from your application are *features*. Each feature has a unique number that is defined in a separate file, described later in this chapter.

The simplest `process()` accepts a feature number, a human-readable feature title, and a human-readable feature description. The other variant of `process()` allows for a byte array payload as well. The method returns a *transaction identifier*. Multiple calls to `process()` will return identifiers that are unique on this device.

```
String title = "Bobble Head";
String description = "Rod Tidwell bobble head.";
int tid = tm.process(1, title, description);
```

The `process()` method returns immediately, but the device takes some action as a result. First, the device is likely to show some prompts on the screen to ask the user questions like the following:

- Are you sure you want to buy this feature?
- Which payment method do you want to use?
- What's your credit card number and expiration date?

The exact prompts the user sees depends on the device, but the feature title and description that you supply to `process()` will show up somewhere. On the Sun Java Wireless Toolkit, the `process()` call first displays a confirmation screen where the user can select an appropriate payment method (see Figure 26.1).

If you choose **Yes**, the emulator shows you another screen where you enter your credit card information (see Figure 26.2).

If the user supplies all the right answers, the implementation attempts to process the payment, usually with some type of network connection. Whether the transaction succeeds or fails, the implementation calls the `processed()` method of your `TransactionListener`.

Figure 26.1 Choosing how to pay for the Rod Tidwell bobble head

Figure 26.2 No, it's not my real credit card number.

The `processed()` method receives a `TransactionRecord`, a simple object that represents a single payment. The `TransactionRecord` contains the following information:

- `getState()` returns the transaction state, represented by constants in `TransactionRecord`. `TRANSACTION_SUCCESSFUL` means that the payment occurred as expected. `TRANSACTION_FAILED` means that something went wrong, like a bad credit card number or a communication failure. `TRANSACTION_REJECTED` means the user chose to cancel the payment before it was attempted.

- `getFeatureID()` returns the same number that you passed to the `TransactionModule` with `process()`.

- `getTransactionID()` returns the same identifier you received from `process()`.

- `getFinishedTimestamp()` indicates when the payment was accepted.

- Finally, `wasMissed()` indicates whether this payment has already been processed.

In your application, whenever you are notified that a transaction is `TRANSACTION_SUCCESSFUL`, you know that money is in your pocket and you can give the user whatever it is he or she just bought.

26.2 Matching Applications to Payment Providers

How does money transfer from your users to you? The answer depends on what mechanism your device supports. The Payment API implementation on a device has one or more *payment providers* that know the nuts and bolts of making payments. The mechanism could be Premium Priced SMS (PPSMS), credit card transactions, or something else, possibly involving the wireless carrier. When your application submits a payment using the Payment API, the implementation selects an appropriate provider to make the transaction happen.

The business of finding an appropriate payment provider is probably the most complicated part of the Payment API. A gaggle of properties in the descriptor, MIDlet suite JAR file manifest, and a *payment update file* map out all the relationships. The payment update file looks like a descriptor file, but it is separate and can be updated to reflect new prices for application features. The payment update file can be retrieved from a server at runtime to provide the most up-to-date pricing information possible.

Taken together, the payment properties in the descriptor, MIDlet suite manifest, and payment update file are the *payment provisioning information*. In essence, the payment provisioning information describes the features that are for sale in your application and how much they cost.

From the top level looking down, the payment provisioning information includes these items:

- The payment adapters your application can use describes the *kinds* of payments you can accept. PPSMS payment is one, credit card payment is another.
- The payment providers your application can use are more specific. For example, you can specify that your application can use SONERA, a specific type of PPSMS provider.
- Pricing information is listed for each provider.

When your application initiates a payment using the Payment API, the device tries to match its supported providers to the providers listed in your application's payment provisioning information. Assuming a match is found, the device will show one or more dialogs to the user confirming that the user wants to make a purchase. If more than one provider matches your application's provisioning information, the device will offer the user a choice.

26.3 Editing Payment Provisioning Information

Fortunately, you do not need to edit the payment provisioning information directly. Your development tool allows you to enter payment information in a window and handles the details of writing the properties to the appropriate files.

In the Sun Java Wireless Toolkit, choose **Project > Settings...**, then click on the **Payment** item in the left column (see Figure 26.3).

This particular application has two items for sale, called *features*. The information for each provider puts a price on each of the features. In Figure 26.4, the

Figure 26.3 Editing payment provisioning information

Figure 26.4   Provider settings

VISA provider information shows that the X-CCARD (credit card) adapter should be used and that U.S. dollars are the currency, and it shows the prices for each feature. Some other information related to the X-CCARD adapter is also provided; consult the specification for the full details.

26.4 Security and Payments

Applications that use the Payment API must be signed. If you are doing your primary development and debugging on a desktop emulator, this is usually possible using test keys and a test root certificate. In addition, the JSR 229 specification allows development tools to use various debugging features that, if they are supported by your development tools, make your life quite a bit easier.

Once you get everything running well on the desktop, the move to real devices is full of the usual challenges of signed MIDlets.

Applications that use the Payment API need the `javax.microedition.payment.process` permission.

26.5 Summary

The Payment API provides MIDlets with a simple API for making payments. The underlying infrastructure is flexible enough to handle a variety of payment mechanisms, from PPSMS to credit cards and more. At the API level, making a payment is simply a matter of obtaining an appropriate `TransactionModule` and calling its `process()` method. A registered `TransactionListener` is notified of success or failure. Payment provisioning information is used to match up the MIDlet suite's payment capabilities with the capabilities of the device. The payment provisioning information is stored as properties in the descriptor, the MIDlet suite JAR file manifest, and possibly also a payment update file.

27

Know Where You Are

$\mathbf{A}$s mobile phones continue to get smaller and cheaper, manufacturers are able to cram more into them. One interesting capability that is making its way into mobile phones is Global Positioning System (GPS). A GPS receiver provides the mobile phone a way to know its own location. This means that your MIDlets can now combine the awesome power of the Internet with the awesome power of GPS. From a programming perspective, it's easy to write applications to find the nearest Starbucks or display your current location on a map at a social networking Web site.

GPS isn't the only way to determine location, but it's probably the most popular. Mobile phones can also use the location of the nearest cell tower to determine location, but it's not as precise. For more information on this technique and its relationship to wireless 911 service, see Wikipedia:

   http://en.wikipedia.org/wiki/Enhanced_911

The JSR 179 Location API is a standard interface to location hardware. It is required on MSA devices that have location hardware. The API is located in `javax.microedition.location`.

On many of today's devices, only signed MIDlets can use the Location API. If you intend to develop a Location API application, check your target devices and target wireless carriers to find out what you must do to make your application run.

27.1 The Short Story

Retrieving the device's current location is relatively simple. You need a LocationProvider, but first you must ask for an appropriate one. It is possible that a device supports more than one method of locating itself. For example, a device could have one LocationProvider that uses GPS hardware and one LocationProvider that uses cell tower positioning.

Ask for a LocationProvider from its factory method getInstance() by specifying the criteria it must meet. For example, you might want to retrieve only a LocationProvider that does not incur any cost, or one that is able to return information about the orientation of the device.

If you just create a brand new Criteria object, it has default values that will match any available LocationProviders. This is also equivalent to passing null for the Criteria argument.

```
Criteria c = new Criteria();
LocationProvider lp = LocationProvider.getInstance(c);
```

If getInstance() cannot find a matching LocationProvider, it returns null. If no LocationProviders are available currently, getInstance() throws LocationException.

Once you've got a LocationProvider, call getLocation() for the device's current location. Pass a timeout value in seconds. The method blocks until the location is determined or time runs out, in which case LocationException is thrown.

```
Location l = lp.getLocation(10);
```

The returned Location object can contain all sorts of useful information. The first thing to check is isValid(), which indicates if the object contains any useful information. Next most interesting is getTimestamp(), which tells when the location measurement was retrieved.

For the location itself, call getQualifiedCoordinates(), which returns an object containing longitude, latitude, altitude, and the accuracy of each measurement.

```
QualifiedCoordinates qc = l.getQualifiedCoordinates();

double lat = qc.getLatitude();
double lon = qc.qc.getLongitude();
```

27.2 An Even Shorter Story

LocationProvider's static getLastKnownLocation() returns whatever location value was last measured by the device. Make sure you check the returned Location's isValid() method. Also, check getTimestamp() to make sure that the measurement isn't too old to be useful.

27.3 Receiving Periodic Location Updates

To receive ongoing updates from a LocationProvider, your application can register a LocationListener by using setLocationListener(). You need to specify how often you want updates (in seconds), how late an update is allowed to be, and how old a location measurement can be.

Here is a call that registers a listener for 4-second updates, which can be at most 1 second late, at most 1 second old.

```
// LocationProvider lp = ...
// LocationListener ll = ...
lp.setLocationListener(ll, 4, 1, 1);
```

The whole LocationListener mechanism is really just a scheduling convenience to save you the trouble of setting up your own periodic updating mechanism.

LocationListener has two methods you must implement. Every time a location is read, the device calls the listener's locationUpdated() method. Furthermore, if the provider's state changes (becomes unavailable, for example), the provider-StateChanged() method is invoked.

27.4 Getting Close

A different kind of listener, ProximityListener, is useful for applications that want to know when they are near a certain location. ProximityListeners are registered and unregistered using static methods in LocationProvider. All you have to do is pass in the location that interests you and a radius that describes how close to that location the device has to be before the ProximityListener is notified.

When the device enters the area you have described, the ProximityListener's proximityEvent() method is invoked.

27.5   Landmark Databases

The other major component of the JSR 179 Location API is *landmark management*. A landmark is a location with an associated name. Specifically, a Landmark in the Location API has a name, a description, a QualifiedCoordinates object, and an AddressInfo object.

A LandmarkStore is a simple database of landmarks. Each LandmarkStore has a name, except for one *default* LandmarkStore, which has no name. LandmarkStores are shared among all Java ME applications on a device but may or may not be shared with other (native) applications.

Static methods in LandmarkStore control adding, removing, and listing LandmarkStores.

```
LandmarkStore.createLandmarkStore("Jonathan");
String[] stores = LandmarkStore.listLandmarkStores();
LandmarkStore.deleteLandmarkStore("Jonathan");
```

To open an existing LandmarkStore, pass its name to the factory method getInstance().

Inside a LandmarkStore, Landmarks can be associated with *categories*, which are simply names. A Landmark can also have a null category, meaning it is not associated with any category.

Categories are managed using addCategory() and deleteCategory(). An Enumeration of categories is returned from getCategories().

Use addLandmark() to either add a new Landmark to the LandmarkStore or to associate a Landmark with an additional category.

You can retrieve landmarks from the LandmarkStore either by category or by geography. For example, the following code returns an Enumeration of Landmarks that match the category Sports and any landmark name (signified by null):

```
// LandmarkStore ls = ...
Enumeration ce = ls.getLandmarks("Sports", null);
```

This code retrieves landmarks in the rectangle defined by the minimum and maximum latitude and longitude values, matching any (null) category name:

```
// LandmarkStore ls = ...
Enumeration ge = ls.getLandmarks(null,
    35.963280, 36.010783,
    -78.555336, -78.483582);
```

27.6 Orientation

Some devices know if they are horizontal, vertical, tilted left, tilted right, or some combination of angles. Like the controllers on the Nintendo Wii, devices that understand their own orientation can be used for all sorts of interesting applications.

The `javax.microedition.location.Orientation` class encapsulates this information. Retrieve the current orientation by calling the static `getOrientation()` method. If the device does not know its orientation, `LocationException` is thrown.

27.7 Simulating Device Location

When you develop Location API applications on a desktop computer, the emulator does not have access to actual GPS hardware and cannot know the location of your computer. Instead, it pretends to know. You can tell the emulator where it should pretend to be. The procedure is the same regardless of whether you use NetBeans Mobility Pack or the Sun Java Wireless Toolkit because the underlying emulator is the same.

When the emulator is running your application, choose **MIDlet > External events** from the emulator window's menu. On the **Location** tab, you can fill in the emulator's current simulated location and other properties related to the Location API (see Figure 27.1).

The emulator also offers the opportunity to run a *location script*, which is a simple XML file that describes the movement of the emulator over time. This is great for testing applications that use `ProximityListeners` or match the current location against known landmarks.

The `CityGuide` sample application (part of the Sun Java Wireless Toolkit and NetBeans Mobility) is a great demonstration of using the Location API and also includes a sample location script.

`StandMIDlet` is part of the example code for this book. It is easier to understand than `CityGuide` and includes many of the code snippets that are presented in this chapter. See the book's Web site to get `StandMIDlet`:

http://kickbutt.jonathanknudsen.com/download.html

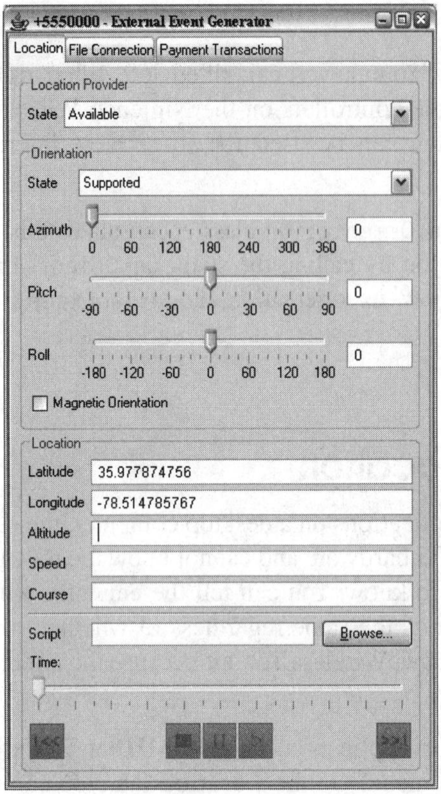

Figure 27.1   Adjusting the emulator's location

27.8 Summary

The JSR 179 Location API is a standard API for devices that know their own location. Use it by retrieving a `LocationProvider` that meets your needs. You can get the device's location directly from a `LocationProvider`, or you can register a `Location-Listener` to receive periodic updates. Another type of listener, `ProximityListener`, is notified when the device comes close to a certain geographic point. The Location API also includes a simple database of named landmarks, the `Landmark-Store`. `LandmarkStores` have names and can store landmarks associated with one or more named categories. Finally, some devices also understand their own orientation, represented by the `Orientation` class. The emulator for the Sun Java Wireless Toolkit and NetBeans Mobility Pack has a supplemental window where the simulated location can be adjusted. For more rigorous testing, a location script can be used to change the simulated location over time.

28

Application Architecture

APPLICATION design is art as much as it is science. As with anything else, your skill at MIDP application design is a product of your knowledge, experience, and talent. The best way to improve is practice.

This chapter presents ideas to help you with your application design. There are no absolutes. What works well for one application might be a disaster for another. The purpose of this chapter is to help you get in the right frame of mind to design your own application effectively and imaginatively.

28.1 Use the Strengths of Java ME

Most applications these days span multiple platforms, so the trick is taking advantage of the best features of the platforms you're using.

The Java ME platform is great for creating clients that are rich and pretty. Your Java ME client should be fun to use, sparkly, and highly responsive. Spend some time and money on this. If you are not a graphic designer, find a good one to make a user interface that people *want* to use.

Use threads to keep the interface responsive even when your application is thinking about something else. If you must show a wait screen while making network connections, consider a design that allows the user to continue working or playing.

28.2   Use the Strengths of the Internet

The other thing that makes Java ME clients so powerful is their ability to connect to the Internet and other networks. I'll assume that the Internet is the ultimate destination, but you can build powerful applications based on SMS, MMS, or Bluetooth as well.

The strengths of the Internet are computing power and storage. Based on a request from a Java ME client, the server side of your application can search through massive databases and perform complicated analysis, sending a simple reply to your Java ME client.

In the near term, most mobile data networks are painfully slow. Faster networks are coming, but any application design for current mobile phones should keep network traffic to a minimum and put a lot of effort into effective background network access. Effective failure handling is also important, because there will always be problems with spotty reception.

Google Maps is a great example of a well-designed application. The Java ME client is attractive and highly responsive. The server side consults a large geographic database and creates compact map images on behalf of the client. The server can also combine the power of large databases to find businesses or specific addresses and flag them on the map. The map client remains responsive and useful while requests for more map images are sent to the server.

28.3   Don't Cram the Desktop into a Java ME Application

This is really the same as *use the strengths of Java ME*. Don't take a desktop application or a Web application and try to cram it into a Java ME client. It doesn't make any sense, and you will end up with something that no one wants to use. It's like trying to put a trailer hitch on a bicycle or adding a luggage rack to a kite.

The screen size is a big factor in this. Desktop and Web applications are designed to run on a screen that is much larger than a typical mobile device. Keep the screens of your Java ME applications as simple as possible. Users don't want to be scrolling through lots of data.

The other big factor is *input*. Desktop computers and browser applications take advantage of a keyboard, which makes it easy to enter text. Mobile phones don't have this kind of keyboard and, texting jocks notwithstanding, text entry on a phone keypad is painful and slow for most people. Your Java ME client should keep text entry to a minimum or eliminate it entirely.

28.4 Developing for Multiple Devices

Part of the point of MIDP was to finally deliver on the promise of Write Once, Run Anywhere. Unfortunately, reality has intruded on this idyllic vision. It is possible to write an application that will run on many different devices, but you'll need to work at it. Testing is crucial.

You can choose from three basic approaches for making an application that runs on multiple types of devices:

1. Use code to adapt to different runtime conditions. In this scenario, you attempt to create a single set of source code that runs correctly on all devices.

2. Use a single set of source code, but create multiple application bundles with different attribute values for different types of devices. You might also use this approach to put different sizes of artwork (images) in application bundles destined for devices with varying screen sizes.

3. Use a preprocessor to embed device-specific or device class–specific code. When you build the application, you'll use the preprocessor to create multiple application bundles for multiple types of devices.

For simple types of applications, especially those that use the prepackaged screens of LCDUI, you'll have a shot at making a single application bundle that runs on all devices. Custom business clients and other boring applications fall into this category.

As soon as you start getting fancy, with artwork, custom screens, sounds, and other snazzy features, you'll probably need to build multiple bundles using the second or third approach described above.

28.5 Stretchy Screens

Stretchy screens are one way you can insulate your application from the perils of running on multiple screen sizes. When I say stretchy, I mean a screen that can adapt to different screen sizes without requiring custom artwork.

The prepackaged screens of LCDUI are already stretchy: you can expect to use them without any changes in code from one device to another.

Custom `Canvas` or `GameCanvas` screens, however, require some more creative planning. One of the simplest things you can do is display an image centered on a `Canvas`. This is possible because, at runtime, you can find out the size of the screen as well as the size of the image. Assuming that your image size is not larger than your smallest expected screen size, you can display an image in the center of the screen on a variety of devices. For devices with especially large screens, however, you might need to use a larger image.

A more elaborate scheme would display a border around the entire screen, regardless of its size. In this case, you need to create separate border images for the corners, top, bottom, and sides. At runtime, based on the available screen size, you can place the corners and tile the top, bottom, and sides to create a border that just fills up the screen.

Although you and your artist will need to do a little more work to create this kind of stretchy screen, it is probably less work than either of you would have to do to create multiple versions of artwork to accommodate different screen sizes.

Another alternative to `Canvas` trickiness is to use Scalable Vector Graphics (SVG), which is stretchy right out of the box. The interactive nature of SVG means that an SVG document can be the entire user interface of your application. NetBeans Mobility even includes support for SVG in its visual designer tool. For more information, try these links:

> http://www.netbeans.org/kb/55/svg-tutorial.html
> http://blogs.sun.com/lukas/entry/tip_using_svg_menu_in

28.6 Make It Just Work

Making applications that *just work* is a huge and worthwhile challenge. You can build a powerful, flexible application, but without a great user interface it will not be successful. Consumers have very short attention spans, so if your Java ME application is not immediately useful or entertaining, users are likely to not try it again.

The usability of desktop applications is often measured by the number of *clicks* it takes to accomplish a task. Consider observing a similar measurement in your Java ME applications. How many button presses does it take to get something done? Are all those presses really necessary? What can be eliminated?

Think about the task your users accomplish with your application and simplify ruthlessly until you're left with the bare essentials. Make it easy to do simple things, and make it possible to do harder things.

Think about the first thing users see when they run your application. Is it a security prompt? Find out if you can cryptographically sign your application to eliminate the security prompt. Does the first screen ask for an account name or number? Consider having users enter account information in a desktop Web browser or providing personalized MIDlet suites that embed account information as an application property. Is your first screen a network wait indicator? Show something more interesting or useful. Is the first screen a legal notice? Fire your lawyers.

Part of making applications that *just work* is consistency. Make sure that similar gestures always work the same way. If your application is based on screens, make sure that moving forward one screen or back one screen is always accomplished the same way. If your users navigate through your application using the arrow and select keys, don't confuse them by throwing in soft button Commands.

28.7 Summary

This chapter presents some of the art and philosophy of Java ME application design. In many cases, a Java ME client connects to an Internet-based server. The Java ME client provides a rich and engaging user experience. The server has hefty computing muscle and can package complex data or analysis as simple results for the Java ME client. Repackaged desktop or Web browser applications will not work well with the small screen sizes and limited input capabilities of Java ME devices. Remember that consumers have a short attention span and will respond well to applications that *just work*.

Understand the problem you are solving and simplify ruthlessly until only the bare essentials remain. Then make it look pretty.

Index

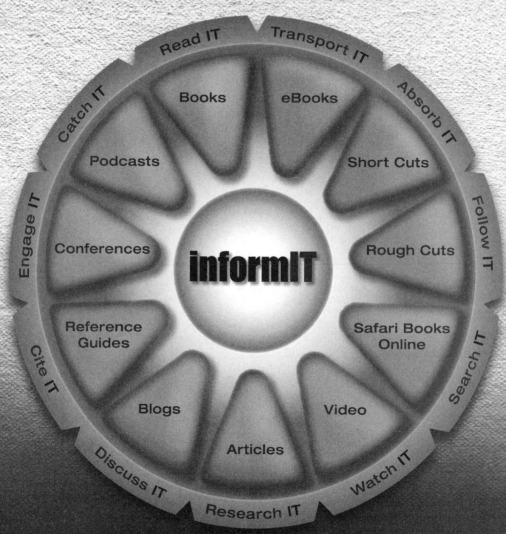